THE ORTHODOX BIBLE STUDY COMPANION
SERIES

The GOSPEL of JOHN

BEHOLDING THE GLORY

by Fr. Lawrence R. Farley

Conciliar Press
Ben Lomond, California

THE GOSPEL OF JOHN:
BEHOLDING THE GLORY
© Copyright 2006 by Lawrence Farley

one volume of *The Orthodox Bible Study Companion* Series

Published by   Conciliar Press
P.O. Box 76
Ben Lomond, California 95005-0076

Printed in the United States of America

ISBN 1-888212-55-1

Dedicated to the memory of
the Rev. Dr. R. K. Harrison,
scholar, teacher, and friend.

Table of Contents and Outline

❦ Introduction ❧

The Character of John's Gospel

In the ongoing first-century polemic between the believing Church and the unbelieving world, the Gospel of St. John comes like the thrust of a sword. This Gospel presents itself as a vigorous attack on unbelief, a bold attempt to persuade the hearts of those who had heard the Church's gospel, a solid and compelling witness to the truth of the Church's proclamation.

It does not claim or pretend to present a Life of Christ, or even to narrate the basic facts of His ministry. Being written (as we will suggest) a generation after the first three Gospels of Matthew, Mark, and Luke, it takes for granted a certain familiarity with those facts. Thus, Christ's Baptism itself is not narrated, nor is His temptation in the wilderness, nor His Transfiguration, nor the events of the Last Supper. John's account assumes that his hearers know these basic events.

This assumed familiarity is apparent in several Johannine passages. In 3:24, John assumes his hearers know that John the Baptist was imprisoned; in 7:42, he assumes they know Christ was born in Bethlehem (hence the subtle and otherwise undetectable irony). In 6:70, he assumes his hearers know that Christ appointed the Twelve, though he nowhere narrates such an appointment himself. In 11:2, he reveals that it was the otherwise anonymous Mary of Bethany who anointed Christ prior to His last earthly week (see Mark 14:3–4), even before narrating that event in 12:1–2. Throughout his Gospel, St. John presupposes his audience knows the basic Gospel narrative.

Why then does he write another Gospel at all? He writes to compel belief, to present a case for the divinity of Jesus. This is his own stated purpose (20:30–31), and it is confirmed in the data he presents. Like one making a case, he stresses over and over again his own role as firsthand and reliable witness (see 19:35). His material is selected to further this specific purpose, and this is why he concentrates so heavily on Christ's controversies with His opponents. John and the Church in his time are involved in this same polemical controversy; John throws the spotlight on Christ and His debate in order that the outcome of that debate may persuade his own opponents.

John's Gospel is therefore unlike the first three Gospels (the so-called Synoptics) in that it is not a narration of the basic Gospel facts. Rather, it is a tightly argued case, brought by one conscious of his status as witness before the tribunal of God and history; it is a blow struck in the eternal conflict between Truth and error, between faith and unbelief, between Light and darkness. It is soaked in the spirit of this primordial controversy. It purports to narrate history, but does so conscious that human decisions made in history will have eternal consequences in the age to come.

The Author and Date of the Gospel

The Church never at any time doubted that this Gospel was written by John the son of Zebedee, the "beloved disciple" who leaned on Jesus' breast at the Last Supper (13:23). Irenaeus (who died c. 202) writes in his *Against Heresies* that "John, the disciple of the Lord who also leaned upon His breast, himself published a Gospel during his residence at Ephesus" (A.H. 3:1, 1). Eusebius, who also records this tradition in his *Ecclesiastical History*, reports that Irenaeus learned this from Polycarp, who in turn learned it from the apostles. Also, Origen (who died in 254) witnesses that "the man who leaned on Jesus' breast . . . left a single Gospel" (cited by Eusebius, E.H. 6.25).

Granted that this is the received tradition of the Church, what is the biblical evidence to confirm it? For the fourth Gospel nowhere claims to have been written by John, but only by one who "leaned upon Jesus' breast" at the Supper, whom "Jesus loved" (13:23). What is the evidence that this person was John the son of Zebedee?

The beloved disciple is mentioned again in 21:7 as part of a group experiencing a Resurrection appearance beside the Sea of Tiberias. The group consisted of Peter, Thomas, the sons of Zebedee (James and John), and two others (21:2). From the mention of the beloved disciple in 13:22–26, it is apparent that this disciple was a close associate of Peter and was a part of the inner circle. John the son of Zebedee is the obvious candidate: he was part of the inner circle (see Mark 5:37; 9:21; 14:33, where Peter, James, and John constitute an inner circle) and was the special companion of Peter (see Acts 3:1; 8:14, where they are found together as a pair). John alone, of those mentioned in the chapter 21 passage, meets the double criterion of being a member of Christ's inner circle and the special friend of Peter.

But why did John not simply identify himself? Why refer to himself only as the disciple whom Jesus loved (13:23) or simply as "another disciple" (18:15)? I would suggest that John's reluctance to identify himself was a part of his overall purpose in writing the Gospel. John the son of Zebedee was the illustrious and well-known apostle, one who had resided at Ephesus for many years and who exercised immediate pastoral oversight over all the seven churches in Asia Minor (see Rev. 1:4). He was thus a man of authority and power. But John commends his Gospel as having compelling authority *not* because he is now an apostle, but *because he was once an eyewitness.* John the powerful apostle must recede to let John the witness come forward with his testimony. What matters is not his present authority over the churches, but that he himself was the intimate friend of Jesus, the one whom "Jesus loved" and who therefore was privy to all the facts. It is this fact alone that he stresses, because this alone gives credibility to the facts he relates. When John says that Jesus loved him, he is not boasting that he was somehow the Lord's favorite. Rather, he is presenting his credentials: as one who was especially close to Jesus, he was in a position to know things not known by others (such as the identity of the traitor; see 13:23–24). Since he offers his Gospel as a witness to the world, he offers himself in his capacity as eyewitness insider.

When and to whom was this Gospel written? It would seem

that it was written later than the other three, since it presupposes familiarity with the basic facts of Christ's life and ministry. I would suggest that it was written about AD 85, from John's residence in Ephesus. Its immediate audience were the Jews of the Diaspora and other interested persons who had heard of Jesus, such as the Gentile God-fearers who clustered around the Diaspora synagogues. Both the Jews and these Gentiles (who believed in Israel's God but who had not taken the final step of being circumcised) were John's targets in his bid to offer Christ to the world. He wrote his Gospel for the Church so that the Church might reach these people with the saving words of Christ. Jesus of Nazareth was by then a source of controversy between Christian and unbelieving Jew and Gentile. Many in the world had heard of the Nazarene who was executed as a criminal, but whom the Christians worshipped as God. By recording Christ's words and deeds, John strives to win the world for his Lord, letting Christ's testimony speak for itself.

Key to the Format of This Work:

• The translated text is first presented in boldface type. Italics within these biblical text sections represent words required by English syntax that are not actually present in the Greek. Each translated text section is set within a shaded grey box.

> ॐ ॐ ॐ ॐ ॐ
>
> **16 And going along by the Sea of Galilee, He saw Simon and Andrew, the *brother* of Simon, circle-casting into the sea, for they were fishermen.**

• In the commentary sections, citations from the portion of text being commented upon are given in boldface type.

> He concentrates on the abruptness of their call and the completeness of their break with the world. They were in the midst of their daily occupation, **circle-casting into the sea, for they were fishermen.**

• In the commentary sections, citations from other locations in Scripture are given in quotation marks with a reference; any reference not including a book name refers to the book under discussion.

> In Jeremiah 16:16–18, God said He would "send for many fishermen" to fish in Israel—those who would judge them for their sins and "doubly repay their iniquity."

• In the commentary sections, italics are used in the ordinary way—for emphasis, foreign words, etc.

> The word translated *circle-casting* is the Greek *amphiballo*; it describes a particular kind of fishnet.

❧ I ❧

PROLOGUE
(1:1–18)

§I. Prologue

St. John sets his Gospel in a cosmic context, for Christ is not simply the Savior of Israel (as the Jews thought), but the Savior of the whole world (see 4:42). So, unlike Matthew's Gospel, which traces Christ's origin back to Abraham (in order to confirm His claim to be the Jewish Messiah), John traces Christ's origin back to the eternal God. God is the Creator of all men, not just of the Jews, and so Christ belongs to all the world. The duality here is not that of Jew vs. Gentile; it is the more basic and universal duality of light vs. darkness. Christ comes into the world as Light into darkness, to enlighten all and draw all the children of light to Himself. The Prologue (written as prose, though with a poetic feel) sets the stage for the ministry of Christ and allows us to see that ministry against a universal and eternal backdrop.

> ❧ ❧ ❧ ❧ ❧
>
> **1** 1 In *the* beginning was the Word, and the Word was with God, and the Word was God.
>
> 2 He was in *the* beginning with God.
>
> 3 All things came to be through Him, and apart from Him not one *thing* came to be which came into being.
>
> 4 In Him was life, and the life was the light of men.

> **5**   And the light shines in the darkness, and the darkness did not grasp it.

St. John begins his Prologue and Gospel with the words **in *the* beginning** (Gr. *en arche*), thereby summoning the associations of the Genesis account of creation, the Septuagint Greek of which begins with the same two words. God existed "in the beginning" (Gen. 1:1) and Christ **the Word** existed in the beginning too, sharing the eternity of God. The pre-incarnate Word and Christ was always **with God**, sharing all of His divine attributes, and in fact **was God**. All that God the Father was, the Word was also.

(This final clause—**the Word was God**, Greek *theos en o logos*—lacks the definite article for **God**, *theos*. This is theologically correct, for John means to ascribe full divinity to the Word and to affirm that the Word was as divine as the Father, but not to suggest that the Word *was* the Father. If John included the definite article, he would be saying not only that the Word was divine but also that the Word was the Father, which would be untrue. John means both to distinguish the Word from God the Father and also to assert the Word's full divinity. The Greek construction is very precise in order to do just that.)

Gazing back before time to eternity past, John declares that the Word **was in *the* beginning with God** and that **all things came to be through Him, and apart from Him not one *thing* came to be which came into being.** Here we may find echoes of the image of the divine Wisdom in Proverbs 8:22–31. In that passage, the wisdom found in the Law is poetically described as eternal. That is, the wisdom found in the Torah is no mere expression of a human culture, but is transcendent and holy, proceeding from the eternal God. This wisdom is personified as Yahweh's eternal companion (much as the pagan gods had their consorts) and as existing "from everlasting, from the beginning, when there were no depths, before the mountains were settled" (Prov. 8:23–24). Wisdom was there when God "established the heavens" (v. 27), being the instrument through which God made the world (see Wisdom 9:2–3, "by Your wisdom You have formed mankind").

The role played by Wisdom in these Old Testament texts is that
actually played by the Word. He, not merely poetically (as with
Proverbs), but actually and personally, is the One whom the Father
used to create the world, so that every single thing created came
into being through the Word. This understanding of the Word (Gr.
Logos) would resonate for pagan Gentile hearers also. Greek philosophers such as the Stoics were fond of talking about the Logos as
the principle of order pervading the world, as the eternal Reason
and Rationality living in all and giving unity to all things. By describing the pre-incarnate Christ as the Word or *Logos*, John is telling all his hearers that Jesus is the fleshly embodiment of the divine
principle, the perfect expression in human form of the eternal God.

As such, **in Him was life, and the life was the light of men.**
Not just Jews, but all men, are only alive because they partake of life
from Him. Jesus of Nazareth is no mere prophet or holy man, but
the life of God who gives life to all. Thus, He belongs to all, not just
to Israel, and all are called to come to Him. All who have the light
of life have it from Him, for His eternal life-giving **light shines in
the darkness, and the darkness did not grasp it.**

The word translated *grasped* is the Greek *katalambano*. It means
not only to grasp in the sense of "understand" (such is its use in
Eph. 3:18), but also to "seize and overpower" (its use in Mark 9:18).
The thought here is of the untouchability and invincibility of the
light—it remains triumphant and beyond the reach of the darkness. However much the darkness may rage, it can never extinguish
the divine Light, which shines on forever and can never be conquered. Christ the Word was not grasped by the darkness of death;
He lives forever, since He is the life and light of God.

ॐ ॐ ॐ ॐ ॐ

6 There came a man sent from God, whose name
was John.
7 He came for a witness, that he might witness
about the Light, that all might believe through
him.

> 8 That one was not the Light, but *came* that he
>   might witness about the Light.
> 9 He was the true Light that, coming into the
>   world, enlightens every man.

Since John's purpose is to witness to Christ, he focuses immediately on St. John the Baptizer, whose main role was to be himself a forerunner and witness to Christ. (No doubt St. John the Evangelist also hopes to win over those Jews who counted themselves disciples of John the Baptizer, for the Baptizer's movement did not vanish with his death; see Acts 19:1–3.) The Evangelist's purpose is not just to show that John's movement was a mere preparation for the Jesus movement and that John's disciples should now become Christians; it is also to amplify John the Baptizer's voice, because that voice had the same message as the Church. **John** the Baptizer was **a man sent from God** with a message that all should hear. He came not to draw disciples to himself or to start his own movement. Rather, he came only as a forerunner, **for a witness** to Another, **that he might witness about the Light**, about Jesus, **that all might believe** in Jesus **through him**. John himself (the Greek pronoun is emphatic: *ekeinos*, **that one**) was **not the Light**; he only came **that he might witness** to it. That is, all of John the Baptizer's significance was found in Jesus. At the time this Gospel was written, John the Baptizer was an immensely popular figure in Israel (at least among the masses), and the Evangelist would tap into that popularity and use it to further the Gospel.

This was quite necessary at that time. Chronologically, John the Baptizer preceded Jesus, and it was known that Jesus had been baptized by John and that His early disciples were formerly disciples of John. Jesus' ministry really only took off after John's arrest (see Mark 1:14). For all these reasons, it must have looked as if Jesus' ministry was simply an extension of John's—that Jesus was John's disciple and that John was His mentor and master. The Christian movement looked to some suspiciously like a spin-off of John's movement.

For this reason, John the Evangelist had to make abundantly

clear in his Gospel that Jesus' ministry did *not* draw its significance from John's, but the reverse. John was not the master or the original. He was simply the forerunner. John was not the Light; *Jesus* was **the true Light that, coming into the world, enlightens every man.** Again, Christ came not just to Israel, but into the whole world, to enlighten every man.

ॐ ॐ ॐ ॐ ॐ

10 He was in the world, and the world was made through Him, and the world did not know Him.

11 He came to His own, and the ones who were His own did not receive Him.

12 But as many as received Him, to them He gave authority to become children of God, to the ones who believe in His Name,

13 the ones who were born not of bloods, nor of *the* will of flesh, nor of *the* will of man, but of God.

14 And the Word became flesh and *pitched His* tent among us, and we beheld His glory, glory as of the only-begotten from the Father, full of grace and truth.

That Christ "came into the world" (v. 9), however, did not mean that He would be instantly recognized for who He was and welcomed. He was indeed **in the world** and fully incarnate, walking among men. He was present as the true Light and Life of all, the One **through** whom **the world** was first **made**. Nonetheless, because He came in humility, **the world did not know Him** or recognize its true Light. Here was the irony and the tragedy. Christ **came to His own** (literally, "to His own things," Gr. *eis ta idia*), to the home where He should have been welcomed, and **the ones who were His own** (Gr. *oi idioi*) **did not receive Him.** Israel was the place where He should have been welcomed; here was the place where His own things were, such as the Temple and the Law, which all spoke of Him. But Israel did not receive Him into their hearts. Instead they hated Him and handed Him over to be hung on the Tree.

But not all in Israel. Some **received Him**, and **to them He gave authority to become children of God**. These are further described as **the ones who believe in His Name**, who accept Him as the Messiah and Lord and become His disciples in the waters of baptism (see 4:1). When they believe in the divine power that He manifests, they are given the high privilege of ceasing to be children of this age and becoming children of God, sharing God's nature. This is an astonishing claim—that sinners, creatures of dust and ashes who drink iniquity like water (Job 15:16), should have the authority and right to inherit such a status. But Christ freely gave us this authority that we should make such a daring claim.

John clarifies what is this miraculous new birth in which believers become God's children. It is utterly unlike birth in this age, and so the Christians are utterly unlike other men. Their birth as the children of God is **not of bloods**, or from natural biological processes (see Wisdom 7:2, which speaks of the role of blood in the formation of the fetus); it is not **of *the* will of flesh,** or from sexual desire; nor is it **of *the* will of man**, or from the natural desire of parents for children. Rather, it is **of God**, being entirely a supernatural process. Thus those born in the natural way belong to earth, whereas the Christians have a completely supernatural origin and belong to heaven (see 17:14).

This is all possible because **the Word became flesh and *pitched His* tent among us**. The word translated as *pitched His tent* is the Greek *skenoo*, cognate with the noun *skene* or tent. The noun is used of any tent or dwelling (such as the tent Abraham pitched when he made his permanent dwelling in Canaan; see Gen. 12:8 LXX) and especially of the divine Tent or Tabernacle in which Yahweh dwelt among His People in the Old Testament (see Ex. 27:21 LXX). St. John uses the verb here to show how Christ became flesh, like us, sharing all our human nature, and made His permanent dwelling among men. Though He was the high and holy

God, transcendent above all, He came down to us, so that we **beheld His glory**. Before His Incarnation, only angels in heaven could look upon such splendor, but now we mortals can behold it as well. As the hymn of Matins declares, though "God is the Lord," He "has revealed Himself to us." John and the apostles beheld His glory, such glory as was formerly inaccessible to men. This is no human glory, but **glory as of the only-begotten from the Father, full of grace and truth**.

The word rendered *only-begotten* is the Greek *monogenes*, which here means "special, unique." (Isaac is described in Heb. 11:17 as Abraham's "only-begotten," though biologically speaking Abraham begot Ishmael as well; Isaac was "only-begotten" in that he was special and alone carried the covenant promises.) Christ's glory is thus the glory of One inseparable from the Father, so that His glory is the glory of God the Father Himself. Thus it is full of grace and truth, radiant with God's favor and faithfulness to His promises. In experiencing Christ's glory as His disciples (see John 17:22), we experience the favor and love of God as He fulfills all that He promised to His People.

> 🦋 🦋 🦋 🦋 🦋
>
> 15 John witnesses about Him, and cried out, saying, "This was He of whom I said, 'He who comes after me has become before me, for He was prior to me.'"
> 16 For of His fullness we *ourselves* have all received, even grace upon grace.
> 17 For the Law was given through Moses; grace and truth came to be through Jesus Christ.
> 18 No one has ever seen God; the only-begotten, the One who is in the bosom of the Father, that One has explained *Him*.

This is the glory of which John the Baptizer was aware. **John witnesses about Him** (the present tense is used to show how John's witness remains in the Church forever), and during his ministry he **cried out, saying, "This was He of whom I said, 'He who comes after me** (that is, as John's disciple) **has become before me** (that is, has attained to a higher rank than John)**, for He was prior to me.'"** Here John is cited as affirming the superiority of Jesus, even though Jesus first appeared on the stage of public history as John's disciple. John was told by God that his ministry would manifest the Messiah (see 1:33), and so it came about.

John the Evangelist, as an apostle and one who saw the Lord, relates that he and his fellow apostles (the pronoun **we** is emphatic in the Greek) all experienced this same glory. John the Baptizer proclaimed, and they can confirm it too. They **all received** of that divine **fullness** and abundant life, **even grace upon grace**, as it washed over them in endless waves. Their time with Jesus was an unceasing experience of the divine glory.

There was nothing in their former experience to compare to it. **The Law** which was **given through Moses** was the most glorious thing they had known prior to that. Yet even that glory was nothing compared to Jesus. God's **grace and truth**, His covenant favor and faithfulness, **came to be** realized **through Jesus Christ**. It was through Him alone that they truly knew what glory, grace, and truth were. God remained invisible; indeed, **no one has ever seen God.** Throughout all Israel's history, God never revealed Himself to the eyes of men, for no one could see that blinding and blasting glory and still live (Ex. 33:20). But God has now revealed that glory through human flesh, for **the only-begotten** (some manuscripts read "the only-begotten God"), **the One who is in the bosom of the Father** and who is inseparable from Him, has come down and has **explained** all.

The word translated *explained* is the Greek *exegeomai*; it is cognate with the English noun "exegesis" or explanation. The verb is used in Acts 10:8 for Cornelius explaining his vision to his attendants. By using the verb here, John tells us that in Christ alone, the transcendent Father is fully revealed; in Him alone is the Father made visible and tangible. Christ is the fullness of God, and everything that is in the Father is made plain to us who come to Christ with faith. This is the One witnessed to by John the Baptizer and experienced by the apostles—the glory of God Himself revealed to the eyes of men.

❧ II ☙

A WEEK OF WITNESS
(1:19—2:11)

After his prologue, which sets Christ in a cosmic and eternal context, John begins to set forth his case for the Christian Faith by narrating a week of witness to Jesus. Just as the opening words of the first creation story in Genesis 1:1 are followed by a week of creation, so John begins his Gospel with a week of testimony to Jesus as Giver of the new creation.

§II.1. Day 1: John the Baptizer's Witness

☙ ☙ ☙ ☙ ☙

19 And this is the witness of John, when the Jews sent to him priests and Levites from Jerusalem to ask him, "Who are you?"

20 And he confessed and did not deny, and he confessed, "I *myself* am not the Christ."

21 And they asked him, "What then? Are you Elijah?" And he says, "I am not." "Are you the Prophet?" And he answered, "No."

22 They said then to him, "Who are you, that we may give an answer to the ones who sent us? What do you say about yourself?"

23 He said, "I *myself am* a voice of one shouting in the wilderness, 'Make straight the way of *the* Lord,' as Isaiah the prophet said."

24 Now they had been sent from the Pharisees.

25 And they asked him and said to him, "Why then are you baptizing, if you are not the Christ, nor Elijah, nor the Prophet?"
26 John answered them, saying, "I *myself* baptize in water; in the middle of you stands One whom you *yourselves* do not know,
27 "even He who comes after me, the strap of whose sandal I *myself* am not worthy to loose."
28 These things happened in Bethany beyond the Jordan, where John was baptizing.

Once again, the Evangelist begins with **the witness of John** the Baptizer, citing John's own words. The **Jews sent to him priests and Levites from Jerusalem to ask him, "Who are you?"** John's ministry had become well known even in the capital, and his seemingly unorthodox practices were arousing suspicion, for he was baptizing Jews.

This was immensely controversial. Baptism was the method by which Gentiles were received into the Jewish faith and made into Jews. Even whole families were sometimes received in this way. After publicly stating their desire to become Jews and their intention to keep all the Law, the males were circumcised (doubtless with the necessary privacy!). Then, after a time for healing, all in the converting family were baptized. The rite of baptism was borrowed and adapted from within Israel: just as a Jew might bathe himself to wash away the stain of ceremonial uncleanness (see Lev. 14:8), so the converting Gentiles would immerse themselves to wash away the stain of the Gentile world.

John had taken this rite of conversion and applied it to the Jews, thereby saying that they stood in the same need of God's mercy and forgiveness as did the godless Gentiles. This was truly scandalous, for it was an article of faith among some that all Israel had a share in the world to come, and would be saved simply by virtue of being Israel. John denied all this and called all in Israel to repentance. No wonder those in Jerusalem who considered themselves guardians of orthodoxy sent priests and Levites to challenge John and ask him by what authority he was baptizing Jews!

Their question, **"Who are you?"** was therefore not simply a request for his name: it was an imperious demand for his credentials. The sense of it is, "Just who do you think *you* are that you are doing this?" What was his authority? John **confessed and did not deny, and he confessed** (John the Evangelist states it twice, to make it doubly clear) that he was **not the Christ**. (The pronoun John the Baptizer uses is emphatic in the Greek; the Forerunner emphasizes his subordinate position—something John the Evangelist is keen to stress.)

If he is not the Messiah, with authority to do such unprecedented things in Israel, **"What then?"** Is he **Elijah**? Popular expectation was that Elijah the prophet, carried up to heaven before his death (2 Kin. 2:11), would reappear personally on earth prior to the end. Elijah, a great prophet, had the requisite authority for such an innovation. Is he Elijah? Once again, John replies, **"I am not."**

Perhaps, they continue, he is **the Prophet**? This again was a figure of eschatological authority, and one expected before the coming of the Kingdom. (Perhaps the figure is to be identified as Jeremiah returned to earth as a harbinger of the final days; see Matt. 16:14. Certainly Jeremiah featured in times of crisis in Israel's history; see 2 Macc. 15:1–15.) Whatever his identity, John denies that he is that Prophet.

The authorities are stymied. **"Who are you?"** they ask, requiring some sort of reply that they **may give an answer to the ones who sent** them, for they will be in trouble if they return with no further information.

In reply, John refuses to draw attention to himself, but reserves all the attention to his message. He and his person are unimportant; what is important is what he has to say. He himself (once again the Greek pronoun is emphatic) is but **a voice**—the sound of **one shouting in the wilderness, 'Make straight the way of *the* Lord.'** *Here* is his authority to baptize: he is the fulfillment of the prophecies of **Isaiah the prophet** in Isaiah 40:3. That is, he is a forerunner to the messianic Kingdom of God.

John the Evangelist adds that the questioners **had been sent from the Pharisees** and therefore could be expected to be hostile to such new things. This is indeed the case: they challenge him openly to justify **why then** he is **baptizing** since he is **not the Christ, nor Elijah, nor the Prophet**. (They either have not caught John's implicit claim to be the Forerunner spoken of by Isaiah the prophet, or more likely do not accept it.) John sweeps away such pedantic small-mindedness and does not answer it directly. They are so concerned about his water baptism—what will they say about the Messiah for whom it prepares? If they cannot accept John, how will they deal with his Messiah? John himself (the pronoun is emphatic) merely **baptizes in water**, but Messiah is at hand, and is even now standing **in the middle** of them and ready to be revealed, even though they do **not** yet **know** or recognize Him. Though He succeeds John and **comes after** him, He is so great that John is **not worthy** even to **loose the strap** of His **sandal**—a work so menial that even slaves were not required to do it. Messiah's greatness is John's justification for baptizing, for John has to make Israel ready to receive such a great Deliverer.

John the Evangelist, concerned for historical veracity and eyewitness detail, adds the note that **these things happened in Bethany beyond the Jordan.** Its exact location cannot now be determined, but John differentiates this Bethany from the more famous one next to Jerusalem by saying that this site was beyond the Jordan. A location to the east of the Jordan River and some miles north of Jericho may be indicated.

❧ EXCURSUS

On the Term "the Jews"

The term "Jew" (Gr. *ioudaios*) is a term with a history. Originally it meant simply a member of the tribe of Judah. After the return from the Babylonian Exile, the restored community was confined mostly to the area occupied by that tribe, centered in Jerusalem with its Temple. Thus the name came to denote one whose life centered in the Temple at Jerusalem, whatever his tribe. Nehemiah 5:8 refers to "Jewish brothers" exiled afar (presumably from many of the Twelve Tribes), and Zechariah 8:23 uses the term "Jew" to denote any member of the covenant community. St. Paul's usage is consistent with this, for by the term "Jew" he means not simply one belonging to the southern portion of Palestine (Judea proper, as distinct from Galilee), but anyone who practices Judaism (see Rom. 2:17–24; Gal. 2:14).

In St. John's Gospel, the meaning is somewhat elastic. It does *not* mean simply someone from southern Judea (as opposed to northern Galilee), for when John speaks of "the cleansing of the Jews" in 2:6, he does not mean the way of purifying specific to those in southern Judea, but the way of purifying common to all followers of Judaism. Christ too, in saying that "salvation is from the Jews" (4:22), manifestly includes Himself in that category, even though He was from Galilee in the north and not from Judea in the south. Thus the term is not strictly a geographical one (though all geographical elements cannot be excluded, because the Temple, which defined Judaism, was in southern Judea).

John's use of the term is colored by the controversy that existed in his day between disciples of Jesus (whether ancestrally Jewish or not) and the mass of the Jewish nation, which did not believe in Him. By the term "Jew," John often seems to mean *one who practices Judaism as opposed to the Christian Faith.*

It is true that, in Jesus' own day, most of those who opposed Him were in the south, in Judea proper, since many Galileans supported Him (see 7:52 for the assumption that belief in Jesus implies Galilean ancestry). But that is not because the term "Jew" was geographical *in itself*; rather it just happened that most of those who opposed Jesus lived in that southern geographical area. Thus, when referring to "the Jews" as Christ's opponents, those in Judea are often the focus (see 5:18; 11:8). But the term can also denote *any* who practice Judaism in contradistinction to Christianity, even if they are from the north (such as those who resisted Him after He multiplied the loaves near the Sea of Tiberias; see 6:1, 41).

In St. John's Gospel, the use of the term is part of John's polemic, and that is why he uses it far more than the Synoptic writers. Matthew, Mark, and Luke have a more strictly narrative purpose than John, and they rarely use the term (and even then mostly to describe Jesus as "the King of the Jews"). John, on the other hand, uses the term "Jews" seventy times, in keeping with his controversial purpose.

§II.2. Day 2: God's Witness

29 The next day he sees Jesus coming to him and says, "Behold the Lamb of God, who takes away the sin of the world!

30 "This is He of whom I *myself* said, 'After me comes a man who has become before me, for He was prior to me.'

31 "And I *myself* did not know Him, but I *myself* came baptizing in water that He might be manifested to Israel."

32 And John witnessed, saying, "I have beheld the Spirit descending as a dove out of heaven, and He remained on Him.

33 "And I *myself* did not know Him, but He who sent me to baptize in water, that One said to me, 'Upon whomever you see the Spirit descending and remaining on Him, this is the One who baptizes in *the* Holy Spirit.'

> **34** "And I *myself* have seen and witnessed that this is the Son of God."

On **the next day**, the second day in the week of witness, John the Evangelist brings forward the witness of God, spoken during Jesus' Baptism. John the Baptizer has witnessed (obliquely, as far as his interrogators are concerned!) that he is the Forerunner (and that Jesus is therefore the Messiah). Now God Himself will confirm the same.

This begins when John the Baptizer **sees Jesus coming to him and says, "Behold the Lamb of God, who takes away the sin of the world! This is He of whom I *myself* said, 'After me comes a man who has become before me, for He was prior to me.'"** (The occasion of this utterance is not further elaborated; it was perhaps when John next saw Jesus after His return from His forty-day temptation in the wilderness.) John the Baptizer thus identifies Jesus as the One of whom he spoke before, when he predicted that his ministry would manifest the Messiah. John said that Messiah was coming, and here He is!

Jesus is further identified by John the Baptizer as **the Lamb of God, who takes away the sin of the world**. It is difficult for us now not to read into this title substitutionary significance, and to understand it in light of the Cross as saying that Jesus takes away the world's sin through His death. For John the Baptizer, however, it need have had no such significance. Indeed, given his later doubts about Jesus arising from His humility (see Matt. 11:3), it is doubtful that John understood the title in this way. Jewish apocalyptic literature spoke of the warrior Messiah as a Lamb, and it is likely that this is what John means. Jesus will take away the sin of the world by rooting out sinners and bringing in the age of righteousness to come. Thus a symbolic parable in Enoch 90:38 speaks of Messiah in terms of "a lamb that became a great animal and had great black horns on its head, and the Lord of the sheep rejoiced over it."

John the Evangelist, however, records the Baptizer's utterance with a fuller understanding of its ultimate significance than the

Baptizer had himself. John and the Church know that Jesus is the Lamb of God because He will offer Himself as a Sacrifice on the Cross to take away the sin of the world. They know that the age of righteousness to come proclaimed by the Baptizer is to be built on the forgiveness of sin.

John the Baptizer further explains to his hearers on that second day of witness that he himself (the pronoun is emphatic in the Greek) **did not know Him** or recognize Him as Messiah when He first came to him. He of course knew who Jesus was (John's mother knew the Mother of Jesus; see Luke 1:39–56), and he knew that Jesus was holier than himself and needed no baptism of repentance. (That was why he protested when he first saw Jesus come to him for baptism; Matt. 3:14.) But at that time he did not know that Jesus was to be Messiah.

John witnesses here of what God said to him, and how God Himself gave the witness that Jesus of Nazareth is Messiah and is therefore the reason that John himself **came baptizing in water**. It is all so that Jesus **might be manifested to Israel**; John's ministry is to focus and culminate in Him. John witnesses to his hearers that day that he **beheld the Spirit descending as a dove out of heaven, and He remained** on Jesus. After Jesus was baptized and left the water of the Jordan, as He stood praying on the banks (Luke 3:21), John had a vision of the heavens opened and the Spirit in the form of a dove alighting on Him. This was the sign that God had given to John to designate His Messiah; the very same One **who sent** him **to baptize in water, that One said to** him, "**Upon whomever you see the Spirit descending and remaining on Him, this is the One who baptizes in** *the* **Holy Spirit**," the Messiah. Therefore John himself (the pronoun again is emphatic) saw this vision and **witnessed** that this very One was **the Son of God**, the designated Messiah. What John the Evangelist stresses in this passage is not just the witness of John the Baptizer. That was dealt with in vv. 19–28. What is stressed here is the witness of God Himself, given to John through the vision of Jesus and the dove.

ॐ ॐ ॐ ॐ ॐ

§II.3. Day 3: Andrew's Witness

> ৡ৾   ৡ৾   ৡ৾   ৡ৾   ৡ৾
>
> 35 Again the next day, John was standing with two of his disciples
> 36 and looked at Jesus as He walked and says, "Behold the Lamb of God!"
> 37 And the two disciples heard him speak, and they followed Jesus.
> 38 And Jesus turned and beheld them following and says to them, "What do you seek?" And they said to Him, "Rabbi (which translated says 'Teacher'), where are You remaining?"
> 39 He says to them, "Come and you will see." They came therefore and saw where He was remaining; and they remained with Him that day, for it was about *the* tenth hour.
> 40 One of the two who heard John and followed Him was Andrew, Simon Peter's brother.
> 41 He finds first his own brother Simon and says to him, "We have found the Messiah" (which translated is "Christ").
> 42 He brought him to Jesus. Jesus looked at him and said, "You are Simon the son of John; you will be called Cephas" (which is translated "Peter").

The third day of that extraordinary week contains the witness of **two of** John's **disciples**. These were there when their teacher John again **looked at Jesus** with a riveting stare as **He walked** (the Greek for *look at* is *emblepo*; compare its use in Mark 10:21) and called out to designate Jesus as **the Lamb of God. Two** of his **disciples heard him** say this, and **they followed Jesus.** (In this way John the Evangelist shows his hearers how the movement of John the Baptizer should join the Jesus movement, for John himself directed his own disciples to follow Jesus.)

Jesus turned and beheld them following Him. He stops and
says to them, "What do you seek?" (The historic present is used, so
that we can almost hear the voice of the Lord ourselves.) The disciples respond with great deference, addressing Him as **Rabbi** (John
translates the term as **Teacher** for any Gentiles who might read the
account). The term "rabbi" did not yet have an official flavor, as
designating an ordained religious functionary. At this time it was
used as a term of respect for any whom the speaker wished to honor
as a teacher. By using it here, the disciples mean to honor Jesus and
secure a hearing for themselves. This is all the more important, for
they do not just want to ask a question. They want to stay with
Him for a while and talk at great length, hoping to become His
disciples. With trembling hearts, they ask, **"Where are You remaining?"** hoping for permission to share His lodging. The One whom
their teacher John has designated as Messiah grants their request,
saying, **"Come and you will see."** They followed Him to the house
where He was staying and **remained with Him that day**, sharing
His evening meal, **for it was about *the* tenth hour** (i.e. four P.M.)

John the Evangelist then reveals the identity of **one of the two**
disciples: **Andrew, Simon Peter's brother.** In his excitement, before
He joins the Lord for the evening, **he finds first his own brother
Simon and says to him, "We have found the Messiah"** (again St.
John provides a translation, **Christ**, for the non-Jews). **He brought
him to Jesus** (we can imagine Andrew grabbing his brother Simon
by the arm and hustling him to meet his new Master) with the
excited explanation, "We have found the Messiah!" (In saying that
Jesus is the Messiah, he is of course not stating his own settled conviction—he does not yet *have* his own settled conviction, since he
has not yet come to know the Lord. Rather, he is simply repeating
what his teacher John the Baptizer said.)

Jesus looked at Simon with a riveting stare of His own (the Gr.
emblepo is again used) and with prophetic insight proceeded to re-
name him, giving him the nickname **Cephas** (Aramaic for "rock")
by which he would later be known in the Church. (Again St. John
explains that this translates into **Peter**, *Petros* in the Greek.) This
renaming is no thoughtless quip. Rather, it represents Christ's

acceptance of Simon as His disciple, for to give a person another name is to exercise authority over him and his destiny (see Gen. 17:5, where God renames Abram as Abraham). From this moment on, Andrew and Simon are the Lord's disciples, in that they have committed themselves to learn from Him as their Teacher.

A final word may be added about the identity of the other two disciples. Andrew is named as one; who is the other? Ancient tradition identifies him as John the Evangelist himself, who characteristically leaves himself unidentified (compare 18:15). John and his brother James were partners with Simon and Andrew (Luke 5:10), and it would be natural for Andrew to be found in the company of his business partner and friend.

§II.4. Day 4: Philip and Nathanael's Witness

ॐ   ॐ   ॐ   ॐ   ॐ

43 The next day he wanted to go out into Galilee, and he finds Philip. And Jesus says to him, "Follow Me."

44 Now Philip was from Bethsaida, of the city of Andrew and Peter.

45 Philip finds Nathanael and says to him, "We have found Him of whom Moses in the Law and the Prophets wrote, Jesus son of Joseph, from Nazareth."

46 And Nathanael says to him, "Can any good thing come out of Nazareth?" Philip says to him, "Come and see."

47 Jesus saw Nathanael coming to Him and says of him, "Behold a true Israelite, in whom is no guile!"

48 Nathanael says to Him, "How do You know me?" Jesus answered and said to him, "Before Philip called you, when you were under the fig tree, I saw you."

> 49 Nathanael answered Him, "Rabbi, You *Yourself* are the Son of God; You *Yourself* are the King of Israel!"
> 50 Jesus answered and said to him, "Because I said to you that I saw you under the fig tree, do you believe? You will see greater things than these."
> 51 And He says to him, "Amen, amen, I say to you, you *all* will see heaven opened and the angels of God ascending and descending on the Son of Man."

The next day in this week, the list of witnesses and disciples continues to grow. Andrew **wanted to go out into Galilee,** and having done so, **he finds** his friend **Philip**. (This **he** of v. 43 has Andrew as its immediate antecedent; it was Andrew who brought Simon to Jesus in v. 42. The thought here seems to be that Andrew continues to bring his friends to his new Teacher.) Jesus accepts his friend Philip also, saying to him, **"Follow Me."** (St. John, with his eye for historical accuracy and detail, adds that **Andrew and Peter** knew of Philip because both were raised in **Bethsaida**.)

Philip himself is impressed by his new Teacher, and immediately **finds** his friend **Nathanael**. (This Nathanael is probably the same person known as Bartholomew [a patronymic meaning "son of Tolmai"] in the Synoptics, for the Synoptics mention Bartholomew but never Nathanael, whereas John's Gospel mentions Nathanael but never Bartholomew. Nathanael is obviously one of the Twelve, since he is present for the Resurrection appearances in John 21, and Bartholomew is paired with his friend Philip in the Synoptic lists of Matt. 10:3, Mark 3:18, and Luke 6:14.)

Philip enthusiastically bubbles that he has **found Him of whom Moses in the Law and the Prophets wrote**—that is, the Messiah—namely, **Jesus son of Joseph, from Nazareth.** (In quoting Philip's description of Jesus as the son of Joseph, John the Evangelist does not mean to imply he disbelieves the account of the Virgin Birth. Rather, he simply quotes Philip as giving Jesus' usual and legal name, for Jews were named after their legal fathers.) Mention that the designated Messiah comes from such a small and insignificant town as Nazareth prompts the incredulous reply, **"Can any good thing come out of Nazareth?"** Such a town has produced nothing good or noteworthy—it can hardly be imagined to produce the Messiah Himself! (It could be that Nathanael, coming from nearby Cana [see 21:2], feels the natural antipathy of rivalry toward Nazareth.) Philip does not attempt to argue. He knows that experience is the best and only teacher. He simply invites his friend to **"Come and see"** for himself.

As the pair approach Jesus, the Lord takes the initiative. Before Nathanael can even be introduced or make his own inquiries, when **Jesus saw Nathanael coming to Him**, He greets him with the acclamation, **"Behold a true Israelite, in whom is no guile!"**

It is high praise, hailing Nathanael as a true and worthy representative of the Chosen People, one in whom there is no love of deceit—a straightforward man of steadfast integrity. Nathanael is suspicious of such praise coming from one who has never met him and who (as he thinks) can know nothing about him. Carefully he asks, **"How do you know me?"** and we can almost hear the suspicion and ring of challenge in his voice.

The Lord, knower of the hearts of men and possessor of a prophet's knowledge (see 2 Kin. 5:26), is equal to the challenge. **Before Philip called** Nathanael, when he was alone and in secret communion with God **under the fig tree**, Christ **saw** him. He knows of his integrity, for by God's power He saw him pouring out that true heart to the Father.

Upon hearing this, Nathanael is completely won over, and now believes all that his friend Philip has said. He exclaims, **"Rabbi, You** *Yourself* **are the Son of God; You** *Yourself* **are the King of Israel!"** That is, he now believes that Jesus, from lowly (and rival) Nazareth, is the true Messiah. The Lord, however, would not have his faith stop there. His ministry has not yet begun. There will come a time when He will do miracles, when He will open blind eyes, make the lame walk, and even raise the dead. Does Nathanael **believe** so easily, just **because** He **said** to him that He **saw** him **under the fig tree**? Can a mere word produce such faith? His messiahship is to be more glorious than that! Indeed, He says (sealing His word with the oath **Amen, amen,** to indicate its certainty), they *all* (the verb changes from the singular in v. 50 to the plural in v. 51) **will see heaven opened and the angels of God ascending and descending on the Son of Man.**

The reference evokes the image in Genesis 28:12, where Jacob saw a ladder stretching from earth to heaven and the angels of God ascending and descending on it. By using this image, Jesus indicates that He is the One through whom men find access to heaven. He is the revelation of the Father on earth. Through Him, heaven will be permanently opened (the verb is in the perfect tense) and salvation made accessible to men. It is through Him that all may go to the Father and be saved (14:6). Nathanael must not think of messiahship in such lowly terms (as most Israelites did). It is something far more glorious than they can imagine.

§II.5. Day 7: The Witness of the First Sign: Turning Water into Wine

ॐ ॐ ॐ ॐ ॐ

2 1 And on the third day there was a wedding in Cana of Galilee, and the mother of Jesus was there;

2 and both Jesus and His disciples were called to the wedding.

3 And *when* the wine was lacking, the mother of Jesus says to Him, "They do not have wine."

4 And Jesus says to her, "Woman, what *is that* to Me and to you? My hour has not yet come."

5 His mother says to the servants, "Whatever He says to you, do."

6 Now there were six stone waterjars lying there, for the cleansing of the Jews, each having room *for* two or three measures.

7 Jesus says to them, "Fill the waterjars with

> water." And they filled them to *the* top.
>
> 8 And He says to them, "Draw *it* out now, and bring *it* to the head-butler." And they brought *it*.
>
> 9 And when the head-butler tasted the water which had become wine and did not know where it came from (but the servants knew, the ones who had drawn the water), the head-butler calls the bridegroom
>
> 10 and says to him, "Every man sets out the good wine first, and when all have gotten drunk, *he sets out* the poorer *wine*; you have kept the good wine until now!"
>
> 11 This beginning of the signs Jesus did in Cana of Galilee and manifested His glory, and His disciples believed in Him.

The final day of this first week of witness takes place **on the third day** after the event narrated in 1:43–51, that is, on the seventh day from the events of 1:19. Having narrated how John the Baptizer witnesses to Jesus' glory as Messiah, how God Himself witnesses to it, and how on successive days His new disciples witness to it, John the Evangelist concludes his narration of that glorious week by showing how Christ's miraculous power witnesses to it as well. It is **in Cana of Galilee** that Christ **manifested His glory** so that **His** new **disciples believed in Him** (2:11).

This is the **beginning of the signs** and miracles which **Jesus did**, and it sets the tone for all the signs He will later perform. For it is not a public miracle, but one which is only manifested and known to His disciples. *They* know of the miracle; the others at the wedding feast do not. To be sure, Christ's subsequent miracles will indeed be seen by all and not just by His disciples. But these later miracles will have this in common with this first sign: they will not fully disclose His messianic glory, but only point to it. That is why John calls them **signs**—for like signposts, they point to something. Christ's miracles point to His status as Messiah, but they only carry such conviction to those who, like the disciples, approach them with faith. For His disciples, the miracles are manifestations of His glory as Messiah. For the Pharisees, however, they are no such thing, but only evidence that "He casts out demons by the ruler of the demons" (Mark 3:22). Thus, Christ's messianic status is veiled in this age, and disclosed only to those with faith. It is this characteristic of Christ and His miracles that St. John stresses in this account, and throughout his Gospel—that His glory is at the same time both revealed and hidden. The fullness of His messianic glory must wait until His hour has come—the hour of His Cross and Resurrection (2:4; 17:1).

John sets the scene by saying that **there was a wedding in Cana of Galilee** and **both Jesus and His disciples were called** and invited to it. Also, **the mother of Jesus was there.** Perhaps she was a close friend of the bride, which would account for her knowing about the social catastrophe of them running out of wine before anyone else knew.

This was indeed a social catastrophe. In a culture which placed such high value on public honor, to run out of wine at such an event would have been to place a cloud over the bridal pair's marriage such as would not pass away. Wedding banquets lasted for days, and the wine was expected to flow freely. To have the wine **lacking** meant that the invited guests would begin to leave—and would have nothing good to say about the newly married ever after! When **the mother of Jesus** learns of this (from the bride?), she whispers to her Son, **"They do not have wine."** That is, she knows He is the chosen Messiah and is calling Him to publicly work a miracle, to take this as the moment to declare His messiahship and reveal Himself to Israel.

Jesus refuses to acquiesce. His **hour** for such open and undeniable demonstration of His messianic glory has **not yet come**, and He refuses the summons from His Mother. He addresses her respectfully but formally, calling her not "Mother" (the usual warm and filial title), but **"Woman."** (This does not sound as rude in the original as the English translation does; He calls her "woman" when consoling her from the Cross in 19:26. Rather, it is like our English title "madam," being polite, but also formal and distant.) Thus, there is a definite rebuff in the way He addresses her, and in His reply as well, **"What *is that* to Me and to you?"** In other words, "Why talk to Me about that?" Though not rude, His reply is unexpectedly abrupt, as He distances Himself from her. Mary accepts His word, and **says to the servants, "Whatever He says to you, do."**

What is going on here? Some suggest that this is an example of the powerful intercession of the Mother of God—though Jesus is reluctant to do the miracle, yet He is persuaded to do so by His Mother. Though the Theotokos is indeed a powerful intercessor, that is not the meaning of the present story. The point is not that Jesus first refuses to do a miracle and then changes His mind and does it anyway. It is that Jesus is asked to *openly manifest all His glory as Messiah by a public miracle and refuses to do it*. He does the miracle secretly instead, so that none see it but His faithful disciples. When this is understood, we can understand too why John focuses attention on the Mother of Jesus and why Jesus distances Himself from her.

Prior to this, Jesus was under her authority, as any dutiful son was under the authority of his mother and surviving parent. His Mother first assumes that He will continue to be under her authority, as He always was as a child. But the time for such submission is past. In these days, Jesus is beginning His work and gathering His disciples. Now He is under the authority only of the Father, and Mary, like everyone else in Israel, is called to accept this and become His disciple. That is, she is called to cease being an authority *over* Him and become one who is *under* Him. That is why Jesus distances Himself and rebuffs her request. He is not rejecting *her;* rather He is rejecting *her authority over Him* and calling her to accept His authority over her as His disciple.

In this way her task mirrors the task of all in Israel. All in Israel see in Jesus simply another Jew, another son of Israel, one who like them is subject to all the limitations imposed by Jewish law (such as keeping the Sabbath; compare 5:16–18). Jesus calls them, like Mary, to see Him as One who has authority and to bring themselves under this authority. That is why John focuses on Mary early in this story, in v. 1. She is mentioned not simply because she is the one who gives Jesus the news that the wine has failed. She is mentioned because she is an image of Israel—she accomplishes the role-reversal that all in Israel are called to accomplish. When Jesus begins to assert His authority and gather disciples, she submits to that authority.

Thus, as His newest disciple, she tells **the servants** of her friend the bride to **do whatever He says to you.** Though not knowing what her Son might do, she is confident He will help, for she (of all people) knows His heart.

Her insight is correct, and He comes to the aid of the bridal pair. In that place **there were six stone waterjars lying there,** which were used **for the cleansing of the Jews.** This water would have been used for the ceremonial washing of the guests' hands, which formed part of the ritual of every meal. **Each** waterjar had **room** *for* **two or three measures** (Gr. *metretes*), twenty or thirty gallons. He instructed the servants to **fill the waterjars with water** (perhaps adding some to the jars which had been partially emptied?) and then to **bring** some of that newly filled "water" **to the head-butler** (that is, to the one who was charged by the bridegroom with the task of coordinating the feast). St. John, ever with the eye for detail, says that they **filled** them right to *the* top.

The servants **brought** it as the Lord ordered, and the head-butler was delighted to taste this unexpected supply of good wine. He **did not know where** the wine **came from.** He only knew when he **tasted** it that it was good! He **calls the bridegroom** over to him and congratulates him on the vintage—though he comments on the bridegroom's strange arrangements! "Usually," he says (doubtless taking another long sip!), "**every man sets out the good wine first, and when all have gotten drunk** (and can't tell the good wine from the bad) *he sets out* **the poorer** *wine;* **you have kept the good wine until now!**" "What odd festal arrangements," he says (as he drains his cup).

John delights in the irony of the story. The head-butler (who had charge of the feast) did not know, though **the servants knew,** since they were **the ones who had drawn the water**. The bridal pair doubtless knew too—as did the Lord's **disciples**. It is to them, with their faith, that He **manifested His glory**, so that they now truly **believed in Him**. They could see how the water of Judaism (imaged by the six stone waterjars for Jewish rites of purification) was to be transformed by Christ into the rich heady wine of the Kingdom. As Christ changed water into wine, so would He change the lives of those in Israel (who knew only the Law) into lives replete with the glory of God.

ॐ ॐ ॐ ॐ ॐ

12 After this He went down to Capernaum, He and His mother and brothers, and His disciples, and there they remained not many days.

After this sign, Christ **went down to Capernaum**, doubtless to visit the families of Simon and Andrew, James and John, since that is where they lived and had their business (Mark 1:16–20, 29). He probably went by way of Nazareth, since John mentions that **His brothers** went with Him. It would seem as if **His disciples** Simon, Andrew, James, and John prevailed on Him and His Mother to come visit their families, and bring His own kin along too. Having become enthusiastic disciples of the Master, the One able to do such wonders, they wanted their families to be as close as possible. Christ obliged them with a visit, though a short one, since they **remained not many days**.

Why does John the Evangelist mention this? By mentioning Jesus' **disciples** as joining with His **mother and brothers**, John wants to make the point that discipleship to Christ means becoming part of His family. That is why, at the end of His ministry, Christ entrusts His Mother to the Beloved Disciple, John himself (19:26–27)—all who believe in Him are one family, and the closest of familial ties bind them all in one.

❧ III ❧

CHRIST'S MINISTRY TO ISRAEL
(2:12—12:50)

§III.1. First Visit to Jerusalem: Passover

§III.1.i. Cleansing the Temple and the Ensuing Controversy

St. John relates a cleansing of the Temple during this early time, occurring even before Christ came into Galilee and began His ministry in earnest. That is, it is related as occurring a good three years before the cleansing of the Temple recorded in the Synoptic Gospels, which is recorded as happening during the final days of the Lord's life prior to His crucifixion (e.g. Mark 11:15–18).

Though some have thought it unlikely that such an event would happen twice (and that therefore either John or the Synoptic Gospels have erred in recording when it happened), it is apparent that these were two different events. The Synoptic Gospels all record Christ as quoting Isaiah 56:7, about the Temple being a house of prayer for all nations, and saying that the Temple had been made into a thieves' cave; the Johannine account does not mention this. John mentions that Christ made a scourge from ropes (2:15); the Synoptics do not mention this. In John's account of the early cleansing, the reaction of those in the Temple is simply to challenge Jesus (2:18–20); in the Synoptic accounts, their reaction is a determination to destroy Him (Mark 11:18).

These reactions are quite consistent with the timing. When this first cleansing occurred, Christ had not yet begun His own ministry. That occurred only after John had been imprisoned (Mark 1:14). When Christ cleansed the Temple this first time, He was considered by most to have been John the Baptizer's disciple, and John's immense popularity doubtless protected Jesus from more extreme consequences from the Temple authorities. At the time of His second cleansing of the Temple at the end of His ministry, Jesus had been antagonizing the authorities for many months, and it was to be expected that His cleansing of the Temple would result not just in their challenging His authority to do so, but in their determination to destroy Him.

Some have thought it unlikely that if Jesus cleansed the Temple, the abuses would return. But nothing is more likely. After Jesus returned to Galilee, the moneychangers would doubtless return, probably immediately and certainly within an interval of three years. Also, if it had been three years since Christ uttered His enigmatic saying about raising up the sanctuary after it had been torn down, it would be reasonable that those who heard it such a long time before would not be able to accurately remember at His trial (compare Mark 14:57–59). If He had uttered this saying a mere week before, the failure of the witnesses to report it accurately would be harder to account for. In short, everything in the Gospels points to this event being a separate one from the later cleansing narrated by the Synoptics.

ॐ ॐ ॐ ॐ ॐ

13 And the Passover of the Jews was near, and Jesus went up to Jerusalem.

14 And He found in the Temple the ones selling oxen and sheep and doves and the coin-dealers seated.

15 And having made a scourge out of ropes, He cast out all from the Temple, both the sheep and the oxen, and He poured out the coins of the moneychangers and overturned their tables,

16 and to the ones selling the doves He said, "Take these things from here; do not make My Father's House a house of trade."

17 His disciples remembered that it was written,
     "The zeal for Your House will eat me up."
18 The Jews therefore answered and said to Him,
     "What sign do You show us, that You do these
     things?"
19 Jesus answered and said to them, "Destroy this
     sanctuary, and in three days I will raise it up."
20 The Jews therefore said, "Forty and six years
     was this sanctuary *in* building, and You *Your-
     self* will raise it up in three days?"
21 But that One was speaking of the sanctuary of
     His body.
22 When therefore He was raised from *the* dead,
     His disciples remembered that He said this; and
     they believed the Scripture and the word which
     Jesus had spoken.

Jesus **went up to Jerusalem** for **the Passover of the Jews** (Gr. *Pascha*). He **found in the Temple** courts **the ones selling oxen and sheep and doves and the coin-dealers seated** at their tables, changing local currency into the currency accepted in the Temple.

This was a comparatively recent abuse. Animals were also sold on the nearby Mount of Olives for use in sacrifice, and coin-dealers were available to convert the various currencies into the coinage accepted in the Temple. The existence of animal-sellers and coin-dealers was not the problem. The problem was the presence of these things *within the Temple courts themselves*. The authorities had allowed these stalls to be set up within the Court of the Gentiles, which was the only place the Gentiles had to pray within the Temple courts. The presence of such commerce turned the sacred place of prayer into an oriental bazaar and made their prayer there impossible. The **House** of the **Father** had been thus degraded into a common **house of trade** and haggling business (Gr. *emporion*). No wonder Christ was incensed at this recent abuse!

So it was that He made a **scourge out of ropes** and used it to **cast out all from the Temple**, whipping the animals, **both the sheep**

and the oxen, to drive them away. These stampeding beasts were followed by their owners, who chased after them (which is why the **all** is in the masculine in the Greek—*pantas* and not *panta*—for it refers to all the people there, along with their sheep and oxen). This is not an act of anger or violence directed at the animals, but rather is the only way to make the animals leave—as anyone who has tried to herd such creatures knows!

He then **poured out the coins of the moneychangers and overturned their tables** to drive them out as well. He directed the astonished coin-dealers (who no doubt rose up incredulous from their seats) to **take** those things **from here** in the Temple courts, and stop making the House of His Father into a common emporium. (We note that Christ refers to God as "**My Father**," and not "our Father" or "your Father," for He is claiming a special relationship to God not shared by anyone else. It is as the Son of God that He dares to cleanse the House of His Father.)

In narrating this story, St. John recounts the first time Christ entered into public controversy with the Jews. He does so to show how the certainty of the Cross was there at the beginning, and how it cast its long shadow over all Christ's ministry. The crucifixion was not a late development; it was foreordained from the beginning and was inevitable as soon as He began to do the Father's will. When the divine Light came into the darkness, there could be no other final result (compare 3:19). Thus the **disciples** later, after His Resurrection, **remembered that it was written** in Psalm 69:9: "**The zeal for Your House will eat me up.**" That is, His final destruction, that which would later eat Him up and consume Him at the Cross, was beginning even then. His zeal to do His Father's will and care for His House made it inevitable.

As He stood in the Temple courts, surrounded by surprised worshippers, some **Jews** came to challenge Him. Only a prophet had the right to overturn the decisions of the high priest and the Temple authorities. **What sign** did He **show** them that He was in fact such a prophet, that he dared to **do these things?**

The Cross was even then showing itself as a future certainty through their challenge. The hardheartedness which allowed the abuse and prompted the challenge would later cause them to **destroy** and crucify **the sanctuary of His body**. Yet even after they did this, **in three days** He would **raise it up**. His Resurrection would prove once and for all His authority to cleanse the Temple.

They did not understand the saying at all. In what would become a pattern (see 3:3–4; 4:10–12; 6:51–52; 7:34–35; 8:22, 32–36, 56–57), they insisted on understanding His words carnally, in the crassest, most physical way. When He challenged them to **destroy this sanctuary**, promising that in three days He would raise it up, they assumed that He was referring to the Temple He had just cleansed. That Temple was **forty and six years *in* building** and was even then not finished. And Jesus was claiming He could build it Himself in a mere three days! They thought this to be insane pride.

They also thought He was evading their challenge. They had demanded that He perform a miracle right there and then to vindicate and prove His authority. This He would always refuse to do (see Mark 8:11–12), for that would be to confirm them in their delusion that He was accountable to them in their wickedness. Yet He was not refusing their challenge, nor failing to give proof: His Resurrection, when it came, would be proof enough for any! However, when He said, "Destroy this sanctuary and in three days I will raise it up," it must have seemed to them as if He chose this test for the express purpose of avoiding the test—as if to say, "If you would just destroy the Temple, I would rebuild it; but since you can't destroy the Temple—well, obviously I can't rebuild it!" The confrontation therefore ended in a stalemate, since they did not understand that **that One** (the emphatic pronoun is used in the Greek) **was speaking of the sanctuary of His body**, not the Temple buildings themselves.

His disciples did not understand the meaning of His saying any more than the other Jews did, but later on, when **He was raised from *the* dead** and they were enlightened by the Spirit (compare 14:26), they **believed the Scripture and the word which Jesus had spoken**. These two things (the Old Testament Scripture and Jesus' word) are mentioned as one unit and one object of faith, for the Old Testament only finds its meaning and fulfillment in Jesus and

His Word. For John, it is only in the light of Christ's Resurrection that the Old Testament becomes comprehensible. The Jews who reject Christ are therefore incapable of understanding their own Scripture.

One final chronological note may be added. At the time of this Passover, Herod's Temple had been in the process of being built for forty-six years. Assuming, as is commonly thought, that work began on the Temple in about 19 BC, this Passover cleansing must have taken place about AD 27.

ॐ ॐ ॐ ॐ ॐ

23 Now when He was in Jerusalem at the Passover, in the festal *crowd*, many believed in His Name, observing His signs which He did.

24 But Jesus Himself was not entrusting Himself to them, for He knew all men,

25 and because He had no need that any witness about man, for He *Himself* knew what was in man.

St. John continues to discuss the result of this visit to **Jerusalem at the Passover**, when Jesus stood amidst **the festal *crowd***. The result of **His signs which He did** was that **many believed in His Name**. That is, they became His disciples, in that they identified themselves with Him and considered themselves as followers of His teaching. (This "believing in His Name" refers to the external act of becoming His disciples and adherents, and does not pronounce upon the internal state of those believing. Compare 8:31–37, where Jews who "believed Him" and had become His external followers were still uncomprehending, so that His word had "no place in them.")

What these signs were is not explained; perhaps they were miracles of healing. But Christ was not deceived into thinking that the external adherence these miracles produced meant that men gave Him their steadfast and immovable loyalty. John is clear that the fickleness of men, and the Cross which would result from it, were no surprise to Christ. **He *Himself* knew what was in man** and how they would finally turn against Him. He was no victim of circumstance, but freely embraced His ultimate death (compare 10:18). Though many **believed** and trusted in Him (Gr. *pisteuo*), He **was not entrusting Himself** (Gr. *pisteuo*) **to them** in return. As God, He could see what was to come (compare 16:30).

§III.1.ii. Conversation with Nicodemus

ॐ ॐ ॐ ॐ ॐ

3 1   Now there was a man of the Pharisees named Nicodemus, a ruler of the Jews;

2   this one came to Him by night and said to Him, "Rabbi, we know that You have come as a teacher from God; for no one is able to do these signs which You do unless God is with him."

3   Jesus answered and said to him, "Amen, amen, I say to you, unless one is born from above, he is not able to see the Kingdom of God."

John next records a conversation Jesus had with Nicodemus at some time during this visit to Jerusalem. Nicodemus is described as **a man of the Pharisees** and as **a ruler of the Jews**—that is, one of the Jerusalem Sanhedrin, though following the teachings of the Pharisees (most of the Sanhedrin were Sadducees). It is stressed that he came to Jesus **by night**. This was apparently so that he might have a long and uninterrupted conversation with Him (since Jesus was often busy during the day with teaching and healing). This seems to have been his motivation rather than fear of being detected, for certainly he had no compunction in standing up to his brothers in the Sanhedrin when Christ was being attacked (7:50–52), and later he joined Joseph of Arimathea in burying Him (19:39). But he seems to have been a man who had trouble in making up his mind and declaring himself. He was a good and fair man, but a bit muddled and ineffectual. (The external night around him therefore mirrored the interior darkness and confusion of his mind; compare 13:30, where the night's darkness mirrors Judas's inner darkness.)

Nicodemus approached Christ with great deference, addressing Him as **Rabbi**. He acknowledged that the Sanhedrin (or some of them!) knew that He had **come as a teacher from God**, being sent to enlighten Israel as a true prophet. How else could He **do these signs** which He did unless **God** were **with Him** and had sent Him as His prophet? Nicodemus thus presented himself as someone sent from the authorities to discuss ideas and receive instruction. The Sanhedrin were willing to be further taught: what would the prophet from Nazareth say to them about how to keep the Law?

Jesus knew only too well how much—or how little!—the Sanhedrin Nicodemus purported to speak for was willing to be taught. Jesus' teaching would cut through and overturn all their Jewish legalism. For them, salvation was in the Law, and they were asking for further illumination in how better to keep it. But salvation was not in the Law, but in humbly receiving new life through the Messiah. Christ therefore bypassed their whole concern with the Law and declared that salvation was a matter not of better keeping the Law, but of receiving new life. He stressed the certainty of it by prefacing His teaching with His customary oath, **Amen, amen, I say to you**. He told Nicodemus that **unless one is born from above, he is not able** even **to see the Kingdom of God** which was then breaking into the world through Him.

The phrase translated *born from above* is the Greek *gennethe anothen*. The word *anothen* is used in 3:31 and 19:11, where it also means "from above." The emphasis is not on the fact that it is *another* birth (being "born again"), though it is in fact another birth. The emphasis is rather on the *divine source* of the birth—one must receive life directly from heaven, so that one belongs no longer to the earth but to heaven. Nicodemus and his colleagues were concerned with how to keep the Law and with creating a godly social order; Christ informed them that such things were irrelevant to entering the Kingdom. The Kingdom of God was even then coming to men through Jesus, but they would not see and experience it if they rejected Him and confined their attention to mere Law-keeping.

༆ ༆ ༆ ༆ ༆

4   Nicodemus says to Him, "How is a man able to be born when he is old? Is he able to enter into his mother's womb a second time and be born?"

5   Jesus answered, "Amen, Amen, I say to you, unless one is born of water and *the* Spirit, he is not able to enter into the Kingdom of God.

6   "That which is born of the flesh is flesh, and that which is born of the Spirit is spirit.

7   "Do not marvel that I said to you, 'It is necessary for you to be born from above.'

8   "The wind blows where it wants and you hear the sound of it, but do not know where it comes from and where it is going to; thus is everyone who is born of the Spirit."

Nicodemus was baffled by such things. To him as a good Pharisee, the Law meant everything, and the idea of receiving life directly from God apart from the Law seemed preposterous. Besides, he believed that when the Kingdom of God came, it would come to all Jews equally, for it was a commonly held tenet that all Israel had a share in the age to come. To be born a Jew was all that was necessary. Christ's words seemed to deny that basic Jewish truth. For Nicodemus, the only birth that mattered was the physical one—the one that meant one was a Jew and not a Gentile. All Jews already had that birth—why did they need another? And how could they get it anyway? Could one get another Jewish birth **when he is old** or somehow **enter into his mother's womb a second time and be born?**

Jesus strives to teach Nicodemus that He is not talking about a physical birth, nor about salvation by race. **That which is born of** the flesh—such as pious Jews born from Jewish mothers—is still simply transient **flesh** and so cannot inherit the Kingdom, which consists of things which are **spirit** and eternal. To **enter into** that **Kingdom of God** with its eternal realities of spirit, one needed to be **born of water and *the* Spirit**. Thus Nicodemus should **not marvel** that He said to him that it was **necessary** for him to be **born from above** if he would enter the Kingdom, for only this new birth from above bestows a status of **spirit** through which one can enter the spiritual and eternal Kingdom. (The term *spirit* here means not simply that which is immaterial, but also that which is eternal—compare the use of the term in Is. 31:3.) Nicodemus should not hesitate to accept such realities, even though they transcend his reason. After all, he accepts the intangible reality of the unseen **wind**. It **blows where it wants**, so that he **hears the sound of it**. He does **not know where it comes from** nor **where it is going to**. But though the origins of the wind (Gr. *pneuma*) are beyond his power to fully understand, Nicodemus accepts the existence of the wind. It is even **thus** with **everyone** who is **born of the Spirit** (Gr. *pneuma*; the word for "wind" and "Spirit" being the same): their supernatural birth and origins might transcend his understanding as well, but he should accept this reality nonetheless.

The reality of receiving life from above is described by Christ as being "born of water and the Spirit." This is a reference to baptism, and would have been understood by John the Evangelist's hearers to denote nothing else. This was not anachronistic, for this whole discussion is placed within the larger context of John the Baptizer's ministry. This conversation with Nicodemus happened before John was thrown into prison, when Jesus was considered by many to be John's disciple or protégé. It is followed by John the Evangelist's description of Jesus coming into Judea and baptizing (3:22). Obviously, Nicodemus would have understood Jesus' reference to water to be a reference to the baptism He was administering, whereby He made disciples (see also 4:1). By saying that one must be born of water and the Spirit, Jesus is saying that one needs to repent and become His disciple, for it is only so that one will receive life from God.

ॐ ॐ ॐ ॐ ॐ

9 Nicodemus answered and said to Him, "How can these things be?"

10 Jesus answered and said to him, "Are you *yourself* the teacher of Israel, and do not know these things?

11 "Amen, amen, I say to you, we speak that which we know and witness that which we have seen, and you *all* do not receive our witness.

12 "If I told you earthly things and you do not believe, how will you believe if I tell you heavenly things?

13 "And no one has ascended into heaven but He who descended from heaven, the Son of Man.

14 "And as Moses exalted the serpent in the wilderness, thus also it is necessary for the Son of Man to be exalted,

15 "that all who believe may have eternal life in Him."

Once again, Nicodemus stumbles at such novelties and responds by asking, **"How can these things be?"** A Kingdom that bypasses all Jews who have not become disciples of Jesus flies in the face of all that he has been taught as a Jew. But Christ expects that Nicodemus's past experience as **the teacher of Israel** and a distinguished expert in the Scriptures would have prepared him to **know** and understand **these things** that He is speaking of. It is not that Nicodemus should have known them already; rather his reading of the Scriptures should have led him to the place where he could **receive** Christ's **witness** of these new realities.

But this is not the case. With some wistful sadness, Christ declares (prefacing it with His solemn **Amen, amen, I say to you**) that both He and John the Baptizer **speak that which** they **know** and **witness that which** they **have seen**, and yet Nicodemus and his Pharisee colleagues (the **you** is in the plural) do **not receive** their

witness. At this point in His ministry, Christ's work was not yet clearly differentiated from that of John the Baptizer, and many considered Him to be John's coworker, if not his disciple. So it is that Christ speaks of John and Himself as together constituting one witness, using the first person plural **we.** The Pharisees are rejecting John's work (see Luke 7:30; 20:5), and Christ here tells Nicodemus that his refusal to accept His words about the new birth means that he is rejecting His work too. But both John and Christ are declaring reliable truth, and are simply speaking and witnessing of realities they both **know** and have **seen.** Nicodemus should not balk at John's words, nor at Christ's apparently novel teaching.

Indeed, Christ is simply speaking of **earthly things,** of realities that can be experienced in this life and this present age. If Nicodemus does **not believe** these things, how could he possibly believe if Christ were to give further revelations and declare **heavenly things,** speaking to him about such transcendent realities as the joy and work of the angels (compare Luke 15:7, 10; Matt. 18:10)?

For Jesus is no mere religious teacher, dependent on human wisdom for His teaching. He is the messianic **Son of Man,** He **who descended from heaven,** and thus is able to declare heavenly realities. No one on earth has access to such knowledge, for **no one has ascended into heaven** from earth to visit there and return with such wisdom. Jesus alone is able to impart such wisdom, as the Son of God.

And this descent from heaven was not simply to teach. Christ descended from heaven to give life to the world—even through offering up His Body in death (compare 6:51). Using the Old Testament image of the life-giving **serpent** that **Moses exalted** and lifted up **in the wilderness** (Num. 21:9), Christ declares that His death also will give **eternal life** to **all who believe** and become His disciples.

It is doubtful that Nicodemus fully understands the import of this image—just as many of the Jews later will not understand Christ's words about His death (see 7:33–36). Nicodemus would remember the Old Testament story of Israel dying as a result of their sins, having been bitten by fiery serpents as God's judgment (Num. 21:6–7).

He would remember how Moses made a bronze image of the serpent and lifted it up on a pole as a sign of God's mercy, and how those who looked at it were healed (Num. 21:9). Jesus uses this image as a veiled prophecy of His own death, of the time when He will be lifted up on the wood of the Cross (compare John 12:32–33), giving life to those who look to Him with faith. For He has come not to bestow political and military liberation, but to bestow eternal life. He is not to be a military Messiah come to kill Israel's enemies; He is a spiritual Messiah come to die, and this death is **necessary** if He is to give eternal life to the world. But as with much of Christ's teaching, His words here are not understood.

This eternal life and blessedness in the age to come are given only **in Him**, for Christ is Himself the eternal life of the Father, so that to have Him is to have life and not to have Him is not to have life (1 John 5:12). This was very different from normal Jewish expectation, which thought that eternal life in the age to come would come to all Jews indiscriminately, simply because they were Jewish. Christ says, on the contrary, eternal life is in Him; to reject Him is to forfeit their hope of eternal life.

(Some versions translate v. 15 "that all who believe in Him may have eternal life," attaching the phrase "in Him" to the verb "believe." But this is contrary to John's use of the Greek, for when St. John uses the phrase "believe in Him," he always uses the preposition *eis*, "to believe *eis* Him," whereas the Greek of v. 15 here reads *en auto*, "*en* Him." John's point in v. 15 is thus not that the one who believes in Jesus has eternal life—though that is in fact true. John's point is that the eternal life the believer has is *in Jesus* and that eternal life is only given to Israel through faith in Christ.)

ℰ EXCURSUS

ON THE TERM "BELIEVE"

The word *believe* (Gr. *pisteuo*) occurs very often in John's Gospel—ninety-eight times, compared with eleven in

Matthew's Gospel, ten in Mark's Gospel, and nine in Luke's Gospel. This is consistent with John's polemical and aggressively evangelistic purpose. His aim is to convert those who do not believe and bring them to faith in Christ (20:31), and so he keeps the issue of believing/refusing to believe squarely in the forefront. "To believe or not to believe"— for John, that is the question!

The term *believe* is basic to John's Gospel, and describes the irreducible core of Christian commitment. It means to become Christ's follower, to acknowledge that one accepts His teaching, to become His disciple and to identify oneself with the other disciples. The word *believe* does not just refer to the inner psychological act of placing one's trust in Christ. Rather, it describes the outer commitment one makes with one's entire life. To believe, for John, means to join Christ's other followers as His disciple and to strive to live like one.

Many modern evangelical Protestants use the term somewhat differently. For them, "to believe" indeed means the psychological and volitional act of placing one's trust in something. "To believe" describes the moment of saving faith, and this mental act and commitment is to be radically distinguished from anything bodily that might accompany it (such as, for instance, baptism). Believing, according to this teaching, refers to the cerebral and inner processes alone; it describes the moment of inner assent.

It is an error to read this reduced meaning into John's use of the term. For John, to believe in Jesus refers not just to a moment of assent, or even the fact of assent. It refers to *the quality of one's life as a disciple*. It means to live as one of Christ's followers and as a part of His Church. This corporate (one may almost say ecclesial) dimension of believing is never far from John's mind. Believing in Christ is almost synonymous with *confessing* Him.

The term is, however, somewhat elastic. It can describe one who follows Christ in sincerity and zeal, as well as those who follow Him without truly committing themselves from the heart. (See 2:23 and 8:31 for examples of those who "believed" in Jesus without being truly converted within.) Just as it is possible to confess Christ outwardly and to be a part of the confessing group of disciples without having a deep and abiding loyalty to Him within, so it is possible to "believe" and yet not be truly His dedicated disciple.

That is why Christ challenges those who believe in Him to continue in His teaching and not turn back. It becomes not simply a matter of believing, but also of remaining, of abiding, of possessing "staying power." It is only as those who believe Him also "continue in His Word" that they will be "truly His disciples" and will find true freedom (8:31–32). It is only as those who believe Him also "abide and remain in Him" that they will "bear fruit" (15:4). During Christ's ministry, there were many who "believed" and heard Him gladly. The challenge was to continue to believe and to persevere as one of His followers when all others turned away (6:67–69).

§III.1.iii. John's Commentary on the Conversation with Nicodemus

Though there were no quotation marks in ancient manuscripts, what follows in vv. 16–21 is almost certainly St. John the Evangelist's commentary on the words of Christ, and not a continuation of His words. This may be seen in the vocabulary (the term "only-begotten" is elsewhere used only by John, as in 1:14, 18; 1 John 4:9) and by the fact that in v. 16, Christ's being given up to death on the Cross is spoken of in the past tense.

ॐ ॐ ॐ ॐ ॐ

16 For God loved the world thus, that He gave His only-begotten Son, that everyone who

> believes in Him might not be destroyed, but
> have eternal life.
> 17 For God did not send the Son into the world
> that He may judge the world, but that the
> world might be saved through Him.
> 18 He who believes in Him is not judged; he who
> does not believe has been judged already, be-
> cause he has not believed in the Name of the
> only-begotten Son of God.

Christ spoke to Nicodemus of His future lifting up on the Cross as giving eternal life to all in Israel who would believe in Him (vv. 14–15)—for certainly that is how Nicodemus would have understood Him. Their discussion was about Jesus' significance as a teacher come from God to Israel (v. 2) and how the Kingdom would come to His People who waited for it (3:3). The nation of Israel formed the unconscious parameters for any Jewish discussion of salvation. What St. John does is to bring out the meaning that was latent in Christ's words. Though Christ spoke of all those in Israel who believe being given eternal life (v. 15), this principle of salvation by faith means that *any* who believe in all the world will also be saved. St. John is not adding to Christ's meaning; he is simply illuminating its full significance in a wider and cosmic context.

Thus, John declares that **God loved** not just His chosen people, but the whole **world**, and that the gift of **His only-begotten Son** on the Cross means that **everyone who believes in Him**, whether Jew or Gentile, will **not be destroyed** and have his life end in mortal death and dissolution, but will **have eternal life**. The death of the body will not be the final word, nor will it last forever into the coming age. Rather, the one who trusts Jesus' word as His disciple will be raised up to eternal life and joy.

That is, **God did not send the Son** to destroy sinners. The Jews may have thought the Messiah was to come primarily **that He may judge** the Roman **world** and the oppressors of Israel and destroy them. On the contrary, Messiah has come **that the** whole **world**—Jew and Gentile—**might be saved through Him**. He has come not as a military conqueror, but as a Life-giver and a Savior.

And yet, because He has come with life for all, there is judgment in His coming in the flesh. All the world lies in the power of death and sin, and He has come to liberate them. Therefore, to accept Him and His word of forgiveness is *to accept in advance* the final verdict and forgiveness of God. In Christ, God has already, in this age, spoken His word of forgiveness, and to **believe in** Christ is to be **not judged** at the Last Day; it is to experience *even now* the future divine word of forgiveness that will lead to blessedness in the age to come. This means, of course, that to refuse Christ's word of forgiveness is to experience *even now* the divine word of judgment and condemnation. He who does **not believe** in Him, but rejects His claim to be Messiah and pushes away His proffered pardon, is **judged already,** for such a one rejects **the Name** and saving authority of **the only-begotten Son of God,** thereby rejecting the Father as well.

> ॐ ॐ ॐ ॐ ॐ
>
> 19 And this is the judgment, that the light is come into the world, and the men loved the darkness rather than the light, for their works were evil.
> 20 For everyone who practices base *things* hates the light and does not come to the light, lest his works should be exposed.
> 21 But he who practices the truth comes to the light that his works may be manifested as having been worked in God.

Thus, in the ministry of Christ, **the** final **judgment** is even now taking place, in that men's acceptance or rejection of Jesus determines how they will be judged on the Last Day. And such a verdict is not arbitrary. Rather, it is simply a mirror and result of the light or darkness that dwells in men.

Christ has come as **the light** of God **into the world**—and all are judged by how they react to the coming of this light. If they experience the judgment and condemnation of God, that is only because they **loved the darkness rather than the light**, since **their works were evil**. They instinctively shy away from the light, to shroud the base *things* they practice under cover of darkness. They do **not come to the light** of Christ, but reject Him, lest their **works** and hypocrisy **should be exposed**. They do not reject Jesus because *He* is an evildoer (compare 18:30), but because *they* are! The one who **practices the truth comes to the light** and accepts Jesus **that his works may be manifested as having been worked in God**. Such a one does not fear the light; rather, he welcomes it!

Jesus of Nazareth therefore forms the standard by which all will be judged. The righteous and humble of heart come to Him, and the evil and hardened of heart reject Him. It might seem to superficial eyes that the Cross is the world's judgment on Jesus, but this is not so—it is the world's judgment on itself.

§III.2. Into Judea

§III.2.i. The Witness of John the Baptizer

ॐ ॐ ॐ ॐ ॐ

22 After these things, Jesus and His disciples came into the land of Judea, and there He was spending *time* with them and baptizing.

23 And John also was baptizing in Aenon near Salim, because there was much water there, and they were coming and were being baptized.

24 For John had not yet been thrown into prison.

25 A debate occurred therefore between John's disciples and a Jew about cleansing.

26 And they came to John and said to him, "Rabbi, He who was with you beyond the Jordan, to whom you witnessed, behold, this One is baptizing and everyone is coming to Him."

St. John continues his narrative, saying that **after these things** and His time in Jerusalem that Passover, **Jesus and His disciples** then **came into the land of Judea**, perhaps near Jericho, and were **baptizing.** That is, He was proclaiming the imminence of the Kingdom, even as John the Baptizer did, and no doubt many thought of Him as John's disciple, successor, and protégé. Those who accepted Jesus' word of the coming Kingdom also accepted baptism from Him, and these would thereby consider themselves as His disciples to some extent. (One should not regard this baptism as full Christian baptism, such as later would be administered by the Church; that later baptism would bestow the Spirit, and John the Evangelist explicitly tells us that the Spirit could not yet be given, for Jesus had not yet been glorified; see 7:39.) Thus, Jesus' popularity continued to grow.

Not far away, John the Baptizer was working, **baptizing in Aenon near Salim** (exact modern location unknown). Some of **John's disciples** got themselves into a **debate** with **a Jew about** the topic of **cleansing** and purification. The nature of the debate is difficult to determine, but it seems to have involved Jesus' baptism, since John's disciples immediately brought this matter to John in the wake of the debate. Perhaps the Jew was comparing John's baptism to the cleansings and daily ablutions of the Qumran community and minimizing John's baptism as no more eschatologically significant than those daily immersions of the other desert dwellers. "After all," he might have reasoned, "why accept John's word? Why not accept the baptism of Jesus instead? He's baptizing too! The desert is full of these supposed prophets—what's so special about your John?" If this was the gist of the Jew's argument with the disciples of John, no wonder **they came** in perplexity to their teacher **John** to complain about the rising popularity of the Nazarene! **He who was with** John **beyond the Jordan** was threatening to overshadow His (supposed) mentor, and **everyone** was now **coming to Him!**

ॐ ॐ ॐ ॐ ॐ

27 John answered and said, "A man is not able to receive anything unless it has been given to him from heaven.

28 "You yourselves witness of me that I said, 'I
    myself am not the Christ,' but 'I have been sent
    before that One.'
29 "He who has the bride is *the* bridegroom; but
    the friend of the bridegroom, the one who
    stands and hears him, rejoices with joy because
    of the bridegroom's voice. Therefore this joy
    of mine has been made full.
30 "It is necessary for that One to grow, but for
    me to diminish."

John the Baptizer was not in the least distressed. Indeed, he
rejoiced. He responded to his disciples' well-intentioned but misguided indignation by reminding them that **a man is not able to
receive anything unless it has been given to him from heaven**. In
that context of messianic fulfillment, the popularity and rise of Jesus
represented the will and blessing of God. After all, John's disciples
had heard him say often enough that he himself (the pronoun is
emphatic) was **not the Christ**, but only one who had **been sent
before that One** as His Forerunner. Jesus of Nazareth was the designated Messiah, the One who would one day liberate Israel. Of course
His rise in popularity must be expected! John did not resent such
popularity, nor the fact that the hearts of all would (as he thought)
turn to Him. Such resentment would be absurd—like **the friend of
the bridegroom,** his "best man," resenting the bridegroom's good
fortune in having **the bride!** The bridegroom's "best man," **the one
who stands and hears him** take the bride, **rejoices with joy** (a
Hebraism for "rejoices greatly") because he hears the **bridegroom's
voice** and observes him fulfilling his destiny and taking his bride.
Therefore John's **joy**, he tells his disciples, also **has been made full.**
Jesus is the designated Messiah; it is **necessary for that One to grow**
and increase in popularity in Israel, while John himself must neces-
sarily **diminish** and step back when his task as Forerunner is com-
pleted. His time at center stage must pass away as the Kingdom
draws near.

§III.2.ii. John's Commentary on the Witness of John the Baptizer

Once again, St. John the Evangelist follows the words he narrates (in this case, the words of John the Baptizer) with his own Gospel commentary. (That the verses which follow are not the words of John the Baptizer may be seen from the vocabulary, for the vocabulary of "Father-Son" and of "witness" are characteristically Johannine.)

ॐ ॐ ॐ ॐ ॐ

31 He who comes from above is above all; he who is of the earth is from the earth and speaks of the earth. He who comes from heaven is above all.

32 What He has seen and heard, of this He witnesses; and no one receives His witness.

33 He who has received His witness has *set his* seal *to this*, that God is true.

34 For He whom God has sent speaks the words of God, for He does not give the Spirit by measure.

35 The Father loves the Son and has given all things into His hand.

36 He who believes in the Son has eternal life; but he who disobeys the Son will not see life, but the wrath of God remains on him.

Once again, John the Evangelist reflects on the contemporary significance of the conversation he has reported. John the Baptizer has confessed his own inferiority to Christ. John the Evangelist continues to elaborate this contrast between the two men, showing that it is of more than local and temporary significance, but is cosmic and eternal in scope. It is not just that Christ was more popular on the local stage of Israel, winning the hearts of that generation as the fashion of the day ebbed and flowed. His popularity and rise happened because those who heard Him recognized something divine and transcendent in His words.

Thus, John the Baptizer, though a true prophet, was nonetheless **of the earth**, in that his origins were merely earthly. He was **from the earth** in that his experiences were limited to earthly realities, and the message he **speaks** is also **of the earth**. This is not to denigrate him. He spoke the message God gave him to speak—of repentance from sin and living a life of righteousness (see Luke 3:10–14). And though this was truly God's message given to His prophet John, yet it was still but a message revealing the only reality John himself experienced—that of a life of holiness in this age and on this earth.

It is otherwise with Christ, **He who comes from heaven**. Christ is **above all**, and speaks the heavenly realities **He has seen and heard** from the Father in heaven. It is of these transcendent realities—things normally beyond discovery by earthly man—that **He witnesses**, even though **no one receives His witness**. Thus Jesus is not John's protégé or his successor. He is altogether different from him, for Jesus is of heavenly and eternal origin, not earthly or temporal. Jesus was **sent** by **God** into the world with the fullness of revelation from the Father, so that He **speaks** the very **words of God**. Jesus is not like the rabbis, offering His own insights into God's Law and will. All of His words are the Father's words, and thus are spirit and life (8:28; 6:63). The one who hears the words and **receives His witness**, accepting His teaching, *sets his* **seal** to it, and knows in himself **that God is true**. That is, the one who receives Christ's teaching does not just know that Jesus' teaching is true; he recognizes it as the true words of God spoken through Him. God **does not give the Spirit by measure** to Jesus, as He does to mere men. Rather, God pours the fullness of His infinite Spirit upon Him, since He is His own Son. **The Father** thus **loves the Son**, and **has given all things into His hand**; there is nothing He does that He does not share with His coequal and coeternal Son. Thus, **he who believes in the Son has eternal life**, for the Son has the life of the

Father to give to those who believe in Him. Likewise, **he who disobeys the Son will not see life**; rather, **the wrath of God remains on him**, for such a one has rejected the true Son of God.

☙ EXCURSUS

ON THE RELATIONSHIP OF JESUS AND JOHN THE BAPTIZER

The relationship between Jesus and John the Baptizer is difficult to trace with accuracy since so little is mentioned in the Gospels, and what is mentioned (especially in the Synoptic Gospels of Matthew, Mark, and Luke) focuses almost entirely on John's role as Forerunner. Nonetheless, if we "connect the dots" between the few facts given to us, the following outline emerges.

John was called by God to bring Israel to a state of spiritual readiness, to call them to repentance so that they would not be destroyed with the world's sinners in the imminent messianic cataclysm. Messiah was coming to bless the righteous and destroy the unholy—let unholy Israel repent if they would not be destroyed! John's ministry was thus not confined to revealing Jesus as the designated Messiah, though naturally this is the main focus of the Gospels. John also was charged by God with the transformation of Israel, to prepare the nation for the coming messianic redemption (Luke 1:17). Thus, he would continue with his prophetic work even after the baptism of Jesus, for the nation had not yet been transformed. (This transformation had a political element as well, which is why John rebuked the ruler Herod for his sins; see Mark 6:18.)

Jesus identified Himself with John and his movement, even to the point of seeking baptism (though this was not for His own sins—for He was sinless—but out of solidarity with sinners, whom He came to save). John knew Jesus prior to His coming to him for baptism, for when He came for baptism, John protested that Jesus was more righteous than himself, and that He needed no baptism (Matt. 3:14). (This prior knowledge was only to be expected, since Jesus' Mother knew the mother of John; see Luke 1:36–56.) It was during Jesus' baptism that John had his vision, in which he saw the Spirit descending as a harmless and pure dove upon Jesus. This was the prearranged sign John had been given by God, by which he would know who was to be the future Messiah.

It is important not to anachronistically read a fully formed and later Christology into John's understanding of the role of Messiah. It seems that, like many of his generation, he expected Messiah to have a political role (for had not John himself been given a political role in rebuking Herod?). He seems to have expected Jesus, as the One designated to later fulfill the role of Messiah, to challenge the powers of His day, and he was perplexed when He did not do so. That was why, after John's imprisonment, he sent messengers to Jesus to challenge Him to act (see Matt. 11:2–6)—for if He *was* the Messiah as John had thought, why did He not begin to challenge the status quo and destroy the sinners?

The early chapters of John's Gospel focus on the early works of Jesus *before* John the Baptizer was imprisoned (3:24). As such, these chapters narrate a time earlier than that narrated by the Synoptics, for they begin their story of Christ's ministry *after* John had been imprisoned (Matt. 4:12; Mark 1:14). (This is pointed out by Eusebius in his *Ecclesiastical History*, 3, 24.) In these early days, it would seem that Christ's ministry was not greatly differentiated from John's— for it was only after John's imprisonment that He came into Galilee and settled in Capernaum, calling the disciples and supporters He had made (see John 1:35—2:12) to leave everything and follow Him (Mark 1:14–20). Prior to His settling in Capernaum, it must have seemed to outsiders that His cause and message and John's were the same, as they both worked on parallel tracks.

That is why the baptism Jesus gave is not contrasted as being of a different kind from John's—for both baptisms were at this stage simply the prescribed way of publicly assenting to Jesus' (and John's) message. That is also why John the Evangelist does not stress Jesus' work of baptizing during His earthly ministry (and why the Synoptics do not mention it at all). For the readers of the Gospels had all been baptized with a fully Christian, post-Pentecost baptism—one in which they were immersed thrice in the Name of the Trinity, in which they received the new birth and gift of sonship and the Pentecostal Spirit. None of these blessings was given through baptism during Christ's ministry, for these blessings depended on Christ being raised and glorified—as John the Evangelist himself reminds us (7:39). If the Gospels stressed Christ baptizing during His ministry, the readers would inevitably—and anachronistically—conclude that people then received the same kind of baptism during Christ's ministry that they themselves had received after Pentecost—which was not the case. Therefore the Gospels do not stress the pre-Pentecost baptisms of Christ, lest this give the readers the wrong impression.

At this early stage of ministry, therefore, John and Jesus appeared to many to be two prongs of one messianic movement—related perhaps as teacher to successor, as mentor to protégé. It was only after John's imprisonment that it became apparent that Jesus was something more, and that He had a message and work unique to Himself. For though Christ's message of the imminent Kingdom was the same as John's (compare Matt. 3:2; 4:17), He was not simply continuing John's work. Rather, He was Himself the bringer and embodiment of the Kingdom, the Messiah (as John the Baptizer had said to his intimate disciples; see John 1:35) and the Savior of the world.

The following is presented as an aid to integrating the chronology of John's Gospel with those of the Synoptics.

1.   Jesus is baptized by John (Mark 1:9; Matt. 3:13–17).

2.   Jesus spends forty days being tempted in the wilderness (Mark 1:12; Matt. 4:1–11).

3.   The "Week of Witness" occurs (John 1:19—2:11), beginning at the end of Jesus' forty days, with Jesus returning during Day 3 of the week (John 1:35f). Jesus gathers disciples of His own; He secretly turns water into wine at the wedding in Cana (John 1:43f; 2:1f).

4.   Jesus goes to Jerusalem with His newfound disciples (John 2:13); He cleanses the Temple (John 2:14f), does miracles (John 2:23), and speaks with Nicodemus (John 3:1f).

5.   Jesus returns to Judea and continues working as part of John's movement (John 3:22).

6.   John is arrested and imprisoned.

7.   Jesus returns home to Galilee and settles in Capernaum, calling disciples to radical commitment to Himself (Mark 1:16f; John 4:43).

8.   At some later point, John in prison sends messengers to Jesus to challenge Him to political action (Matt. 11:2f).

9.   John is later executed; Jesus withdraws and continues His ministry (Mark 6:29–31).

§III.3. Into Samaria

§III.3.i. The Conversation with the Samaritan Woman

ॐ ॐ ॐ ॐ ॐ

4 1   When therefore the Lord knew that the Pharisees had heard that Jesus was making and baptizing more disciples than John

2   (although Jesus Himself did not baptize, but His disciples *did*),

3   He left Judea, and departed again into Galilee.

John the Evangelist calls attention to the beginning of **the Phari-sees'** opposition. **The Lord knew** the rumors they had heard—that **Jesus was making and baptizing more disciples than John!** In order to avoid an immediate conflict with them, **He left Judea** (where the opposition was centered) and **departed again** into the relative safety of His own land of **Galilee**. (It is possible that John was taken in custody by Herod about this time. If that is true, then Christ's withdrawal into Galilee had the advantage of preventing a confron-tation with Herod also.)

With his customary concern for historical accuracy, John the Evangelist adds that the rumors were not entirely correct—**Jesus Himself did not** actually **baptize** any of His supporters, **but His disciples** *did* the baptizing. The Lord perhaps left the disciples to do the actual work of baptizing for the same reason that in Mark 6:41 He gave the miraculous bread to the crowds through His dis-ciples' hands and not directly Himself—because He willed to use His disciples and the Church as the instruments of His own power. Just as He would use His Church as His hands to bless the world after His Ascension, so here He accustomed His disciples to be employed in this way.

ॐ ॐ ॐ ॐ ॐ

4   And it was necessary for Him to pass through Samaria.

5   So He comes to a city of Samaria called Sychar, near the plot *of land* that Jacob gave to his son Joseph;

6   and Jacob's fountain-*fed well* was there. Jesus therefore, being wearied from His journey, was sitting thus by the fountain-*fed well*. It was about the sixth hour.

7   There comes a woman of Samaria to draw water.

On His way from Judea to Galilee, **it was necessary for Him to pass through Samaria**, for that was the direct route. On the way through, **He comes to a city of Samaria called Sychar** (present location; it is possibly to be identified with modern Askar). (The present tense is used in the following narrative, allowing us to follow our Lord in His conversation with the woman at the well.) In this city, there was a **plot *of land* that Jacob gave to his son Joseph**, and on this plot of land there was **a fountain-*fed well*** (the Gr. word is *pege*, the usual word for fountain or spring; compare its use in Rev. 8:10 and for the internal fountain of blood within the hemorrhaging woman in Mark 5:29). Jesus was **wearied from His journey**. It was **about the sixth hour** (that is, about noon), and the sun was beating down on Him. The disciples therefore left Him by Himself, **sitting by the fountain-*fed well*** to rest, while they went away into the nearby city to buy food (see v. 8). Like all travelers, they would have had with them a skin-bucket to use to draw water, but this was with the disciples and not available for Jesus to use when He wanted it. As He rested by the well, **there comes a woman of Samaria to draw water.**

John the Evangelist records their conversation at some length—which fact also requires comment. He recorded other conversations of Christ with His adversaries (in chs. 6–12) so that the Christians might learn how to deal with their own arguments with unbelievers, and he records Christ's conversations with His disciples (in chs. 13–16) that the Christians might be comforted in the midst of their afflictions. But why does John spend so much time recording this conversation with an otherwise insignificant person, a foreigner and a woman at that?

The answer is that John records Christ's conversation at such length precisely because He spent such time and care talking to a foreigner (that is, a Samaritan) and a woman. Such things were not done in Israel—the Jews hated the Samaritans (to call a Jew a Samaritan was to curse him; compare 8:48) and pious rabbis certainly did not speak with women in public. But John makes the point here that Christ came to transcend the limitations of Israel and Judaism. The limitations and exclusivity of Judaism were indeed of divine appointment—but they had served their purpose, and now their time was over. Formerly men were called to worship as Jews, and to commune with Israel's God in Jerusalem. But now Christ was calling Israel and all the world—even the hated and foreign Samaritans—to a new way of access to God (v. 21). John records Christ's conversation with the Samaritan woman in such detail and at such great length because it witnesses to the inbreaking of this new spiritual reality.

ॐ ॐ ॐ ॐ ॐ

7   Jesus says to her, "Give Me a drink."
8   For His disciples had gone away into the city to buy food.
9   The Samaritan woman therefore says to Him, "How is it that You, being a Jew, ask a drink from me, being a Samaritan woman?" (For Jews do not use the same *vessels* as Samaritans.)

As One who came to seek the lost sheep, Christ makes the first move—and a shocking one. The woman was no doubt going about her daily task of drawing water, pointedly ignoring this Jew sitting close to her, pretending that He didn't exist. Jesus startles the woman by saying to her, **"Give Me a drink."** It was, in one sense, a natural thing to do: He was thirsty, He did not have the skin-bucket with Him, and the woman did have a bucket.

The woman, however, was shocked—and perhaps a little hostile. As a Samaritan, she would have had no more love for Jews than they had for her. It was highly irregular for a man to address a woman like that in public, especially a Jewish man addressing a Samaritan woman. And to ask to use her bucket to drink from! Jews considered Samaritan drinking vessels ritually unclean and would never use one. (St. John explains that **Jews do not use the same *vessels* as Samaritans.**) What was going on? In responding, **"How is it that You, being a Jew, ask a drink from me, being a Samaritan woman?"** the woman was not so much asking a question as rebuking His supposed presumption.

> 10 Jesus answered and said to her, "If you knew
> the gift of God, and who it is who says to you,
> 'Give Me a drink,' you *yourself* would have
> asked Him and He would have given you liv-
> ing water."
> 11 She says to Him, "Lord, You have no bucket to
> draw with, and the well is deep; from where
> then do You have the living water?
> 12 "Are You greater than our father Jacob, who
> gave us the well and drank of it himself and his
> sons and his cattle?"
> 13 Jesus answered and said to her, "All who drink
> of this water will thirst again;
> 14 "but whoever drinks of the water which I *My-
> self* will give him will never ever thirst, but the
> water which I will give him will become in him
> a fountain of water leaping up to eternal life."
> 15 The woman says to Him, "Lord, give me this
> water, that I may not thirst, nor come here to
> draw *water*."

The Lord is not offended at her refusal. He simply counters
that if she knew what **the gift of God** is (and how close it is!) and
who it is who says to her, **"Give Me a drink,"** she **would have asked
Him and He would have given** her **living water.** (One can almost
see the smile beginning to play on our Lord's lips as he places the
divine bait of truth before this Samaritan fish.)

The woman's answer is instantaneous, self-confident—and re-
tains a bit of her Samaritan hostility to this strange Jew. It seems to
her as if Jesus is talking jingoistic Jewish nonsense—as if the Jews
were so good they could provide water from a well without a bucket!
Is this Jewish one-upmanship or what? She quickly calls Him to
account, reacting to what she takes to be Jewish pride. **"Lord,"** she
says (Gr. *Kyrie*, meaning "Sir" in this context), **"You have no bucket**

to draw with, and the well is deep; from where then do you have access to this **living water?**" In other words, she is (she thinks) calling His bluff. Is He **greater**, she demands, **than our father Jacob, who gave us the well** himself? (We note how the Samaritan woman appropriates the Jewish Patriarchs to herself, saying the Samaritans, not the Jews, are the true heirs of the Fathers.)

The Lord then begins to clarify. He is not talking about the water in the well—that is no divine gift, for **all who drink of this water will thirst again.** No, He is speaking of a different kind of water—spiritual, not physical. (We note that the Samaritan woman misunderstands Him in the same way as Nicodemus did; see 3:4.) **Whoever drinks of the water** Jesus alone can give (the pronoun is emphatic in the Greek) **will never ever thirst**, for that **water will become in him a fountain of water leaping up to eternal life.** Christ is speaking of the Holy Spirit, the divine life all His disciples will receive at baptism (compare 7:37–39). The water the Samaritan woman has to offer can slake thirst only for a few hours. Water is indeed life, but the mere physical and biological life of this age, and all that life is doomed to end in death. The water Christ has to offer is the spiritual water and new life of the age to come, a life eternally renewed and unfailing.

The Samaritan fish takes the bait, and the woman is hooked. She still, however, thinks that Christ is speaking of physical water and physical thirst, and thinks only of how this miraculous water will save her any more trips to the well. She responds, "**Lord** (that is, "Sir"), **give me this water, that I may not thirst, nor come here** to the well **to draw** *water*."

ॐ ॐ ॐ ॐ ॐ

16 He says to her, "Go, call your husband and come here."

17 The woman answered and said, "I do not have a husband." Jesus says to her, "You have well said, 'A husband I do not have,'

18 "for you have had five husbands, and the one

> whom you now have is not your husband; this
> you have said truly."
>
> 19 The woman says to Him, "Lord, I observe that
>   You *Yourself* are a prophet.
> 20 "Our fathers worshipped in this mountain, and
>   you *yourselves* say that in Jerusalem is the place
>   where it is necessary to worship."

If the woman is indeed to experience new life, it is necessary for her to come to repentance, and to offer all her life to God. So, to bring her to repentance and self-knowledge, the Lord tells her first to **go** and **call** her **husband**. Only then can He begin to give her new life.

Her matrimonial status is not something the woman wants to dwell on. She has either a sinful or a very unfortunate past, having **had five husbands** before and being now attached to one who is **not** her **husband**. Doubtless that is why she comes to the well to draw water during the sixth hour, at the hottest part of the day—for then she is the least likely to meet other women drawing water. She is apparently notorious in her village, and probably shunned by the respectable women there.

Her reply to the Lord is very short, a mere three words in the Greek: *ouk exo andra*, and we can almost hear her voice drop as she quietly mutters the words. She is anxious to change the subject and hopes that her negative reply will draw a veil over her past.

But it is not to be, for Christ can see into the hearts of men, and is determined to draw the fish into His saving net. He reveals His knowledge of her past in a few words—while agreeing with her! **You have well said**, He replies (with a wry smile?), "**A husband I do not have**" (the word order here in the Greek is different than in the woman's reply, with the word *husband* coming at the head of the sentence for emphasis), **for you have had five husbands, and the one whom you now have is not your husband; this you have said truly**. By her short three-word reply, the woman wants to avoid the topic; by His long reply, Christ opens wide the unwelcome subject. We can almost see the woman's face redden as He speaks. But the Lord does not simply reveal her past, He also stresses the truth-fulness of her reply, saying that she has spoken truer than she knew. He thus wants to commend her for her confession of the truth (even if made reluctantly) in order to encourage her to continue speaking the truth. She has spoken well and truly—let her continue to face her past and find the way to repentance!

Christ's supernatural knowledge of her hidden past leads the woman to recognize Him as a **prophet**, for only a prophet could know such things (compare Elisha's supernatural knowledge of Gehazi's hidden sins in 2 Kin. 5:25–26). Turning from her past to a more welcome subject, she addresses the central controversy sepa-rating the Samaritans from the Jews—the question of access to God. The Samaritans had a rival view of sacred history. For them, the whole progression of history from David onward was one long wrong turn, leading to a dead end. For them, God had not made any cov-enant with David, nor sent the prophets Isaiah, Jeremiah, or the rest, nor authorized the transfer of the Ark to the Temple in Jerusa-lem. No access could be had to God's Presence through the Temple in Jerusalem. The **fathers** had **worshipped** God **in this mountain** of Gerizim, near where they are now standing, building altars there in Samaria (Gen. 12:7; 33:20). Access to God and His true temple could only be through this place. The Jews, however (the plural **you** is emphatic in the Greek), in contradiction to these obvious facts, alleged that **Jerusalem is the place where it is necessary to worship** and to access the saving Presence of God. Jesus obviously is a prophet—what does He have to say about this central controversy?

ॐ ॐ ॐ ॐ ॐ

21 Jesus says to her, "Woman, believe Me, an hour is coming when neither in this mountain, nor in Jerusalem will you worship the Father.

22 "You *yourselves* worship what you do not know; we *ourselves* worship what we know, for salva-tion is from the Jews.

23 "But an hour is coming and now is, when the

> true worshippers will worship the Father in
> Spirit and truth, for indeed the Father is seek-
> ing such ones to worship Him.
> 24 "God *is* spirit, and it is necessary for those who
> worship Him to worship in Spirit and truth."

The woman is talking about religion, about realities of this age. Christ has come to transcend religion and bring in the realities of the age to come. He preempts and refuses to enter into the debate separating Jew and Samaritan. The time for religious realities is quickly passing away. He addresses her with the respectful title **Woman** (or "Madam" as we should say) and urges her to **believe** Him that such debates are fruitless. For **an hour is coming when neither in this mountain** of Gerizim **nor in Jerusalem** will they **worship the Father.** Soon the time for all earthly temples will pass, and animal sacrifices on stone altars will not be required to gain access to the saving Presence. That does not mean, however, that the sacred history of the Jews is invalid (as the Samaritans allege). On the contrary, the Samaritans (the **you** is emphatic in the Greek) **worship** what they do **not know**; their interpretation of sacred history is erroneous and their attempted worship on Gerizim futile. The Jews (the **we** is emphatic also) **worship** what they **know** and have saving experience of, for **salvation** is indeed **from the Jews.**

But though Israel's history and Scriptures are true, another page is being turned. **An hour is coming** and is **now** upon them, **when the true worshippers will worship the Father in Spirit and truth**, for **the Father** is even now, through Jesus, **seeking such ones to worship Him.** Through Jesus, God is seeking true worshippers, those men and women who can experience true communion with God and to whom God can reveal Himself. Soon (and through close discipleship to Jesus, even now) there will be access to God in the Spirit and in truth. **God *is* spirit** Himself—that is, He is transcendent and above all earthly realities and limitations. Thus it is fitting and **necessary** that to truly experience His Presence in all its fullness, the worshipper must himself **worship in Spirit and truth.**

Spirit and *truth* are not used here as mere synonyms for interiority and sincerity; the Lord is not simply saying that those who approach God must do so from their deepest heart, and not merely in word alone. That is true, but it is not much of a revelation. Every devout Jew and Samaritan already knew that, and they approached God from their deepest heart and in true sincerity already. The issue here is not the attitude one must bring to worship; it is the question of *access*. The question separating Jew and Samaritan was, "How does one access the Presence of God—in Gerizim or in Jerusalem?" Christ says that the new reality He brings makes that question outdated and moot—one now is to access the Presence of the Father by the Holy Spirit He will give (see Eph. 2:18) and through the truth of the Father's word and promise given by Jesus (see John 17:14, 17). The transcendent and spiritual God will be approached through these transcendent and spiritual realities, not through physical altars and animal sacrifices.

ॐ ॐ ॐ ॐ ॐ

25 The woman says to Him, "I know that Messiah is coming" (He who is called Christ); "when that One comes, He will announce all things to us."
26 Jesus says to her, "I *Myself* who speak to you am *He*."

The woman finds this a bit overwhelming, as her whole world is being turned upside down. She declines to discuss it further with Him. Such controversies will only be solved when **Messiah** comes (John translates this as **Christ** for his readers). **When that One comes,** she says, **He will announce all things to us.** Like the Jews, the Samaritans also anticipated a coming Deliverer. They referred to Him as the *Taheb*, the Restorer. He was to come as a teacher (not a king, as in the Jewish expectation), and when He came, He would **announce all things** and unravel such mysteries. Jesus replies, "**I** *Myself* (the pronoun is emphatic) **who speak to you am** *He*." The

Samaritan hopes also are to be fulfilled in Him, and His word about such things can be taken as definitive and final.

ॐ ॐ ॐ ॐ ॐ

27 And at this *time* His disciples came, and they marveled that He was speaking with a woman; however, no one said, "What do You seek?" or "Why do You speak with her?"

28 So the woman left her waterpot and went into the city and says to the men,

29 "Come, see a man who told me all the things I ever did. Surely this is not the Christ?"

30 They went out of the city and were coming to Him.

31 In the meanwhile the disciples were asking Him, saying, "Rabbi, eat."

32 But He said to them, "I *Myself* have food to eat which you *yourselves* do not know about."

33 The disciples therefore were saying to one another, "Surely no one brought Him *anything* to eat?"

34 Jesus says to them, "My food is to do the will of Him who sent Me, and to perfect His work.

35 "Do you *yourselves* not say, 'There are yet four months, and *then* the harvest comes'? Look, I say to you, lift up your eyes and behold the fields, that they are already white for harvest.

36 "He who reaps is receiving a reward and is gathering fruit for life eternal, that he who sows and he who harvests may rejoice together.

37 "For in this *instance* the word is true, 'One sows and another harvests.'

38 "I *Myself* sent you to harvest that for which you *yourselves* did not toil; others have toiled, and you *yourselves* have entered into their toil."

As the Lord was finishing His discussion with the Samaritan woman (given the name Photina by the Church, meaning "one who has been enlightened"), the disciples returned from the Samaritan village where they had gone to buy food. They **marveled that He was speaking with a woman**, for pious rabbis did not speak with women like this in public. Despite their astonishment (and amidst their suppressed muttering to each other?), **no one said** to the woman, **"What do you seek?"** or challenged her, nor did they say to the Lord, **"Why do you speak with her?"** Instead, they kept silence while their Lord finished speaking with the woman.

The woman was equally astonished at discovering that the strange Jew who had asked to share her waterpot was a prophet—and one who claimed to be Messiah. In great excitement, she **left her waterpot** there by the well and **went into the city** nearby to tell the men of her discovery. She could scarcely believe it herself. **"Come, see a man who told me all the things I ever did,"** she cried out breathlessly to those sitting in the public square. **"Surely this is not the Christ?"**

She did not intend to be away for long, which is why she left her waterpot behind in her excited haste. She would soon return with men from the city, who would themselves (she hoped) confirm what she scarcely dared hope. The Lord, therefore, did not want to begin the planned-for long and leisurely meal with the disciples. When they offered Him some of the food they had come back with, and urged Him, saying, **"Rabbi, eat,"** He would not settle down to eat with them. He still had work to do, for the woman would return soon, bringing others from the Samaritan city. The disciples might find satisfaction in eating the food they had bought; *He* has **food to eat which** they (as spiritual outsiders; both the pronouns I and **you** are emphatic in the Greek) **do not know about**.

As the Samaritan woman could not grasp spiritual realities (v. 11), so the disciples misunderstand Christ's words as well, and suppose that one of them somehow sneaked back to bring Him something to eat. Christ, however, speaks of the spiritual satisfaction and joy of obedience, saying that His **food is to do the will of Him who sent Me, and to perfect His work**. That work is not yet finished or perfected—He is in the midst of gathering in the Samaritan souls who are even now streaming down the road to see Him.

The disciples are concerned for their own comfort (and hungry for their meal!). They think they have plenty of time to rest and still do their apostolic work. Are they thinking, the Lord asks, of the popular proverb, "**There are yet four months, and *then* the harvest comes**"? (This seems to have been a popular saying justifying procrastination, like our modern cry, "We've still got lots of time!") Christ denies that this is so. The time for harvesting is not far off—it is upon them already! Now is the time to work, not to eat and rest! He bids them **lift up** their **eyes and behold the fields**. They are **already white for harvest**, and there is work to do.

The phrase *white for harvest* needs some explaining, for grain turns golden when it is ready to harvest, not white. It seems our Lord was not speaking of the realities of agriculture they had seen in the fields, but the realities of spiritual harvest that were before their eyes then. What He bade them lift up their eyes to behold was the many men who were even then streaming out of the city to approach them, with their white robes glistening in the noonday sun. Now was the time to talk with them (even though they were Samaritans) and to harvest, for this would bring **a reward** in the Kingdom of God. If they would do this, they would **gather fruit for life eternal**. Their task as His disciples was even then to reap the harvest that had been long prepared. The time for reaping had come—but only because the harvest had been sown long ago.

For the harvest had indeed been long in the preparation. Even as the old proverb said, "**One sows and another harvests**," so it was in this case. (The proverb doubtless celebrated an uncommon happenstance. Usually, the same farmer both sowed and reaped his own harvest, but sometimes another would have to finish his work for him. It was this occurrence that popular wisdom celebrated.) In this case, the disciples were called to finish the work begun by others—that is, the saints and sages and prophets who came before them. Throughout all Israel's long history, they had prepared for this final harvest. These others **toiled**, and the disciples were now called to **enter into their toil**. That is, Christ's work was the culmination and goal of Israel's long salvation history. Thus the saints of old who **sowed** and the disciples who now **harvested** could **rejoice together**, for they were engaged in the same holy task. (Compare 8:56, where Abraham is said to rejoice in the work of Christ.)

§III.3.ii. Witness of Samaritans

ॐ ॐ ॐ ॐ ॐ

39 And from that city many of the Samaritans believed in Him, because of the word of the woman who witnessed, "He told me all that I did."
40 So when the Samaritans came to Him, they were asking Him to remain with them, and He remained there two days.
41 And many more believed because of His word;
42 and they were saying to the woman, "It is no longer because of your speaking that we believe, for we have heard for ourselves and know that this One is truly the Savior of the world."

The following discussions with the men of the city are not related in any depth. John simply says that **many of the Samaritans believed in Him** (that is, they came to listen to His teaching; a formal and dedicated discipleship is not envisioned in v. 39). They believed and came to hear Him **because of the word of the woman** that she first said when she hurried into the city. They **were asking Him to remain with them** in their city, that they might hear for themselves, and when He did, **many more believed because of His word**. And they admit this to the woman themselves. They no longer have to take her word for it; they have **heard for** themselves **and know that this One is truly the Savior of the world**. That is, He was indeed the promised *Taheb*, the messianic restorer they were expecting. John stresses the title *the Savior of the world,* for he is concerned to show the universality of Christ's mission. Jesus was not just the Messiah of the Jews; He was sent to save the whole world—Samaritans and even Gentiles as well (see 10:16).

§III.4. Into Galilee

§III.4.i. Journey to Galilee

ॐ ॐ ॐ ॐ ॐ

43 And after the two days He went out from there into Galilee.

44 For Jesus Himself witnessed that a prophet does not have honor in his own home town.

45 Therefore when He came into Galilee, the Galileans welcomed Him, having seen all the things He did in Jerusalem in the festal *crowd*, for they themselves also went to the feast.

After two days staying with the Samaritans, Jesus continued from Samaria **into Galilee**, His original destination (vv. 3–4). His experiences there would fulfill what He **Himself witnessed** and bore testimony to—**that a prophet does not have honor in his own home town.**

In referring to Jesus' witness that a prophet is usually dishonored and unrecognized among his own people, John was evidently referring to a saying of Christ that his readers already knew by heart (compare Mark 6:4; Luke 4:24). John does not report Jesus as saying this directly, nor does he narrate the occasion that prompted Him to say it. John does, however, assume that his readers know of this saying, and he uses it to introduce the Second Sign, for he wants to show how this Sign illustrates the unbelief of those in Galilee—and of the Jews in general. In doing so, John digs a little deeper into the inner significance of this well-known saying of Jesus. All of John's readers knew that Christ said "a prophet does not have honor in his own home town"; John will illustrate the roots of that dishonor and unbelief in a way that suits his overall purpose.

The lack of honor Christ experienced in Galilee, according to the Synoptics, was illustrated most dramatically by His rejection at the synagogue of Nazareth, when the Jews challenged Him to perform a sign (Luke 4:23). John delves more deeply into this demand for signs, with his observation that **the Galileans welcomed Him** (i.e. crowded into the synagogue when He was there and followed Him around, gawking at Him like a celebrity) only because they had **seen all the things He did in Jerusalem in the festal** *crowd*. That is, they only responded to Him at all because they observed all the miracles He did in front of the Passover crowds in Jerusalem (2:23).

Here St. John touches on one of his special themes: that it is a mark of unbelief to withhold faith until one has miraculous proof. A true and open heart will respond to Christ and believe in Him because of His words and the quality of divine love they reveal; the miraculous works He does should be unnecessary (14:11). The apostles "saw and believed"—but that was only because they did not then know the Scriptures (20:8–9). If they had known the Scriptures, they would have believed in Him without the necessity of seeing. Thus Thomas also sees and believes (20:25–28)—but more blessed are all they who believe without having seen (20:29). The Galileans are for John an image of the unbelieving Jews generally, for the Galileans reject Christ even as the Jews as a whole reject Him (1:11). The Jews demand signs (1 Cor. 1:22) and will not believe in Jesus without them. Even though He manifests the glory of the Father's love, they demand that He perform a miracle to authenticate His mission (Mark 8:11).

§III.4.ii. Second Sign: Healing of the Official's Son

ॐ ॐ ॐ ॐ ॐ

46 Therefore He came again to Cana of Galilee, where He had made the water wine. And there was a certain royal *official* whose son was ailing at Capernaum.
47 This one, having heard that Jesus had come

out of Judea into Galilee, went to Him and asked Him to come down and cure his son, for he was about to die.

48 Therefore Jesus said to him, "Unless you *people* see signs and wonders, you will never believe."

49 The royal *official* says to Him, "Lord, come down before my child dies."

50 Jesus says to him, "Go; your son lives." The man believed the word which Jesus spoke to him and he went.

51 And while he was going down, his slaves met him, saying that his child lives.

52 Therefore he inquired of them the hour in which he improved. They said therefore to him, "Yesterday at the seventh hour the fever left him."

53 So the father knew that it was in that hour in which Jesus said to him, "Your son lives"; and he himself believed and his whole house.

54 This is again a second sign which Jesus did when He had come out of Judea into Galilee.

The unbelief of the Galileans was illustrated by the request of **a certain royal *official*** when **He came again to Cana of Galilee**. (This second miracle the Lord would do in Cana is foreshadowed by John's reference to His first miracle there, when **He had made the water into wine**.) This **royal *official*** was probably part of King Herod's court (Herod was popularly styled a king; Mark 6:14); some have suggested that he was Herod's steward Chuza, mentioned in Luke 8:3, though this is impossible to prove. Whatever his name, his **son was ailing** and had been left sick **at Capernaum**, a distance of some twenty-five miles.

The boy **was about to die**, and the distraught father had heard a rumor that **Jesus had come out of Judea** and was somewhere in **Galilee**. In those days before cell phones and televisions, it was no small matter to determine exactly where in Galilee He actually was.

Doubtless the father ran breathlessly from his home in Capernaum, seeking news from anyone he could find on the road. (He perhaps traveled by donkey, though a journey on foot was possible too.) At length he heard that Jesus was in Cana, and found Him there. In what was probably a state of near exhaustion, he pushed his way through the crowd and **asked Him to come down** to Capernaum and **cure his son**. The man was insistent that Jesus drop everything He was doing and begin the frantic twenty-five–mile journey to Capernaum, for he believed that Jesus needed to physically see the boy in order to cure him.

The crowd also wanted to see Him do the miracle, and doubtless regarded it as a kind of test for Him. Here, for St. John, was the root of Jewish unbelief. Christ recognized that the crowd's insistence on seeing this miracle was proof of their defective faith. Though he speaks to the father of the afflicted boy, Christ's words are in the plural (thus it is rendered **you** *people*), and He laments a lack of faith on the part of the crowd. They were a faithless generation that did not honor their hometown prophet (v. 44), and they would **never believe** if they did not see authenticating **signs and wonders**.

The father, however, was beside himself with fear and growing apprehension. All **the royal** *official* could say to the humble preacher from Nazareth was, **"Lord, come down before my child dies."**

The Lord responded to his faith with compassion—and with a challenge. He refused to go with him, yet challenged him to believe that he was healing his boy at a distance, with a mere word. The words **"your son lives"** were not a prediction that he would recover. They were an authoritative word of healing. The challenge to the father was to believe, even though he had not seen (compare 20:29). The faithless of Galilee demanded to see signs and wonders. Would this man believe on the strength of Jesus' mere word alone?

The father, an image of obedient faith, indeed **believed the word which Jesus spoke to him**, even without seeing the boy being healed. The Lord said **"Go"** (Gr. *poreuou*), and **he went** (Gr. *eporeueto*, the same word in the Greek, showing the man's obedience), leaving Christ's presence to start the long journey home.

The confirmation of his faith came soon enough, the next day.

It was the seventh hour (that is, 1:00 p.m.) when Christ spoke the saving words "your son lives." The man was, we may think, in a state of exhaustion when he found Christ, and after he believed Him and had faith that the crisis had indeed passed, he would have rested before starting the return journey home, possibly staying overnight in Cana. Early the next day, he began the journey home, hardly daring to doubt the Lord's words, yet fighting back the fear that haunted the edge of his mind. At some point on the journey, **his slaves met him** and said to him that the **child lives**. After the Lord's words brought healing to the boy and drove the fever away, doubtless they left the house in haste, to track down their master with the good news.

The slaves, however, knew nothing of their master's encounter with Jesus. All they knew was the joyful news that the fever had left the boy. The ran to their master with the good news of his son's recovery. Excitement rose in the father's heart when he heard their words, and he breathlessly **inquired of them the hour in which** his son **improved.** They told him that the fever broke **yesterday at the seventh hour**, and **the father knew** that it was Jesus' word that had healed his son. The father **himself believed** in Him, along with **his whole house.** St. John concludes by saying that this was the **second sign which Jesus did** in Galilee **when He had come out of Judea** (though not the second sign He ever did; compare 2:23). Galilee had twice seen evidence of His power—and the multiplicity of these signs was calling them to faith.

§III.5. Second Visit to Jerusalem

§III.5.i. Third Sign: Healing of the Paralytic

ॐ ॐ ॐ ॐ ॐ

5 1   After these things there was a feast of the Jews, and Jesus went up to Jerusalem.

2   Now there is in Jerusalem by the Sheep *Gate* a pool, which in Hebrew is called Bethesda, having five colonnades.

> 3   In these was lying down a multitude of those who were ill, blind, lame, and withered.
>
> 5   And a certain man was there who had been thirty-eight years in his illness.
>
> 6   When Jesus saw this one lying down, and knew that he had already been *ill* a long time, He says to him, "Do you want to become healthy?"
>
> 7   The ill one answered Him, "Lord, I do not have a man to cast me into the pool when the water is troubled, but while I *myself* am coming, another goes down before me."
>
> 8   Jesus says to him, "Arise, take up your pallet and walk."
>
> 9   And immediately the man became healthy, and took up his pallet and walked.

The next time **Jesus went up to Jerusalem** was for an otherwise unspecified **feast of the Jews**. Though it is impossible to be certain which feast was meant, I would suggest the Feast of Purim as the most likely one. It is unlikely that it is the Passover that was meant, or Booths or Dedication, for John mentions these feasts by name elsewhere (2:13; 7:2; 10:22), and there is no reason for him to omit such a designation here if that were what he meant. Also, the Feast of Weeks, coming fifty days after Passover, would not leave much time for Christ to be in Jerusalem for Passover (2:23), then spend time in Judea (3:22), then go through Samaria (4:4) and spend time in Galilee (4:45; Luke 4:15), and then return again to Jerusalem in time for the Feast of Weeks. Fifty days seems too short a time for Him to have done all that, and so it seems that the Feast of Weeks could not be meant. Purim, however, comes in the following spring, which would allow the necessary time for an extended stay in Galilee. Moreover, its nationalistic nature (compare Esther 9:20ff) qualifies it as a **feast of the Jews**—that is, not just a Jewish feast, but a feast celebrating Jewishness.

St. John sets the stage for Christ's sign by saying **there is in Jerusalem by the Sheep *Gate* a pool**. (The present tense as used here, "there is," may simply be an historic present—i.e. "there *was*," but it is possible too that the pool survived the destruction of Jerusalem in AD 70 and was still in existence at the time when the Gospel was written.) The pool **in Hebrew** was **called Bethesda** (possibly from *Beth Eshda*, "house of the stream"), and it had **five colonnades** or rows of columns. (The location is possibly to be identified with the double pool now known as St. Anne's, which had a colonnade along each side of each of the two pools and a fifth between them.) In these colonnades, a varied **multitude** of people were **lying down**—the **ill, blind, lame, and withered**. An early gloss on the Gospel (in some manuscripts inserted into the text as v. 4) reveals what they were waiting there for. At certain times, the water of the pool was troubled and stirred up, and this was attributed to the descent of an angel of the Lord into the pool. It was said that whoever first descended into the pool after the angel's visit was healed of whatever sickness he had—doubtless because the body of the afflicted one absorbed the divine energy left in the pool by the angel.

In the midst of this large crowd was **a certain man** who had been **thirty-eight years in his illness**. He was a paralytic, and thus unable to hurl himself into the water soon enough after it was stirred up to be the fortunate one who received healing. His age is not stated, but it may be thought that he had spent at least his entire adult life in his illness, hoping for health.

In his mind, the pool was his only hope, and all his attention was fixed upon it. When he awoke in the morning, he wondered if this was to be the day the water would stir and he would be the first one in it; when he went to sleep at night, all his hope was pinned on entering the pool the next day. The pool represented the only hope for salvation and life he knew.

So it was that when **Jesus saw** him and supernaturally **knew** that he had been such **a long time** in his illness, and asked him, **"Do you want to become healthy?"** all he could think of was the pool. He **answered Him** as one whose heart was still fixed on the pool, saying to him, **"Lord"** (or "Sir"), **I do not have a man to cast me into the pool."** Doubtless he hoped that Jesus would offer to perform this task, and take His place waiting with him for the supernatural troubling of the waters.

Christ, however, did nothing of the kind. Instead, He called the man to cease looking to the pool for healing and salvation, and to look to Him instead. He, Jesus, was the source of salvation—not the pool. He simply said to the man, **"Arise, take up your pallet and walk."** (The words of Jesus to the man in vv. 6 and 8 are reported in the historic present.) The healing words of Christ took effect **immediately**, and **the man became healthy** and obediently **took up his pallet and walked.**

In St. John's narrative, the story has a deeper significance than a mere healing. It reveals that Christ is the source of salvation for Israel—not the Law. The pool of water symbolized the Law, the great rival to Christ in the hearts of the Jews. They thought that in the Law they had eternal life (v. 39), and they put their hope in the Law even as the paralytic put his hope in the pool. The Law was given by angels (Acts 7:53; Gal. 3:19), even as the water was thought to be stirred by an angel. And the Law of Moses had five books, even as the pool had five colonnades or porticoes (which was, I suggest, John's reason for mentioning this). St. Augustine said regarding this passage, "The five porticoes were significative of the Law, bearing the sick, but not healing them." Salvation for the Jews involved transferring their hope and attention from the Law to Christ, just as salvation for the paralytic involved transferring his attention from the pool to Jesus. The man had been ill a long time, waiting for healing, just as Israel had been waiting for messianic salvation for a long time. By relating the story of the paralytic, St. John means his readers to understand its deeper significance and see how in Jesus alone is salvation for Israel.

§III.5.ii. Controversy over the Healing of the Paralytic

꧁ ꧁ ꧁ ꧁ ꧁

9   Now it was a Sabbath on that day.
10   Therefore the Jews were saying to the one who

had been healed, "It is a Sabbath, and it is not permitted you to take up your pallet."

11 But he answered them, "He who made me healthy, that one said to me, 'Take up your pallet and walk.'"

12 They asked him, "Who is the man who said to you, 'Take *it* up and walk'?"

13 But he who had been cured did not know who it was, for Jesus had withdrawn, as there was a crowd in the place.

14 After these things, Jesus finds him in the Temple and said to him, "Behold, you have become healthy; do not sin any longer, lest something worse happen to you."

15 The man went away, and announced to the Jews that Jesus was the one who had made him healthy.

The ensuing controversy with **the Jews** (that is, those committed to Judaism, not to Jesus) revealed how great was Israel's need to transfer its hope from the ineffectual Law to Christ. St. John introduces the controversy by explaining that **it was a Sabbath** on the day that Christ healed the paralytic. When the Jews saw the man carrying his pallet, they forbade him to do so, saying, **"It is a Sabbath, and it is not permitted you to take up your pallet."** It was forbidden to work on the Sabbath, and according to their rigid interpretations, this carrying of the rolled-up mat constituted work, regardless of the light effort it entailed and of the fact that it witnessed to the glorious healing he had received from God. He was therefore to drop the pallet and continue on his way without it.

The reaction of the man was immediate: he placed the responsibility for his action squarely on the shoulders of Jesus, who had bidden him take up his pallet and carry it home. **He answered** his accusers, **"He who made me healthy, that one said to me, 'Take up your pallet and walk.'"** Let his challengers blame Him! The Jews not unnaturally inquired, **"Who is the man"** who instructed him to (as they thought) so flagrantly break the Law? The man **did not know** and could not point Him out, **for Jesus had withdrawn** and disappeared into the large **crowd** there was **in the place**.

Later on (perhaps the next day, or the day after?), **Jesus finds him in the Temple**, where the man had perhaps gone to offer thanks to God. It would appear that his illness had some connection with sin in the man's life, though whether the sin had caused the illness or whether the illness occasioned the sin (of bitterness?) is not said. Whatever the precise details, Christ is concerned for his spiritual and eternal welfare, and tells him **not to sin any longer, lest something worse happen** to him. That is, the judgment of God that would befall him if he continued in sin after receiving such a healing would be worse than if he had never been healed.

With an economy of words, John narrates that **the man went away** and, having learned Jesus' name, **announced to the Jews that Jesus was the one who had made him healthy**. It is easy for us to perceive the man's ingratitude, but we must remember too how he had been accused by the Jews of being a Law-breaker. The reference to Jesus was his only defense.

ৡ৵ ৡ৵ ৡ৵ ৡ৵ ৡ৵

16 And because of this the Jews were persecuting Jesus, because He did these things on a Sabbath.

17 But He answered them, "My Father is working until now, and I Myself am working."

18 Because of this therefore, the Jews were seeking all the more to kill Him, because He not only was destroying the Sabbath, but also was saying that God *was His* own Father, making Himself equal to God.

After **the Jews** of Jerusalem learned that it was Jesus who had counseled the man to carry his pallet, they **were persecuting** Him. That is, they transferred their hostility from the man who had been healed to Jesus, openly and officially charging Him with desecrating the Sabbath. They were utterly blind to the divine glory of the healing; all they could see was a violation of the Law. (We note that John uses the language of polemic here; the Jewish confrontation with Jesus was not legitimate challenge, it was "persecution.")

Jesus did not enter into a debate with them about the legitimacy of their interpretation of the Sabbath restrictions. The issue here was not about the meaning of the Law. It was about His own authority. Whatever the Sabbath restrictions were, He was above them. Just as God was not bound by the limitations of the rules He gave to Israel, so Jesus was not bound by them. God could do His work of creating, saving, and healing—even on the Sabbath—and therefore Jesus could also, for He was the fullness of the Father and came with all the Father's authority. "**My Father is working until now**," even on the Sabbath, He replied, and so "**I Myself am working**."

The claim to share the authority of God enraged **the Jews**, and they **were seeking all the more to kill Him**. (We note that this was not the first time He had enraged them and made them want to kill Him. Rather, it just gave them fresh incentive to do so all the more.) For He not only **was destroying** and desecrating **the Sabbath**, by healing the paralytic then and bidding him carry his pallet. More scandalously, He **also was saying that God** *was His* **own Father**, and by claiming God's immunity to the Law's restrictions, **making Himself equal to God**.

Jesus' reference to God as "My Father" was truly something new and startling in first-century Judaism. God was acknowledged as the Father of the nation (compare Is. 64:8), but the reference to God as one's individual Father ("*My* Father," and not just "our Father") constituted the claiming of a special and unique relationship to Him. Given the context of also claiming that this relationship with God involved sharing His transcendence above the Law, Jesus' use of the term "My Father" was indeed claiming equality with Him—and therefore essential divinity, for no created being could be equal to God.

ॐ ॐ ॐ ॐ ॐ

19 Therefore Jesus answered and was saying to them, "Amen, amen, I say to you, the Son is not able to do anything from Himself, except what He sees the Father doing, for whatever that One does, these things the Son also likewise does.

20 "For the Father loves the Son, and shows to Him all things that He Himself is doing, and greater works than these will He show to Him, that you *yourselves* may marvel.

21 "For just as the Father raises and makes alive the dead, thus the Son also makes alive whomever He wants.

22 "For not even the Father judges anyone, but He has given all judgment to the Son,

23 "that all may honor the Son even as they honor the Father. He who does not honor the Son does not honor the Father who sent Him.

24 "Amen, amen, I say to you, he who hears My word and believes Him who sent Me has eternal life, and does not come into judgment, but has passed over from death into life.

25 "Amen, amen, I say to you, an hour is coming and now is, when the dead will hear the voice of the Son of God, and those who hear will live.

26 "For just as the Father has life in Himself, thus He gave to the Son also to have life in Himself;

27 "and He gave Him authority to make judgment, because He is *the* Son of Man.

28 "Do not marvel at this, for an hour is coming in which all who are in the tombs will hear His voice

29 "and will come out—the ones who did the good

> **things to a resurrection of life, the ones who practiced the base things to a resurrection of judgment.**

Christ does not shrink from this conclusion, nor say that they have misunderstood His supposed claims to divinity. He does not deny that He is claiming equality with God—instead, He stresses it! He begins His answer with a solemn **Amen, amen**, testifying that this is truth from God. His foes think He cannot possibly share the Father's immunity from the Law's restrictions, and that His actions are contrary to the will of God. Jesus assures them that this is impossible, for indeed **the Son is not** even **able to do anything from Himself**; such is His communion with the Father that He can do only **what He sees the Father doing**. His actions must reflect the will of God because of His unbroken union with and contemplation of the Father. **Whatever that One** (the Father) **does**—the pronoun is emphatic in the Greek—**these** very **things the Son also likewise does**. Thus His healing on the Sabbath was done in exact obedience to the Father's will. There is nothing in the Father's heart that He withholds from the Son, **for the Father loves the Son, and shows to Him all things that He Himself is doing**. That is, Jesus does not have to strive to discover the will of God, seeking it amidst all the doubts and ambiguities which attend normal mortal existence. Like a father showing his apprentice son his craft, the Father pours into Him all His own knowledge and will, so that the Son has perfect knowledge of the Father's will.

Do they marvel at this? But **greater works than** this healing will the Father **show** to the Son for the Son to do so that the Jews themselves (the pronoun **you** is emphatic) **may marvel**. Jesus has made a paralytic walk—if this is not enough, wait until they see Him raise the dead! **The Father raises and makes alive the dead**, for that is within His power as the true God and Judge of all (see 1 Sam. 2:6; Tobit 13:2). The Son shares all His power and authority, and **thus** He **also makes alive whomever He wants**, just as the Father does. Christ's raising of the dead (compare Luke 7:14–15; 8:54–55; Matt. 11:5) testifies to the fullness of His divine authority. Such power over death is a function of judgment—for it involves the decision regarding who shall live and who shall die. Such judgments are solely in the hands of God, as all the Jews know. Jesus says here that now **not even the Father judges anyone,** for **He has given all judgment to the Son, that all may honor the Son even as they honor the Father.** That is, these divine functions of judging and deciding matters of life and death have now been given over by God to Christ, that Christ may share the glory of the Father. To refuse Christ's authority is therefore to dishonor God, for God gave this authority to Him. His adversaries who do **not honor the Son,** but persecute Him, are not thereby honoring God, as they think. Instead, they are insulting and **not honoring the Father who sent Him.**

This authority over physical life and death is but a revelation of Christ's eternal authority as the final Judge of all. Prefacing His promise with a solemn **Amen, amen, I say to you,** He tells what this authority as life-giver means: it means eternal life for those who trust Him. The one who **hears** His **word** with faith and **believes** the Father **who sent** Him (for to believe Jesus' word is to believe the Father's word, since Jesus speaks the words of the Father), this one **does not come into judgment** and condemnation on the Last Day, but even now **has passed over from death into life.** Christ not only bestows physical life on some of the dead now, He bestows eternal life on all who believe and follow Him.

The **hour** for such miracles **is coming** quickly—and **now is** here! Let them watch His acts as **the dead** and buried **hear the voice of the Son of God.** His foes will see that **those who hear** His voice **will live**—proving that He is indeed the Son of God. It will confirm His claim that **just as the Father has life in Himself** and is able to give life, in the same way **He gave to the Son also to have life in Himself** and to have **authority to make judgment** about who shall live, because Jesus of Nazareth was no Law-breaker but was the messianic **Son of Man.**

Christ's response to His foes was an extraordinary one. They had challenged Him as if He were not only merely human, but an impious breaker of God's Law. With untroubled consciousness of His own authority, Jesus does not deign to debate their interpretations of the Law. Instead, He presents a series of startling claims, putting Himself forward as One who shares all the authority and glory of God.

One can almost see their jaws drop and their eyes bug out, and hear them sputter! Jesus cuts short such expressions of incredulity and plunges on. "**Do not marvel at this**," He says. Do not think My authority to bestow life in this age and forgiveness in the age to come is the limit of My power. **An hour is coming**—on the Last Day—when not just some of the dead but indeed **all who are in the tombs will hear** My **voice and will come out** from the tombs—**the ones who did the good things to a resurrection of life, the ones who practiced the base things to a resurrection of judgment**. In this age, He will raise but a few from the dead, as a revelation of His divine authority. On the Last Day, His voice will summon all to resurrection and judgment. All Jews knew that it was only the Voice of God that could raise the dead. Jesus says that His voice is the very one that will bring them alive and trembling before the final and eternal Throne.

ॐ ॐ ॐ ॐ ॐ

30 "I *Myself* am not able to do anything from My-self. As I hear, I judge; and My judgment is righteous, because I do not seek My will, but the will of Him who sent Me.

31 "If I *Myself* witness about Myself, My witness is not true.

32 "There is Another who witnesses about Me, and I know that the witness He witnesses about Me is true.

33 "You *yourselves* sent to John, and he has wit-nessed to the truth.

34 "But the witness which I *Myself* receive is not from man, but I say these things that you *your-selves* may be saved.

35 "That one was the burning and shining lamp,

> and you *yourselves* were willing to exult for a
> while in his light.
>
> 36 "But the witness which I *Myself* have is greater
> than John's, for the works the Father has given
> Me to finish, the very works I do, witness about
> Me that the Father has sent Me.
>
> 37 "And the Father who sent Me, that One has
> witnessed about Me. You have never heard His
> voice, nor seen His form.

Christ continues by speaking of the witnesses that testify to His divine authority. He stresses again that His **judgments** (such as His decision to heal on the Sabbath) are **righteous**, because, unlike the Jews, He Himself (the pronoun is emphatic) is **not able to do anything** on His own initiative, but only as He **hears** from the Father. His judgments are true because they are not His alone, but represent also the judgments of the Father.

He acknowledges that if He *were* to present a solitary **witness** to Himself, such a witness would indeed **not** be **true**. All His authority comes from His union with the Father. It is the fact that **Another**— the Father—**witnesses about** Him that makes Jesus' word and self-witness true. Jesus' witness to Himself thus does not stand alone; it is confirmed by the witness of the Father, as He witnesses to Christ's status through His miracles.

The Jews understand about the value of witnesses. They themselves (the pronoun is again emphatic) **sent to John** the Baptizer to learn the truth (1:19f), and John **witnessed to the truth** by saying that Messiah was coming. He was a **burning and shining lamp**, and they recognized this, and **were willing to exult for a while in his light** and learn from him (compare Matt. 3:7). (The phrase "for a while" seems to indicate that John had been imprisoned by this time.) But **the witness** that Jesus **receives** is **not from man**. John's testimony was indeed valuable, but Jesus has a **greater** witness **than John's**—the witness of the Father. The miraculous **works the Father has given** Him **to finish**—such as healing the paralytic—**the very works** He is doing and which they are arguing about—these works **witness that the Father has sent** Him. Jesus only mentions John at all **that** they **may be saved**, as He condescends to their weakness. Jesus was **sent** by the Father and knows all His will; the Jews have **never heard** the Father's **voice**, **nor seen His form**, and are in no position to know His will as the Son knows it.

ॐ ॐ ॐ ॐ ॐ

38 "And you do not have His word remaining in you, for you do not believe that One whom He sent.

39 "You examine the Scriptures because You *yourselves* think that in them you have eternal life, and it is those that witness about Me,

40 "and you do not want to come to Me that you may have life.

41 "I do not receive glory from men,

42 "but I know you, that you do not have the love of God in yourselves.

43 "I *Myself* have come in My Father's Name and you do not receive Me. If another comes in his own name, that one you will receive.

44 "How can you *yourselves* believe, who receive glory from one another, and do not seek the glory that comes from the only God?

45 "Do not think I *Myself* will accuse you before the Father; the one accusing you is Moses, in whom you *yourselves* have hoped.

46 "For if you believed Moses, you would believe Me, for that one wrote about Me.

47 "But if you do not believe that one's writings, how will you believe My words?"

The Lord continues His counterattack on the Jews. Not only have they never had intimate knowledge of the Father as He has, but also they **do not have** the Father's **word remaining in** them. That is, the truth from the Father has not found a home in them, for they have hardened their hearts to His word. And because Jesus speaks the word of the Father (3:34), if one does **not believe** Jesus whom the Father **sent**, then one cannot receive that word from the Father. The Jews think they can be obedient to God and still reject Jesus, but the Lord tells them this cannot be. To reject Jesus is also to reject the Father, for the Father is inseparable from His incarnate Son.

The Jews, ironically, **examine the Scriptures** and pore over them, multiplying interpretations (such as that which forbids His healing on the Sabbath!). They do this because they themselves think (the pronoun **you** is emphatic in the Greek) that in the Scriptures they **have eternal life.** The irony is that eternal life is not in the Scriptures and in their legalistic use of them, but in Christ, and it is these very Scriptures that **witness about** Him. The Jews center their heart in the Scriptures and the Law while still refusing **to come** to Jesus that they **may have life.**

Jesus does not court human favor, nor strive to **receive glory from men** as they do. Their hearts are wrapped up in pride and fear, so that they **do not have the love of God** in them. Their goal is to **receive glory** and approval **from one another,** and they refuse to **seek the glory that comes from the only God.** Opening their hearts to Jesus and His word would mean unpopularity with their coreligionists, and perhaps even being cast out of the synagogue (compare 9:22). This they are unwilling to accept. While they refuse to risk their reputations, **how** can such as they themselves **believe** in Him? (The pronoun in v. 44 is again emphatic.) He has **come in** His **Father's Name,** seeking only God's glory, and they **do not receive** Him. **If another** were to **come in his own name,** a false Messiah seeking his own glory, **that one** they **will receive!**

Perhaps they think that He is their enemy and is accusing them before God. Let them **not think** that *He* is the one who will **accuse** them **before the Father. The one accusing** them is **Moses**—the very one **whom** they **have hoped** in and relied upon. It was out of their supposed zeal to obey Moses (compare 9:28) that they rejected Jesus for breaking the Sabbath. They think perhaps that Moses will commend them for their faithfulness. Far from it! Moses will accuse

101

them before God for rejecting his word, for Moses wrote about Jesus. If they truly **believed Moses**, they **would believe** Jesus too, for Moses prophesied of His coming. But since they **do not believe that one's writings** (Gr. *gramma*, the divine letters preserved on the Torah scrolls), **how** can they then **believe** Christ's **words**? Having rejected the prophecy, of course they reject its fulfillment!

§III.6. Into Galilee

§III.6.i. Fourth Sign: Multiplication of Bread

ॐ ॐ ॐ ॐ ॐ

6 1 After these things Jesus departed to the other side of the Sea of Galilee (*or* of Tiberias).

2 And a great crowd was following Him, because they were seeing the signs He was doing on the ones who were ill.

3 And Jesus went up into the mountain, and there He sat with His disciples.

4 Now the Passover, the feast of the Jews, was near.

5 Jesus therefore lifting up His eyes, and beholding that a great crowd was coming to Him, says to Philip, "From where are we to buy bread, that these may eat?"

6 But this He was saying to test him, for He Himself knew what He was about to do.

7 Philip answered Him, "Two hundred denarii *worth* of bread is not enough for them, for each one to take a little."

8 One of His disciples, Andrew, Simon Peter's brother, says to Him,

9 "There is a lad here who has five barley breads and two fish, but what are these to so many?"

10 Jesus said, "Make the people sit down." Now there was much grass in the place. Therefore

the men sat down, in number about five thousand.

11 Jesus therefore took the breads, and having given thanks, He gave *it* away to the ones reclining, likewise also of the fish, as much as they wanted.

12 And when they were filled up, He says to His disciples, "Gather up the leftover broken *pieces* that nothing may be lost."

13 And therefore they gathered *them*, and filled twelve baskets with broken *pieces* from the five barley loaves left over by the ones who had eaten.

14 When therefore the people saw the sign He did, they said, "This one is truly the Prophet, the One who comes into the world!"

15 Jesus therefore, knowing that they were about to come and snatch Him to make *Him* king, withdrew again to the mountain by Himself alone.

After this time in Jerusalem (5:1), **Jesus departed** northward to a place by **the other side** (or east side) **of the Sea of Galilee** (John further identifies this for the sake of his Gentile contemporaries as the Sea **of Tiberias,** named for the emperor). Jesus was **followed** by **a great crowd,** because **they were seeing the signs He was doing on the ones who were ill.** That is, they thronged Him not because they truly recognized His significance, but because they wanted to see more miracles (compare 2:23; 4:45, 48). Like the Jews in general, they were incapable of piercing through to the true and inner meaning of His signs. By stressing this, St. John prepares us for their rejection of Jesus in the verses that follow (6:66).

Jesus **went up into the mountain, and there He sat with His disciples.** By comparing this account with those of Matthew 14:33 and Mark 6:31, we learn that Christ had taken His disciples up into the mountain in order for them to rest. But when He saw the crowds gathering expectantly (they saw Him depart from the other side of the lake and ran to this spot to pursue Him; compare Mark 6:33), He abandoned His planned rest in order to descend the hill and teach the crowds that were gathering.

St. John mentions that **the Passover** (Gr. *Pascha*), **the feast of the Jews, was near.** This reference is at first sight somewhat strange, since that feast was kept in Jerusalem, not in Galilee. The people gathering to Jesus were not about to keep the feast, since they would have to leave this area to keep the feast in Jerusalem. Why mention this at all?

St. John mentions the nearness of the Passover feast to set the stage for the impending multiplication of the breads and its lesson. For this sign would show that Jesus was the true Passover, and it was His Flesh that was the true and saving Bread (6:51). At each Passover, the Jews would break the Passover bread, eat the Passover sacrifice, and look forward to the final messianic redemption. John's message is that *here*, in their midst, was the true messianic redemption, the true Paschal Sacrifice. Like all the Jewish feasts, Passover found its fulfillment and meaning in Him.

Toward the end of the day (Mark 6:35), Jesus **lifted up His eyes** and saw the crowd was not dispersing. Rather, **a great crowd** was still **coming,** so that a crisis threatened. To feed such a multitude, they would have to go into various towns about them to buy food, for such an immense throng defied the resources of any one town. Capernaum, for example, had a population of about two thousand five hundred, and this crowd numbered more than five thousand men, plus the women and children (Matt. 14:21). The apostles were alarmed, and some suggested the crowd should be dismissed to the various surrounding villages.

The Lord takes the initiative in this situation. He addresses **Philip,** perhaps because he was a native of nearby Bethsaida (1:44)—or perhaps because he was the one who wondered the loudest what they were to do faced with such a crisis! He asks him (with a suppressed smile?), **"From where are we to buy bread, that these may eat?"** (and when Philip shrugs in bewilderment at such a question, He suggests that *they* could provide the food—see Mark 6:37). St.

John adds the remark that Christ asked this question of Philip not because He Himself was at a loss what to do, but simply **to test him**. John is emphatic that Christ was never at the mercy of circumstances, since He is the sovereign Lord of all, but at all times **knew what He was about to do.**

Philip is stunned at our Lord's response, and replies that **two hundred denarii** *worth* **of bread** would **not** be **enough for them, for each one to take** even **a little** bite. The denarius was the day's wage for the laborer, and two hundred denarii was a sizable sum. Yet even this would be insufficient to buy bread for such a crowd. Philip mentions this amount probably because it is all the money they have with them. Even if they spent their entire sum to feed them, he says, it would not be enough! Christ is testing him to see if he will recognize His messianic power, but Philip is failing the test.

The Lord instructs them to gather all they have. **Andrew, Simon Peter's brother**, perhaps to call attention to the unreasonableness of Christ's order to feed the crowd (Mark 6:37), brings forward the resources of **a lad here**, probably after a quick search of those nearby who had food. The word translated **lad** is the Greek *paidarion*, a diminutive form, which indicates the boy was probably quite young, possibly ten years old. He has **five barley breads and two fish.** Barley loaves were the bread of the poor. Moreover, the word translated *fish* is the Greek *opsarion*, also a diminutive, meaning "cooked food," something eaten with bread. In this case, it was two small fishes—that is, two small pickled fish, to be eaten as a side dish with the barley bread. A small boy with such a humble snack, **what** would **these** resources be to **so many** hungry people?

The apostles are at a loss, but Jesus seems to think that such resources are enough. Taking the food from the wide-eyed boy, He announces that dinner is at hand, and instructs His apostles to **make the people sit down** for the meal. (John adds the eyewitness detail that they were able to sit down because **there was much grass in the place,** so that all that crowd could recline for the feast. **The men sat down, in number about five thousand**, expecting to eat, but perplexed as to where the meal was to come from.

As they were ready to eat, **Jesus therefore took the** five **breads,** and having given thanks, gave away to the ones reclining the multiplied loaves, and likewise also of the fish, until they received as much as they wanted. By His miraculous messianic power, He multiplied the loaves and the fish until all that mighty throng was filled up. There was such an abundance that there were even some leftover broken *pieces*. The English word "leftover" conveys a negative sense to our affluent ears. To eat leftovers is not to dine well. The Greek word contains no such negative connotation: it is from the word *perisseuo*, "to abound, to have an abundance." The thought here is that there was such an abundance that there was even some left over, for they could not eat such a large amount of food. Here was an abundance characteristic of the messianic age!

The Lord tells His disciples to gather up these leftover pieces of bread that nothing may be lost. This detail is not accidental. St. John narrates it to show Christ's abiding concern for preserving His own. For they gathered up and filled twelve baskets (Gr. *kophinos*, small wicker carrying baskets that pious Jews customarily carried about with them as part of the daily attire). These twelve baskets were those carried by His twelve apostles. By narrating Christ's order for them to gather the fragments that nothing be lost, John means to show how Christ cares for His own, and takes care that none of them be lost or destroyed (compare 6:39; 17:12; 18:8–9). This detail illustrates Christ's preservation of His own, that none snatch them out of His hand (10:28).

The effect of the miracle on the people was dramatic. This show of power convinced them that this one was truly the messianic Prophet, the One who comes into the world! It seems they concluded that Jesus was the Prophet (compare 1:21) whose coming into the world heralded the final messianic redemption. A riot was beginning, as they were about to come and snatch Him to make *Him* king. It seems their intention was to raise an army of five thousand men then and there, with Jesus as their military leader. Christ sent the disciples away in a hurry from such a dangerous situation and decisively dismissed the crowd (Mark 6:45). He then withdrew again to the mountain where they first went to rest to be by Himself alone and pray (Mark 6:46).

§III.6.ii. Fifth Sign: Walking on the Sea

ॐ ॐ ॐ ॐ ॐ

16 Now when evening came, His disciples went down to the sea,

17 and got into a boat, and *started* across the sea to Capernaum. And darkness had already come, and Jesus had not yet come to them.

18 And the sea was roused because a great wind blew.

19 When therefore they had rowed about twenty-five or thirty stadia, they observed Jesus walking on the sea and coming near to the boat; and they were afraid.

20 But He says to them, "*It is* I; do not be afraid!"

21 Therefore they were willing to receive Him into the boat; and immediately the boat was at the land to which they were going.

After Christ sent His disciples away, they **got into a boat** to go **across the sea** again. It would seem the prearranged plan was for them to make the four-mile crossing to the other side, then meet Jesus in Bethsaida on the western side (Mark 6:45) before continuing together to their home base in **Capernaum**. However, a sudden storm with **a great wind** swept down on the Sea of Galilee so that **the sea was roused**, and the four-mile journey that should have taken a few hours took all night.

Meanwhile, **Jesus had not yet come to them** to meet them at the other side of the lake because He continued praying until the wee hours of the morning (Mark 6:48). He perceived that they were in distress, rowing vainly against the wind and the waves, about **twenty-five or thirty stadia** out (that is, about three or four miles). He therefore came to them, **walking on the sea and coming near to the boat**.

The disciples had endured a long and extraordinary day. They

were already in a state of near exhaustion before the day began—
that was why they had come to the eastern shore in the first place
(Mark 6:31–32). The long day of teaching ended with the high
enthusiasm of Christ multiplying the loaves and the near-riot that
ensued when the crowd tried to come by force and make Him king.
Now, after they had rowed the entire night, through the darkness,
wind, and waves, they observed a figure walking on the waves and
drawing near to them. For the disciples as for all Jews, the sea was
no friendly place, but the reputed haunt of demons, and it must
have seemed to them as if the dark and supernatural figure approaching were indeed one such. With his usual economy of language,
John simply reports, **they were afraid**. That is, they were terrified to
the point of being unstrung!

The Lord reassured them that He was no dark spirit, shouting
out, "*It is* **I; do not be afraid!**" (The phrase rendered here *It is I* is
the Greek *ego eimi,* rendered "I am" in 8:58. Christ is not simply
identifying Himself; He is also manifesting His saving Presence.)
When they heard that it was He and not a demonic phantom, **they
were willing to receive Him into the boat**. When He entered the
boat, the storm ceased (for the presence of the Lord brings peace to
the storm-tossed) so that **immediately the boat was at the land to
which they were going**. It was as the Psalmist had prophesied long
ago: God "made the storm be still so that the waves of the sea were
hushed; they were glad because they had quiet and He brought them
to their desired haven" (Ps. 107:29–30).

Why does St. John record this sign? It is reported because it
reveals the nature of Christ's kingship. The crowd had recognized
Jesus as a messianic figure and had attempted to make Him King.
That is, they interpreted the messianic redemption in crassly political and military terms. Jesus is indeed a King, but one whose Kingdom is not of this world (18:36). His kingship is spiritual and transcendent, not political and military. His walking on the sea proves
this. Just as He was revealed to transcend the powers of nature, so
His Kingdom transcends this world. By refusing to be made an
earthly king and then walking on the sea, Jesus revealed that His
Kingdom was not earthly, as Caesar's was. His subjects were not

those who would fight, but those who heard His voice of truth (18:37).

§III.6.iii.   Controversy over the Multiplication of Bread: Jesus the Bread of Life

ॐ ॐ ॐ ॐ ॐ

22 The next day the crowd that stood on the other side of the sea saw that there was not another boat there, except one, and that Jesus had not entered with His disciples into the boat, but His disciples had departed alone.

23 Other boats came from Tiberias near to the place where they ate the bread after the Lord had given thanks.

24 Therefore when the crowd saw that Jesus was not there, nor His disciples, they themselves got into the boats and came into Capernaum, seeking Jesus.

25 And when they found Him on the other side of the sea, they said to Him, "Rabbi, when did You come here?"

26 Jesus answered them and said, "Amen, amen, I say to you, you seek Me, not because you saw signs, but because you ate of the breads and were filled.

St. John next narrates the controversy that ensued as Christ explained the inner meaning of His multiplication of the loaves. For Christ is the Giver of life to the world, bestowing a messianic abundance of life even as He bestowed an abundance of bread. If they would eat what He would provide—not simply earthly loaves of bread, but His Flesh and Blood, to be offered on the Cross—they would live forever. They had eaten the bread (with its provision of earthly life) He had provided. Would they so eagerly eat the Bread of His Flesh, with its provision of eternal life?

The controversy is set within the context of their general in-comprehension and superficiality of understanding. That is, **the crowd that stood on the other side of the sea** (on the eastern side of the lake, where the Lord multiplied the loaves) **saw that Jesus was not there.** This perplexed them, since **there was not another boat there, except one.** That is, the only boat available that Jesus could have used was still there. He **had not entered with His disciples into** their **boat,** for **His disciples had departed alone.** How then had He vanished from that side of the lake? These crowds were joined that morning after the multiplication of the loaves by **other boats** that came **from Tiberias** on the western side of the lake. These also came to the eastern side, **near to the place where** the crowd **ate the bread after the Lord had given thanks,** so that the crowd on the eastern side now had boats they could use to travel back across to the western side. These all crossed the lake and **came into Capernaum, seeking Jesus.** At length they **found Him** there, **on the other side of the sea** from where they thought Him to be stranded, and asked Him, **"Rabbi, when did You come here?"** Their question showed their superficial understanding. One who could supernaturally multiply the loaves might have been expected to prove superior to such limitations also.

The Lord's response reveals their unspiritual state and their fail-ure to gain insight from the miracle of the loaves. Jesus chides them with a gentle challenge, ignoring their question and directing their hearts to truth. He tells them that they **seek** Him, not because they **saw signs** and understood the import of His miracles. Rather, they only followed Him across the lake **because** they **ate of the breads and were filled** to satisfaction. They sought Him out for the thrill of such miracles and experiences, not because they recognized Him as the true Messiah. He had fed them with bread yesterday—would He do the same today?

(The Lord's pointed non-answer of their question is significant, for it shows that God speaks only to hearts prepared to hear Him. The crowd did not see the significance of the miracle of the loaves—how could they see the significance of the miracle of His walking on the water? The Lord would only tell them what they were able to hear.)

༄ ༄ ༄ ༄ ༄

27 "Do not work for the food that perishes, but for the food that remains to eternal life, which the Son of Man will give to you, for the Father, *even* God, has sealed this One."

28 Therefore they said to Him, "What must we do, that we may work the works of God?"

29 Jesus answered and said to them, "This is the work of God, that you believe in Him whom that One has sent."

The Lord continued to instruct them after they had gathered in the local synagogue (v. 59). They had come all the way across the sea to seek Him, expending effort in the hope of seeing the miracle of the loaves repeated and being filled with earthly bread. Their effort was commendable, but misplaced. They should **not work for the food that perishes**—seeking merely physical bread—but **for the food that remains to eternal life**. They were right in seeking Him, but were seeking Him for the wrong reason. The food they sought (and the Kingdom they sought) was earthly, carnal, temporal. The bread they hoped He would give them again would not last. It would harden and crumble, and could only provide a physical and temporal life, which would end in death—even as the kingdom they sought was an earthly, political kingdom, one which, like all earthly kingdoms, would be overthrown. They should instead seek the food that would remain—the eternal life that He, **the Son of Man**, would **give** to them. This was the true and lasting sustenance which brought an unfailing, eternal life. They should not marvel that He could give this to them, for **the Father**—the true and life-giving **God**—has **sealed this One** (the pronoun is emphatic in the Greek). Seals were used in those days to authenticate and prove ownership. The Son is the very One the Father sealed, in that He is the One sent by the Father to bring His life-giving power into the world.

When they heard His call to **work** (Gr. *ergazomai*), being good Jews, they thought in terms of performing some commandment or work of the Law, for in their mind, eternal life came only through the Law. They asked Him therefore, **What must we do, that we may work the works of God**, and do what is pleasing to Him? What work of the Law does God require of us that we may have this eternal life?

Christ's reply was instant and emphatic. The eternal life He was offering did not come from striving to fulfill the Law. The Kingdom came through Him, not from Moses (compare 1:17). **This** was **the work of God**, and what God required of them; this was what was necessary for eternal life—that they **believe in Him whom that One**, the Father, had **sent**. That is, discipleship to Jesus was the condition for receiving eternal life and the Kingdom of God—not the accumulation of *mitzvoth* (or commandments), as the Pharisees taught.

ॐ ॐ ॐ ॐ ॐ

30 They said therefore to Him, "What sign then do You *Yourself* do, that we may see and believe You? What do You work?

31 "Our fathers ate the manna in the wilderness; as it is written, 'He gave them bread from heaven to eat.'"

32 Jesus therefore said to them, "Amen, amen, I say to you, it was not Moses who gave you the bread from heaven, but My Father gives you the true bread from heaven.

33 "For the bread of God is that which comes down from heaven and gives life to the world."

This was an extraordinary claim: to think that the carpenter of Nazareth, from a pious but ordinary family (v. 42), should be greater than the Law, and able to give eternal life! Such a claim required proof. **They said therefore to Him, "What sign then do You *Yourself***

do (the pronoun *You* is emphatic in the Greek; they were trying to put Him on the hot seat), **that we may see and believe You? What do You work? Our fathers ate the manna in the wilderness; as it is written, 'He gave them bread from heaven to eat'"** (Ps. 78:24). In their view, Jesus was claiming to be greater than Moses, and must therefore do a sign to substantiate His claim. Moses was willing to perform such signs (compare Ex. 4:1–8), and he proved himself a true prophet by giving Israel **bread from heaven** to eat when they were **in the wilderness** (Ex. 16). If Jesus is indeed greater than Moses, let Him perform a sign right now before their eyes!

Jesus redirected their focus from man to God. He was emphatic (prefacing His words with **Amen, amen, I say to you**) that all life comes from God, not from man. **Moses** indeed was instrumental in providing the manna for Israel, but the bread (and the life it gave) did not come from him. Rather, the manna and life came from His **Father**. It was to Him they should look, not to Moses. In the same way it is the Father who even now **gives** them **the true bread from heaven** and who is offering them eternal life. That **bread of God**, the food that gives true and eternal life, **is that which comes down from heaven and gives life to the world**. They were requesting a repetition of the miracle of bread from heaven—but the miracle had already been done, and was standing before them! For Jesus Himself was that true bread of God that came down from heaven, and would give life, not just to the Jews, but also to the whole world.

☙ ☙ ☙ ☙ ☙

34 They said therefore to Him, "Lord, always give us this bread."
35 Jesus said to them, "I *Myself* am the bread of life; he who comes to Me will not hunger, and he who believes in Me will never thirst again.
36 "But I told you that you have seen Me, and *yet* do not believe.
37 "All that the Father gives Me will come to Me,

> and he who comes to Me I will *certainly* not cast outside.
>
> 38 "For I have come down from heaven, not to do My own will, but the will of Him who sent Me.
>
> 39 "And this is the will of Him who sent Me, that of all that He gave Me, I do not lose *any* of it, but raise it up on the Last Day.
>
> 40 "For this is the will of My Father, that everyone who observes the Son and believes in Him may have eternal life, and I *Myself* will raise him up on the Last Day."

His hearers are still uncomprehending. Even as the Samaritan woman did not perceive His meaning when He offered her the water of life (4:15), so these Jews do not understand Him. Perhaps still thinking of the loaves they ate the previous day, they say, **"Lord** (that is, "Sir"), **always give us this bread."** Let Him multiply the loaves, not just yesterday, but today and every day thereafter!

Again the Lord answers them plainly. He Himself is that **bread of life** (the **I** is emphatic in the Greek—He and He alone is the Bread), and the life that He gives is spiritual and eternal, not physical and fleeting. The one who **comes to** Him as His obedient disciple and **believes in** Him will **never hunger** or **thirst again**. Merely physical life is passing; each meal is succeeded by hunger, and length of days by eventual death. The life He gives will never fail nor end. Nonetheless, it is as He **told** them on the way to synagogue when they first found Him that morning (v. 26)—they **have seen** Him, and *yet* **do not believe**. They have seen the sign of the bread He provided (v. 11) and still have no insight into its meaning.

Their lack of faith is no surprise to Him. They do not believe because they do not truly belong to the Father or know Him (6:45; 8:42; 15:21). They are not those who belong to **the Father** and whom the Father **gives** to Jesus to be His disciples. The truly pious in Israel will **come** to Him, and these He will *certainly* **not cast outside** or reject. On the contrary, He will give them the eternal life of which He speaks, for this is **the will of Him who sent** Him. God's will is that none of Jesus' disciples—however humble, sinful, or outcast (compare 7:49; 9:34; Mark 2:16)—will be **lost**, but that every one of them will be **raised up** to life **on the Last Day**. Indeed, everyone who **observes the Son**, focusing his heart and life upon Him, is to **have eternal life**, and Jesus Himself (the **I** is again emphatic in the Greek) will **raise him up on the Last Day**.

ॐ ॐ ॐ ॐ ॐ

41 Therefore the Jews were grumbling about Him, because He said, "I *Myself* am the bread that came down from heaven."

42 And they were saying, "Is not this Jesus, the son of Joseph, whose father and mother we *ourselves* know? How does He now say, 'I have come down from heaven'?"

43 Jesus answered and said to them, "Do not grumble among yourselves.

44 "No one is able to come to Me unless the Father who sent Me draws him, and I *Myself* will raise him up on the Last Day.

45 "It is written in the prophets, 'And they will all be taught by God.' Everyone who has heard and learned from the Father comes to Me.

46 "Not that anyone has seen the Father, except the One who is from God; He has seen the Father.

Here are more astonishing claims. It is for God alone to raise up all men on the Last Day, and here is Jesus, a mere man (as they think), claiming that He will do that! Just as Israel of old grumbled about the bread from heaven (Num. 11:6), so **the Jews** now **were grumbling about Him**. He claimed that He Himself (the pronoun is emphatic) **came down from heaven**: how could this be? What did He mean, "come down from heaven"? He never came down from heaven—He was born right here on earth, in their midst! They knew Him as **the son of Joseph**, and his **father and mother** were well known in Nazareth. **How does He now say, 'I have come down from heaven'?** Such a claim was patently absurd!

The Lord is again not surprised or rattled by their rejection. He simply bids them **not** to **grumble** in unbelief as they are doing, and calls them to faith. Until they have **heard and learned from the Father**, they will not be **able to come** to Him as His disciples, for the Father will only **draw** to Jesus those who have open and teachable hearts. They must allow themselves to be drawn by the Father.

The word rendered *draw* is the Greek *elko*, used elsewhere for the hauling of a net (John 21:6) and for dragging someone from the Temple (Acts 21:30). Its use always presupposes that there is some resistance to be overcome; its use here shows how the Father overcomes the prejudices of the Jews, teaching them new ways of perception. It is these, His disciples who have learned these new ways, who are assured of eternal life **on the Last Day**—not those who reject Him in their misguided zeal for the Law (such as those of 5:16).

This is what was **written in the prophets** regarding the Kingdom of God—"**they will all be taught by God**" (Is. 54:13). In that day of the Kingdom, it was said, all would know God, as God gave them hearts of flesh and put His Law into them (Ezek. 36:26; Jer. 31:33). Jesus says that this hope of the prophets is fulfilled in those who become His disciples, for it is only those who have been touched by God and learned from Him that are able to hear the Gospel word. (**Not**, Jesus adds, **that anyone has seen the Father** as He has; Jesus alone has **seen the Father** and knows all His will. Learning from the Father does not bestow equality with Jesus. He alone remains the Teacher.)

In limiting His disciples to those who have been taught by God, Jesus does not mean to exclude His hearers. On the contrary, it is a bold invitation for them to repent and open their hearts. They claim to delight in God's will; they pore over the Law to learn what He wants from them. Let them therefore truly learn what He wants, and come to Him!

ॐ ॐ ॐ ॐ ॐ

47 "Amen, amen, I say to you, he who believes has eternal life.

48 "I *Myself* am the bread of life.

49 "Your fathers ate the manna in the wilderness, and died.

50 "This is the bread that comes down from heaven, that one may eat of it and not die.

51 "I *Myself* am the living bread that came down from heaven; if anyone eats of this bread, he will live forever; and the bread also which I *Myself* will give for the life of the world is My flesh."

The Lord continues to encourage them to come to repentance, promising that **he who** will **believe** and become His disciple will **have eternal life**. (To show how secure the promise is, He again prefaces it with a solemn **Amen, amen, I say to you**.) That is because He Himself, amazing as it seems to them (the pronoun **I** is emphatic), is **the bread of life**. The Father gave Him as the true bread and nourishment that could give life to the world (v. 33). Their **fathers ate the manna in the wilderness** (Ex. 16) **and died**. For that bread, though given by God, was earthly bread, able to nourish the body for this life only. Jesus Himself (again the emphatic pronoun) is **the living bread that came down from heaven**. It is not of this world, and is able to give life in the age to come as well. If one will **eat of this bread**, and receive the life Jesus can give, one will **not die**, but will **live forever** in the age to come. And what is this bread He came to give them? The Lord does not flinch: it is His **flesh**, which He will **give for the life of the world**. The reference, obvious to later Christian readers though veiled from the Jewish hearers that day, is to the Cross. Christ came to give up His Flesh and Blood as a saving sacrifice to take away the sins of the world.

ॐ ॐ ॐ ॐ ॐ

52 The Jews therefore quarreled with one another, saying, "How is this one able to give us His flesh to eat?"

53 Jesus therefore said to them, "Amen, amen, I say to you, unless you eat the flesh of the Son of Man and drink His blood, you do not have life in yourselves.

54 "He who devours My flesh and drinks My blood has eternal life, and I *Myself* will raise him up on the Last Day.

55 "For My flesh is true food, and My blood is true drink.

56 "He who devours My flesh and drinks My blood remains in Me, and I *Myself* in him.

57 "As the living Father sent Me, and I *Myself* live because of the Father, so he who eats Me, he also will live because of Me.

58 "This is the bread which came down from heaven, not as the fathers ate and died, he who devours this bread will live forever."

59 These things He said in *the* synagogue, as He taught in Capernaum.

The Jews were perplexed—and aghast. His words, often uttered in parables, seemed hard to fully fathom. But this seemed to be not only unfathomable—for **how** could He **give** them **His flesh to eat?**— but also revolting. When Jesus said this in the synagogue, the whole crowd was stirred, and a debate broke out. They **quarreled with one another**, arguing about what these words could possibly mean. The rabbi from Nazareth seemed to be suggesting cannibalism!

Jesus does not retreat from His words, nor suggest that they are simply misunderstanding a metaphor. Some Christians of later ages would suggest that to eat the Flesh of Jesus simply means to believe in Him and accept His teaching. If that were all Jesus meant, He certainly could have clarified His meaning there and then, and put an end to His hearers' misunderstanding and scandalized reaction.

But in fact He does nothing of the kind. Instead of pacifying them and explaining that He was simply speaking metaphorically, He plunges ahead to scandalize them even more. Before He spoke about giving His Flesh as bread for the life of the world, implying (without stating) that one should eat His Flesh (v. 59). Now He states the matter boldly, prefacing it with His solemn testimony that this is truth from God, **Amen, amen, I say to you**. They must indeed both **eat the flesh of the Son of Man and drink His Blood**, for if they refuse to do so, they will **not have life** in themselves. The only way to be assured of eternal life in the age to come is to eat and drink His Flesh and Blood. He could not have stated the matter more graphically. For the Jews, who had an aversion to any eating of blood (compare Lev. 17:10), such language was disgusting.

There is more. He says they must even eat Him eagerly and voraciously. It is not a question of them overcoming their revulsion and nibbling with cringing reticence. They must be positively enthusiastic in their eating. The word in the Greek is *trogo*, rendered **devour**. It means to "gnaw, munch, to eat audibly," and is used of the voracious devouring action of animals. An animal will devour its food in that it eats hungrily and continuously until all the food is gone. This is the enthusiasm the Lord commends and commands. Only so will the eater **have eternal life** and be **raised up on the Last Day** by the Lord Himself.

This eating is commanded because the Lord's **flesh is true food** and His **blood is true drink**. That is, His Flesh and Blood provide true nourishment and lasting life, to transfigure the soul and body and bring one into the eternal age to come. The one who **devours** Jesus' **flesh** and **drinks** His **blood** will **remain in** Him, and the Lord Himself will in turn **remain in** him. That is, such feasting on the Lord and receiving of His life mean that the disciple has an indissoluble bond with his Lord. The life of Jesus will remain in him forever. The life of **the living Father**, the One who **sent** Jesus and whose life is the life of Jesus (since the Father and the Son remain one), will be in the disciple who **eats** Jesus, so that he will **also live** forever because of his union with Christ. That is why to eat Christ means to **live forever**.

The fathers in the wilderness **ate** the manna and then (in due time) **died**, for they ate a merely earthly bread and received a merely earthly life. But the Kingdom Christ offers transcends anything seen before. It is spiritual, not political. The Bread and Kingdom He offers give a life that will endure. The one who **devours this bread** and receives life from Him **will live forever**.

St. John, with his customary concern for historical detail, adds that **He said these things in *the* synagogue** of **Capernaum**. (It is perhaps ironic that the Jews should have stumbled at Christ's claim to be the true manna from heaven, for there was an image of the manna engraved on the lintel above that synagogue door.)

ॐ ॐ ॐ ॐ ॐ

60 Therefore many of His disciples when they heard this said, "This is a hard word; who is able to hear it?"

61 But Jesus, knowing in Himself that His disciples grumbled about this, said to them, "Does this cause you to stumble?

62 "What then if you should observe the Son of Man ascending where He was at first?

63 "It is the Spirit who gives-life; the flesh does not profit anything; the words that I *Myself* have spoken to you are spirit and life.

64 "But there are some of you who do not believe." For Jesus knew from *the* beginning who they were who did not believe, and who it was that would deliver Him up.

65 And He was saying, "Because of this I have said to you that no one is able to come to Me unless it has been given him from the Father."

The forcefulness with which Jesus claimed to be the world's life-giver and the graphic insistence on what they took to be cannibalism was too much for them. **Many** of them, **when they heard** it, **said, "This is a hard word,"** too difficult to accept. **"Who is able to hear it?"** Jesus had said and done many inspiring and extraordinary things, but this was insane.

The Lord, however, **knowing** supernaturally what was going on inside them, bade them not to **grumble** or harden their hearts. Did His saying that He came down from heaven (v. 58) **cause** them **to stumble** and take offense? What if they **should observe** Him **ascending** back up to heaven, **where He was at first?** If they could not accept His authority now, how could they later accept it after He had been invested with His former glory? They must open their hearts to be led by the Holy Spirit. They were judging Jesus' words as if they were merely human words, when in fact His **words** were **spirit and life**, bestowing new possibilities and life on those who accepted them. They must open themselves to **the Spirit,** to Him **who gives-life** to all flesh. Hearing Jesus with a carnal mindset, with predispositions limited by **the flesh,** could not **profit** them **anything.**

Christ openly acknowledged that **there** were **some** of them present who did **not believe.** For **Jesus knew from** *the* **beginning who they were who did not believe, and who it was that would deliver Him up.** His apparent popularity did not mislead Him into misreading the situation. He knew exactly what went on in men's hearts and what was to happen to Him. This was the inevitable result of man's hardness of heart, and why it was **that no one** was **able to come** to Him **unless it had been given him from the Father.** Their rejection of Him, He told them, proved the truth of what He said to them earlier (in v. 44), that one needed a changed attitude in order to come to Him and inherit the Kingdom.

John is concerned to stress that nothing that happened to Christ—not His rejection in Galilee, not even His being delivered up and betrayed by one of the Twelve—was unforeseen by Him. As the One who was inseparably united to the Father, nothing came as a surprise to Him, but He knew all things (compare 16:30).

66 From this *time* many of His disciples went back and were not walking with Him any longer.

67 Jesus said therefore to the Twelve, "Do you *yourselves* also want to go away?"

68 Simon Peter answered Him, "Lord, to whom will we go? You have the words of eternal life.

69 "And we *ourselves* have believed and have come to know that You *Yourself* are the Holy One of God."

70 Jesus answered them, "Did I *Myself* not choose you, the Twelve, and one of you is a devil?"

71 Now He was speaking of Judas the *son* of Simon Iscariot, for this one, one of the Twelve, was about to deliver Him up.

This controversy in Capernaum proved to be a turning point in His popularity, and **from this *time* many of His disciples went back and were not walking with Him any longer.** They had counted themselves as His disciples and had followed Him from place to place, prepared to give His teaching a hearing. But no more.

Such defections tended to spread. He challenged **the Twelve,** asking if even they (the pronoun is emphatic) **also wanted to go away.** Would they return to their homes and find themselves another teacher? **Simon Peter,** as usual, spoke for them all. The Lord had appealed for their continued loyalty, and Peter, his impulsive heart overflowing with love (compare 13:37), blurted out that such loyalty was inevitable and unfailing. Could they go away from Him? To go where and attach themselves to which teacher? There *was* no other place to go—He only had **the words of eternal life,** the words that promised the Kingdom of God. By being with Him those past months, they of all people (the pronoun **we** is emphatic) had **believed** and **come to know** that He and He alone (another emphatic pronoun) was **the Holy One of God,** the Messiah. Though all might fall away, He could count on the Twelve!

The Lord's response was sobering (as was usual when He encountered overexuberant protestations of loyalty or flattery; compare 13:37–38; Mark 10:17–18). He knew how much—and how little—He could count on the Twelve. For even though He Himself personally **chose** them to be **the Twelve** (the pronoun **I** is emphatic), yet **one** of them was **a devil**, one in whom Satan was at work. John adds that Christ knew even then how **Judas the *son* of Simon Iscariot** (that is, a man from the Judean town of Kerioth) was **about to deliver Him up** and betray Him in due time. The Lord was not misled by Peter's well-intentioned exuberance. As God, He knew that the seeds of defection and sin were even then growing in the heart of Judas.

℀ EXCURSUS

ON THE EUCHARIST

From the days of the apostles and the earliest Fathers, the Church has confessed that the Eucharist (variously called the Divine Liturgy, the Mass, Holy Communion, among other later titles) was the time when the faithful would eat the Body and Blood of Christ. As early as the time of St. Ignatius of Antioch (martyred c. AD 107), the Church confessed that the eucharistic Bread is "the Flesh of our Savior Jesus, which Flesh suffered for our sins" (Ignatius, *Epistle to the Smyrneans*, ch. 6).

This eating and drinking of His Flesh and Blood under the forms of bread and wine was the weekly experience of the Church, and could be expected to color and inform their reading of this chapter of John's Gospel. Indeed, St. John Chrysostom (d. 407), commenting on this chapter, refers it to the Eucharist, saying, "Those men then at that time [the Jews who heard Christ] reaped no fruit from what was said, but we have enjoyed the benefit in the very realities. Therefore it is necessary to understand the marvel of the Mysteries [or Sacraments] . . . Christ has given to those who desire

Him not only to see Him, but even to touch and to eat Him, and fix their teeth in His Flesh" (John Chrysostom, *Homily 46 on John's Gospel*). It will be helpful to examine this chapter in greater detail to discern which elements in it are fulfilled in the Eucharist.

In speaking of Himself as "the Bread of God which came down from heaven," and as "the Bread of Life" (6:33, 35), Christ means that He is the One who gives life to the world. Even as bread was the basic foodstuff in the ancient world ("to eat bread" was a synonym for "to eat food"), the basic form of nourishment and life, so Christ is food for the world. Just as bread keeps men physically alive, so Christ keeps them alive spiritually. He "came down from heaven" when He was born of the holy Theotokos that first Christmas morning. As bread gives life to those who eat it, so Christ gives life to the world.

Christ expands that basic image in 6:51, explaining that He gives that life to the world through the offering of His Flesh. The reference (oblique to His original hearers, but plain to Christian readers of the Gospel) was to the Cross: it was on the Cross that He offered that saving Flesh to God and brought life to the world.

As we have seen in the commentary above, Christ continued to press the point on His hearers, telling them that they had to eat—and even devour—His Flesh and drink His Blood if they were to have eternal life (6:53–54), for His Flesh and Blood were true food and drink (6:55). Only so could they abide in Him, have Him abiding in them (6:56), and live forever (6:58). This eating and drinking was not to take place carnally, however, as if Christ's hearers were to consume the meat on His bones and the blood flowing through His veins. Christ was referring to the sacramental eating and drinking of His Body and Blood in the Eucharist, which He would later establish.

We may still ask, *why* did Jesus say that we had to "eat

and drink His flesh and blood" (v. 53) or (more graphically) to "eat Him" (v. 57)? To eat Christ means receiving all of Him into oneself, so that the life in Him comes to be one's own life. When one eats bread, that bread (and the power in the bread to nourish) actually *becomes one's own self*; so that there is an inmost union of oneself with the bread. This is why Christ said we must "eat Him": the life in Him (which He received from the Father) comes to be life in the believer (6:57). And this is why St. John Chrysostom, in the homily quoted earlier, also says that in the Eucharist we are "blended into Christ's Flesh" and that He has "mixed up Himself with us" and has "kneaded up His Body with ours, that we might be One Thing, like a body joined to a head." We become one with Christ and have an inmost union with Him.

Thus, the phrase "eating His Flesh" expresses an intimate union with Him. This is what "to believe in Him" (6:29, 35, 40, 47) actually entails and what it leads to, for if one is His disciple, one will eat Christ's Flesh and drink His Blood in the Eucharist. That is why Christ not only says "*he who believes* has eternal life" (6:47), but also "*he who eats* has eternal life" (6:54), since the one who believes in Him becomes a part of His Church, and as a part of that Church, constantly partakes of the Eucharist as the defining and characteristic act of discipleship. As a believer, one continually renews one's union with Christ by receiving His Flesh and Blood sacramentally. In this way, one is "blended into Christ" (to use Chrysostom's phrase) and becomes "one Body" (to use St. Paul's phrase; see 1 Cor. 10:17).

The primary meaning of Christ's words in 6:53–58, therefore, was the Eucharist. It did not matter that the Eucharist had not yet been instituted, for Christ was speaking of what would be in store for them if they continued as His disciples. It was the same when He spoke to them of their receiving the Holy Spirit (4:10, 14; 7:37–38), even though this also could not be received until later, after Christ's

Ascension and glorification, when the Holy Spirit would be given (7:39). As John Chrysostom says (in the homily quoted above), "If the people believed Him to be a prophet [compare 6:14], they ought to have believed His words." In speaking of eating His Flesh (and of receiving the living water of the Holy Spirit), Jesus spoke as a prophet of the blessings to come.

This is also why Christ did not retract His words about eating His Flesh and drinking His Blood, even though this caused many to stumble. If He was not referring to a eucharistic eating and drinking, but was simply using a metaphor, then why not explain this? His hearers understood Him to be talking about actually eating His Flesh—if all He really meant was believing in Him, or accepting His teaching, or experiencing a spiritual inner union, then why did He not explain that this was all He meant? For that explanation would have saved them from stumbling. In fact, He could not retract His hard words about eating His Flesh, or redefine them as simply a metaphor, because He meant exactly what He said.

Finally, it should be remembered that the Eucharist was the weekly experience of St. John's first generation of readers, and they could hardly fail to read their eucharistic experience into the text. To eat and drink Christ's Flesh and Blood was the act which continued to constitute them as Christians—and the lens through which they would see Christ's words. St. John recorded those words in such a way that they would identify Christ's reference to eating and drinking with their own eucharistic experience. In doing so, he was not misleading them, for it was to the Eucharist that Christ was referring.

§III.7. Third Visit to Jerusalem: Feast of Booths

§III.7.i. Journey in Secret

ॐ ॐ ॐ ॐ ॐ

7 1 And after these things Jesus was walking in Galilee, for He did not want to walk in Judea, because the Jews were seeking to kill Him.

2 Now the feast of the Jews, the Feast of Booths, was near.

3 Therefore His brothers said to Him, "Leave here, and go away into Judea, that Your disciples also may observe Your works which You do.

4 "For no one does anything in secret when he himself seeks to be in open *view*. If You do these things, manifest Yourself to the world."

5 For not even His brothers believed in Him.

John picks up his narrative **after these things**—that is, after the waning of Jesus' popularity (6:66) and His prediction of betrayal (6:70–71), narrating the building up of the storm which would finally take His life. Things down south in Jerusalem and Judea had become too hot for Him. His healing of the paralytic on the Sabbath led to persecution (5:16), and His response to their challenges (with His renewed claims to divinity; 5:17–18) had led to even more intense opposition as they **were seeking to kill Him**. It was now no longer safe **to walk** and work **in Judea**. Instead, He confined Himself to working in the safety of **Galilee**, where the bulk of His support still resided.

A moment of opportunity came about six months later, however, with **the feast of the Jews** in the autumn, **the Feast of Booths**. This was the great Feast of the Ingathering, the harvest festival (Ex. 23:16). It was a time of great joy in Israel, and commemorated their possession of the plentiful Promised Land. To provoke a sense of gratitude for the land, the people were commanded by God to dwell in booths or tents for seven days, reliving their time of wandering in the desert, when they did *not* possess the land, but had to dwell in tents. In so doing, the people could better appreciate the land with its bounty and rejoice in their harvest as the gift of God.

There were special ceremonies in the Temple as well. There was a daily procession with music to fetch water from the nearby Pool of Siloam. The water was carried in a golden pitcher and poured, along with the customary wine, onto the morning and evening sacrifices. Throughout the weeklong festival, people in the Temple would carry branches of palm, myrtle, willow, and citron in their hands to wave in festive jubilation. In the evening, great lamps were lit in the Court of the Women, which illumined the whole Temple area. It was a time of joy, of reveling in singing crowds—and of exultant nationalism.

When this Feast of Booths was near, and the time approached when the Jews should go as pilgrims to the festival, Jesus' brothers challenged Him. Here, they said, was the perfect opportunity to perform miracles and gather crowds and reveal Himself to all Israel as their Messiah. He should **leave here**, abandoning the relative safety of Galilee, and **go away into Judea** to use the approaching feast as the backdrop for His self-promotion. There He could astound them all with His miracles so that His **disciples** and sympathizers there could **observe** these **works** and prepare for revolution. If He **sought to be in open** and public *view* (Gr. *en parresia*) and to play on the world stage, He must no longer confine Himself to the backwater of Galilee, working **in secret** (Gr. *en krupto*), far away from the applause of the nations. He must step up into the attention of the nations and **manifest** Himself **to the** whole **world** as Messiah and King. But this was not, as we might think, the voice of loyalty. It was the voice of tragic misunderstanding. Like the crowds fed by the loaves, they thought of His authority in worldly, political terms (6:15).

For John, this highlighted once more the nature of unbelief. Jesus' brothers not only did not see the transcendent and unworldly nature of His authority, they also thought that faith could come only after seeing miracles—just as the men of Galilee thought (4:44, 48). For Jesus' brothers, too, seeing was believing, and believing could only come by seeing. That was why they urged Him to do works and miracles which men could observe—only thus, they thought, could He manifest Himself to the world and win the world's support. For John, such an uncomprehending and shallow attitude revealed simply that **not even His brothers believed in Him**. Like the world, they were prisoners of the need to see.

> ॐ ॐ ॐ ॐ ॐ
>
> 6   Therefore Jesus says to them, "My *appointed* time has not yet come, but your *appointed* time is always ready.
> 7   "The world is not able to hate you; but it hates Me because I *Myself* witness about it, that its works are evil.
> 8   "You *yourselves* go up to the feast; I *Myself* do not go up to this feast because My *appointed* time has not yet been fulfilled."
> 9   And having said these things to them, He Himself remained in Galilee.

Jesus refused to be stampeded into worldly ways or to be pushed into acting before God's time. His way was to submit to God's will, not to promote Himself. His *appointed* time (Gr. *kairos*) for self-revelation had **not yet come**. Now was not the hour for joining and leading the crowd and for revealing Himself to them as Messiah. His brothers' *appointed* time was **always ready**; they could always revel with the crowd. They shared the same values and assumptions as that worldly crowd (such as expecting a military Messiah), and **the world** was **not able to hate** them. It was different for Him. The world indeed **hated** Him, because He was the one (the **I** is emphatic in the Greek) who **witnessed about it that its works were evil**. His words about the Kingdom stood in judgment on the world, with the world's insistence on retaliation, strident nationalism, and a military kingdom. Let His brothers be the ones to go to the feast (the pronoun **you** is again emphatic). As for Himself, He (Gr. *ego*, the emphatic **I**) would **not go up to this feast** to reveal Himself as they counseled, for His *appointed* time of glory had **not yet been**

fulfilled. And, consistent with His words, **He Himself remained in Galilee** while they went up as part of the joyful pilgrim throng. They wanted Him to lead that throng and appear in Jerusalem as the messianic Deliverer of all. But He stayed where He was, and missed the beginning of the feast—with its opportunity for self-glorification.

ॐ ॐ ॐ ॐ ॐ

10 But when His brothers had gone up to the feast, then He Himself also went up, not manifestly, but as *it were* in secret.

11 The Jews therefore were seeking Him at the feast, and saying, "Where is He?"

12 And there was much grumbling about Him among the crowds; some were saying, "He is a good man"; others were saying, "No, but *rather* He deceives the crowd."

13 Yet no one was speaking openly about Him for fear of the Jews.

After this, **His brothers** left to join the pilgrim crowd on the way to Jerusalem to keep the feast. They had challenged Jesus not to work **in secret** (Gr. *en krupto*), but to manifest Himself (Gr. *phaneroo*) to the world (v. 4). This Jesus refused to do. So, after they had **gone up to the feast**, Jesus **Himself also went up** quietly with His disciples, separately from the boisterous crowd. He did **not** go up **manifestly** (Gr. *phaneros*) and with great fanfare, as they suggested, to gather and lead the crowd, but rather in secret, traveling as a private person.

In Jerusalem, everyone was **seeking Him at the feast, and saying, "Where is He?"** His absence was noted, for many there had thought this was the time when He would summon the crowds to Himself and begin His revolution. He was still a figure of controversy, however, and **there was much grumbling about Him among the crowds**. That is, the teeming crowds present in the Holy City for the feast were divided. **Some were saying, "He is a good man,"** and were inclined to ignore the denunciations of His enemies, who condemned Him as impious (5:16; Luke 7:34). **Others** sharply dissented, saying, **"No, but *rather* He deceives the crowd."** These latter thought that He could not be the righteous prophet He seemed to be, and that His claims to speak for God and His seeming miracles were simply a deception.

John represents this all as *grumbling* (Gr. *goggusmos*). This is cognate with the word used in Numbers 14:27, where it describes the children of Israel's grumbling at God in the wilderness and rejecting His leadership. In those ancient days, they "did not believe in Him, despite all the signs which He performed in their midst" (Num. 14:11)—even as Jesus' generation did not believe in *Him*, despite the signs which *He* performed. John uses this word to describe the debate that raged over Jesus during the Feast of Booths, for if the Israel of his day had been faithful, there would have been no debate. Rather, all Israel would have accepted Jesus. But as it was, they rejected Him as a figure of controversy. This debate, however, was held in hushed whispers, within huddled crowds. **No one** dared to openly defend Him or confront His foes. The debate was not held **openly** (Gr. *parresia*) **for fear of** the reprisals that might come from **the Jews** and the leaders of the nation.

§III.7.ii. More Controversy over the Healing of the Paralytic: Jesus the Water of Life

ॐ ॐ ॐ ॐ ॐ

14 But when it was already the middle of the feast, Jesus went up into the Temple and taught.

15 The Jews therefore were marveling, saying, "How has this one known letters, not having learned?"

16 Jesus therefore answered them and said, "My teaching is not Mine, but the One who sent Me.

> 17 "If anyone wants to do His will, he will know about the teaching, whether it is of God, or whether I *Myself* speak from Myself.
> 18 "He who speaks from himself seeks his own glory; but He who seeks the glory of the One who sent Him, He is true, and there is no unrighteousness in Him.
> 19 "Did not Moses give you the Law, and none of you does the Law? Why do you seek to kill Me?"

After the Feast of Booths had begun, **when it was already the middle of the feast**, then **Jesus went up into the Temple** (doubtless into one of the colonnades; compare 10:23) **and taught.** John stresses that Jesus arrived in the middle of the feast, the nonsacred part of the festive week. That is, He did not go up in time to keep the whole feast, as His brothers counseled. Nor did He go to perform more signs for the purpose of astounding people and gathering support (as they also suggested). Rather, He simply continued His teaching, awaiting the Father's timing.

The Temple authorities, **the Jews** who presided over the feast, **were marveling** at His teaching. Jesus had not **learned** from any eminent rabbi. He was not technically or rabbinically trained. **How has this one known** the sacred **letters** of the Law with such evident depth and familiarity? How is it that one like *Him* can give such a sustained and powerful discourse on the Law! (We can almost see the sneer on their lips as they refer to "this one"—that is, a mere carpenter from Galilee.)

The Lord **answered them** by referring to His divine origin. The **teaching** He gave in the Temple was not His own—He did not make it up Himself, nor learn it from any distinguished rabbi. Rather, it came from **the One who sent** Him—from the Father. They might deny this and stumble at the notion of Him being sent by God. But they could know the truth about Him if they wanted to. For **if anyone** truly **wanted to do** God's **will** and was open to being taught by Him, they would **know about the teaching** Jesus gave, **whether**

it was of God (as Jesus claimed) or whether Jesus was simply **speaking from** Himself and presenting His own ideas as if they were God's—for God would reveal it to him (compare 6:44).

That Jesus did not speak from Himself, or on His own merely human authority, could be seen by this too—that the one who **speaks from himself**, putting forward his own ideas, **seeks his own glory**. If He did not speak for God, but was simply trying to advance His own notions, He would be doing all He could to court the favor of the powerful. And this was plainly not the case, for He was setting Himself against the powerful and influential and making many enemies. It was apparent then that He cared only for God's favor, since He **sought** only **the glory** of the Father **who sent Him**. This showed that Jesus was **true** and that there was **no unrighteousness in Him**. He was not the false prophet they denounced Him as, nor a breaker of the Law. They prided themselves on their scrupulous keeping of the Law, and condemned Him because He healed a man on the Sabbath, commanding that he carry his bed (5:8). They claimed to be Moses' loyal disciples. **Moses** had indeed **given** them **the Law**, but **none** of them actually **did** and kept that **Law**. Their claims to follow Moses were a sham. Moses had forbidden murder in the Law, and yet here they were, **seeking to kill** Jesus, in clear violation of the Law!

ॐ ॐ ॐ ॐ ॐ

20 The crowd answered, "You have a demon! Who seeks to kill You?"

21 Jesus answered and said to them, "One work I did, and everyone marvels

22 "because of this. Moses gave you circumcision (not that it is from Moses, but from the Fathers) and on a Sabbath you circumcise a man.

23 "If a man receives circumcision on a Sabbath that the Law of Moses may not be destroyed, are you infuriated with Me because I made an entire man healthy on a Sabbath?

> **24** "Do not judge according to appearance, but judge with righteous judgment."

The crowd of festal pilgrims reacts with derision. "**You** must **have a demon** to talk that way," they say. "**Who seeks to kill You?**" Those from Galilee find the possibility of Judean murder plots incredible. The Lord, however, does not stop to debate the matter, but goes to the heart of the Jewish objections and the reason some seek to kill Him: His alleged destruction of the Sabbath. Christ's foes fundamentally misunderstand the intent of the Sabbath—and this is proven even by their own inconsistency.

Jesus **did** but **one work**—that of healing on the Sabbath (5:8–9)—and **everyone marveled because of this**. This single act (the words **one work** come at the head of the sentence in the Greek for emphasis) was enough to astonish and enrage them. You would think they were all so zealous to uphold the Sabbath and do the will of God! But let them **not judge according to appearance**, looking at the matter superficially. Let them **judge with righteous judgment**, discerning what God truly wants and what He truly intends by His Law.

For **Moses gave** them not only the Sabbath, but also **circumcision** (though Christ elaborates that circumcision did **not** come **from Moses** originally, but went further back and came **from the Fathers**—see Gen. 17:9–14). Circumcision, being older than Moses, was thus a matter of great importance, for it meant including the newborn child in the covenant of God. It brought God's blessing to the eight-day-old, and one must **circumcise** a child on the eighth day, even if that day fell **on a Sabbath**. This they all freely admitted. This work was allowed on the Sabbath, for it brought the blessing of God.

How blind they were! For if **a man received circumcision on a Sabbath**—which involved God's blessing on one bodily member—in order to fully keep **the Law of Moses**, how much more could **an entire man** be **made healthy on a Sabbath**? For Christ had brought blessing, not just to one bodily member, but to a man's whole body. How could they be **infuriated** at that? Christ had *kept* the intent of the Sabbath, not broken it, for it clearly honored the Sabbath to do good on it (compare Mark 3:4). If they would **judge with righteous judgment**, they would not condemn Christ as if He were a Law-breaker, but accept Him as One sent from God.

ॐ ॐ ॐ ॐ ॐ

25 Therefore some of the Jerusalemites were saying, "Is this not He whom they seek to kill?
26 "And behold, He is speaking openly, and they are saying nothing to Him! Do the rulers truly know that this is the Christ?
27 "But we know where this one is from; but whenever the Christ comes, no one knows where He is from."

The controversy continued. **Some of the Jerusalemites**—the ones who resided in Jerusalem and therefore knew more of what the authorities in Jerusalem were planning—began to be perplexed. They had heard that Jesus was **He** whom the authorities were **seeking to kill**. And yet there He was, **speaking openly** in the Temple as a kind of defiant challenge to those threats, while His foes went on **saying nothing to Him**! Did it mean that **the rulers** and Temple authorities **truly knew that this was the Christ** after all? But that could not be, for they all **knew where this one was from**—namely Nazareth in Galilee, whereas **whenever the Christ** would **come, no one** would **know where He was from**.

St. John narrates this part of the controversy to focus on the Jewish misunderstanding. Popular Jewish thought of that day held that Messiah would appear suddenly to Israel, as if coming out of nowhere. Thus one of the rabbis taught, "Three things come unawares: the Messiah, a found article, and a scorpion." That is, just as one suddenly comes across a formerly lost article and as one suddenly finds a scorpion where one least expects it, so Messiah will suddenly come on the scene to Israel. Jesus seemed disqualified as Messiah, since everyone knew where He came from. He did not burst on the scene as an unknown. His family and origins in Nazareth were well known. The Jews stumbled over the humility of His Incarnation—a Messiah who was a carpenter from mediocre Nazareth was too much for them!

ॐ ॐ ॐ ॐ ॐ

28 Jesus therefore cried out in the Temple, teaching and saying, "You both know Me and know where I am from! And I have not come of Myself, but He who sent Me is true, whom you do not know.
29 "I *Myself* know Him, because I am from Him, and that One sent Me."
30 They were seeking therefore to take hold of Him, and no one laid a hand on Him, for His hour had not yet come.
31 Many from the crowd believed in Him; and they said, "Whenever the Christ comes, will He do more signs than this one does?"

This Jewish misunderstanding was the crux of the matter, and it could not be allowed to go unchallenged. **Therefore** the Lord lifted up His voice and **cried out in the Temple**. The word rendered **cried out** is the Greek *krazo*; it was used for the shouting of the demoniacs in Mark 5:7 and 9:26, and means to call out loudly—almost (in some contexts) to shriek. Its use here shows that the Lord thundered forth a mighty cry, intent on reaching all within earshot. This matter was of the utmost importance.

They thought that they **both knew** Him and **knew where** He **was from**! Hardly. They were still judging according to appearance, and not with righteous judgment (v. 24). If they would be taught by God, they must see past outward appearances and not stumble at such things as His humble earthly origins. He had **not come of** Himself or as if promoting His own ideas. On the contrary, He had come to them simply because He had been sent from the Father. The Father who **sent** Him was **true**.

In saying that God was **true** (Gr. *alethinos*), the Lord meant more than that God was truthful and did not lie. The use of the word *alethinos* in John's Gospel always denotes the genuine and eternal, as opposed to that which is merely earthly, and therefore transient and fading. Thus Christ is the *true* light (1:9) that abides, as opposed to mere earthly lights that fade. He is the *true* Bread (6:32) that gives eternal life, as opposed to mere earthly bread, which cannot nourish for eternity. He is the *true* vine (15:1), which gives divine life to its branches, as opposed to mere earthly vines, which can wither and die. In all cases, the contrast is between the divine, eternal realm and the earthly realm, which always falls short of such eternal, unfading realities. In describing God here as **true**, Jesus asserts that God lives in the eternal realm, beyond reach of their erring senses. That is why they do **not know** Him. Only Jesus Himself, and He alone (the pronoun **I** is emphatic in the Greek), could know God, because Jesus had His eternal origin **from Him**, and the Father was the very One who **sent** Him—His humble origins in Nazareth notwithstanding. For Jesus' origins were not ultimately from Nazareth, but from God.

These claims to divine origin once again enraged His foes, and they **were seeking** to **take hold of Him**. That is, there were unofficial attempts to seize Him and drag Him before the authorities. These were unsuccessful. Whatever the human causes for their failure (our Lord's popularity and the presence of the crowds), St. John focuses on the underlying divine reason: that **His hour had not yet come**. The time would come for His Cross and glorification, but that time was not yet. Until God willed, Jewish rulers could do nothing. In saying this, John stresses that Jesus' death did not represent His powerlessness before His foes, but the will of God, which Jesus freely accepted.

The Lord's bold and loud claims had their effect: **many from the crowd believed in Him**. But John also reveals the superficiality of this faith, saying that it was based on their seeing **signs** and miracles. They only believed because of the multitude of miracles, not because their hearts were truly open. The controversy would continue.

137

32 The Pharisees heard the crowd grumbling these things about Him; and the chief-priests and the Pharisees sent attendants to take hold of Him.

33 Jesus therefore said, "For a little time yet I am with you, and *then* I go away to the One who sent Me.

34 "You will seek Me, and will not find Me, and where I *Myself* am, you *yourselves* are not able to come."

35 The Jews therefore said to themselves, "Where is this one about to go that we *ourselves* will not find Him? Is He about to go to the Diaspora of the Greeks and teach the Greeks?

36 "What is this word which He said, 'You will seek Me and will not find Me, and where I *Myself* am, you *yourselves* are not able to come'?"

This controversy and **grumbling** came to the attention of **the Pharisees**. Together with **the chief-priests** (that is, the aristocratic priestly families of Jerusalem who controlled the Temple), they **sent attendants**, members of the Temple police, **to take hold of Him**. Jesus' foes resented His growing popularity in the Temple, under their very noses, and sought to remove Him from this public setting.

Jesus sets such plots in their true perspective. His foes might think they have power **to take hold of Him**—but that can only be if and when God allows. For now, **for a little time yet**, He is **with** them. Then, when God wills, He will be taken, and die and return to the Father in ascended glory. Soon He will **go away to the One who sent** Him—and then they will **seek** Him and **not find** Him, for He will be forever safely beyond the reach of such police attendants, at the right hand of God. He will soon go where they and

their kind (the pronouns are emphatic) will **not** be **able to come.**
He is the true Messiah, and their sense of power over Him is completely illusory.

Consistent with the pattern of carnal Jewish incomprehension
(compare 2:19–20; 3:3–4; 6:51–52), they misunderstand His words.
They suppose that His talk of eluding their grasp means that He is
about to go to the Diaspora of the Greeks and teach the Greeks,
far from Palestine. Jerusalem is too hot for Him, and He is planning
to flee to the safety of foreign soil. What else can His words possibly
mean, **"You will seek Me and will not find Me, and where I** *Myself*
am, you *yourselves* **are not able to come"**?

ॐ ॐ ॐ ॐ ॐ

37 Now on the last day, the great *day* of the feast,
Jesus stood and cried out, saying, "If anyone
thirsts, let him come to Me and drink.
38 "He who believes in Me, as the Scripture said,
'From his belly will flow rivers of living water.'"
39 But this He spoke about the Spirit, whom those
who believed in Him were about to receive;
for the Spirit was not yet *given*, because Jesus
was not yet glorified.

Our Lord gave this teaching (vv. 14–34) in the Temple, having
appeared there in the middle of the festal week (v. 14). Several days
passed, and **the last day, the great** *day* **of the feast** arrived. This was
possibly the eighth day of the feast (compare 2 Macc. 10:6), a cul-
minating post-feast in which there were extra sacrifices (Lev. 23:36).
On this day, however, there was no rite of water-pouring, as there
had been on the previous days of the feast.

The Lord therefore **stood** up in the Temple and **cried out** (Gr.
krazo; compare v. 28) with a mighty voice. This standing was significant. The usual posture for teaching was sitting (compare Matt.
5:1). That Jesus stood shows His determination to reach all with
His message.

His message was an invitation to come and find life in Him, for water was an image of life. The water was not poured out in the Temple sacrifices that day, yet the true water of life was still available. As with everything else in the Law, what was foreshadowed and promised in the Temple rites was fulfilled in Him. **If anyone thirsts**, he should **come** to Jesus **and drink**. True life was abundantly available in Him, able to slake the thirst of all who longed for it. More than that, as the Scripture promised, the one who **believed** in Him would himself become a source of life to others, for **from his belly**, his innermost being, **rivers of living water** would **flow** out to the thirsty world around him. Coming to Christ, the disciple would be so filled with life that this life would overflow and spill out to the world, so that others in turn would be drawn to the Lord. In saying **as the Scripture said**, Jesus is referring to the scriptural theme of water as an image of life, which would be abundantly available in the messianic age (see Is. 44:3; 58:11; Ezek. 47:1–12; Joel 3:18). (The quote "From His belly will flow rivers of living water" is a digest and encapsulation of that theme, not an exact citation of a single verse.)

In our modern Western society, with water always abundantly and instantly available, we can have little appreciation of the Lord's words. Water was a precious commodity in the ancient Middle East, and thirst a terrible thing. The desire of the thirsty man for water was overwhelming, and his joy at finding it total. The slaking of thirst therefore was a fit image for the life Christ would supply to His followers. To those who desperately desired life and fulfillment and joy, who tired of toiling in the hard world, who found in the Jewish Law more promise than fulfillment, Jesus was able to satisfy the deepest longings of their hearts. Not only would He pour into their inmost beings water enough to satisfy their thirst, He would pour it in such abundance that they could not contain it!

St. John, writing at a later date, explains how the Lord's promise was to be fulfilled. **This He spoke about the Spirit, whom those who believed in Him were about to receive** as part of His Church. When the seeking soul came to Christ in the waters of baptism, was thrice immersed, and emerged from the water to receive the laying on of hands (compare Acts 19:5–6)—what today would be called baptism and chrismation—then He received the Holy Spirit. At the time of Jesus' words in vv. 37–38, St. John explains, this experience lay in the future. The promise was to be fulfilled later in the sacramental life of the Church. At the time of Jesus' words, **the Spirit** had not yet been sent in Pentecostal power from heaven. This would only happen after **Jesus** had been **glorified** and had sat down at the right hand of God (Acts 2:33).

ॐ ॐ ॐ ॐ ॐ

40 *Some* of the crowd therefore, hearing these words, were saying, "This truly is the Prophet."

41 Others were saying, "This is the Christ." But some were saying, "Does the Christ come from Galilee?

42 "Has not the Scripture said that the Christ is from the seed of David, and from Bethlehem, the village where David was?"

43 A division therefore occurred in the crowd because of Him.

44 And some of them wanted to take hold of Him, but no one laid their hands on Him.

Once again, the Lord's loud proclamation had an effect. *Some* **of the crowd** concluded that Jesus **truly** was **the Prophet**, the eschatological figure expected who would signal the messianic end times (compare 1:21). (The reference to the prophet Jeremiah in Matt. 16:14 makes it probable that this expected Prophet was Jeremiah come again to earth.) **Others** in the crowd concluded that Jesus was indeed **the Christ**, the Messiah Himself. That is, they took Jesus for the one who had been *designated* by God *to become* the Messiah at the proper time. They anticipated that God would soon reveal Jesus as His Messiah, investing Him with power and supernatural might to drive the Roman invader from Israel.

This latter opinion was considered as impossible by yet another group of **some** others. They asked rhetorically, **"Does the Christ come from Galilee?"** Obviously not! The very **Scripture** itself **said that the Christ is from the seed of David**, that He was David's descendant and must therefore come **from Bethlehem, the village where David was** (see Micah 5:2). So **a division occurred in the crowd because of Him**, with vocal opinions being loudly expressed and these several groups all arguing among themselves. Indeed, **some** within that large crowd were so convinced He was not the Messiah that they **wanted to take hold of Him** as a deceiver. Nonetheless, **no one laid their hands on Him**, since His hour had not yet come (v. 30).

St. John, writing for a later and more informed audience, presents the controversy with silent irony. His audience knew that Jesus had indeed been born in Bethlehem, since they were familiar with the traditions embodied in the Nativity stories (Matt. 2:1ff; Luke 2:1ff). These readers would listen to John's account of the controversy with a superior knowledge and see that there was no reason not to accept Jesus as the Messiah.

ॐ ॐ ॐ ॐ ॐ

45 The attendants therefore came to the chief-priests and Pharisees, and those ones said to them, "Why did you not bring Him?"

46 The attendants answered, "Never did a man speak thus!"

47 The Pharisees therefore answered them, "Have you *yourselves* also been deceived?

48 "Has any of the rulers believed in Him, or of the Pharisees?

49 "But this crowd which does not know the Law is cursed."

St. John's comment that no one laid their hands on Him leads him now to narrate the result of the Lord's immunity from arrest. For police **attendants** of the Temple had been sent to take hold of

Him some time earlier, after the Lord began teaching during the middle of the feast (v. 32). Since Jesus was surrounded by a crowd containing many supporters (and since Middle Eastern crowds could be volatile—compare Luke 20:6), the attendants waited to find an opportune time to arrest Him. They did not want to create a riot! They therefore waited on the outskirts of the crowd, listening to His teaching and to the controversy day after day, looking for their window of opportunity.

There were perhaps six or more of them (compare the number sent to arrest Christ in Gethsemane; Luke 22:47), and they first came simply to discharge their duties as Temple police. But as they listened to Jesus hour after hour for several days, His words pierced their hearts. It was not only what He said, but even more, how He said it! For **never did a man speak thus** (Gr. *outos*), in this manner, with such majestic authority. He was manifestly no common rabble-rouser or troublemaker, as they had been led to believe. Perhaps there was something to His claims after all.

So it was that they returned to the Sanhedrin empty-handed, where **the chief-priests and Pharisees** awaited their return. These could see at once that the attendants' mission had failed, and they demanded, **"Why did you not bring Him?"** They were given an order—what had stopped them from fulfilling it?

Their reply is instructive. They might have blamed the presence of the crowd in order to get themselves off the hook. But they did no such thing. Instead, and at some personal risk, they simply stated that their intended prisoner had spoken in such a way as to make their arresting Him impossible. "Never," they stated, "did a man speak thus!" The unanimity of the group is significant too. The crowd had been divided in their verdict (v. 43), but there was no division here. The attendants all agreed that Jesus was a holy man and not to be opposed. (Did they remember the fate of those sent to arrest holy Elijah, in 2 Kin. 1:9–10?)

The simplicity of their reply reveals their sincerity and nobility of spirit. They did not give a long explanation, nor seek to excuse themselves or avoid punishment for disobeying orders. They simply witnessed to their own convictions. For St. John, they are a

foreshadowing of the martyric Church and of those later Christians
who would stand up to Jewish hostility and witness to their loyalty
to Christ.

The reaction of **the Pharisees** (who had long opposed Jesus,
and who were perhaps more bitter enemies of Him than their chief-
priestly partners) was immediate. Scornfully they demanded whether
they, of all people (the pronoun **you** is emphatic in the Greek), **also**
had **been deceived** by the Galilean. Did they suppose Jesus to be a
prophet or the Messiah? No one of any education or sense believed
that! Had **any of the rulers** of the Sanhedrin **or of the Pharisees**—
people who could be trusted to know such things—**believed in Him?**
None that they knew of! Some of the common rabble may have
been swayed by His words, but what of that? **This crowd** that did
not know the Law, and was not rabbinically trained as they were,
was cursed and damned. The curse of God was on such as these.
Who cared for their verdict?

ॐ ॐ ॐ ॐ ॐ

50 Nicodemus says to them (he who came to Him
at first, being one of them),
51 "Does our Law judge a man without first hearing from him and knowing what he does?"
52 They answered and said to him, "Are you *yourself* also from Galilee? Examine and see that no
prophet arises from Galilee."

Nicodemus is part of that Sanhedrin. (St. John reminds us it was
he who came to Jesus **at first** by night, though he was **one of them**,
that is, of the Sanhedrin; 3:1ff.) As might be expected, he was impressed by Christ's words to him, and he undertakes to defend Him.
Objecting to such high-handed and premature condemnation of
Jesus, Nicodemus pointedly asks, "**Does our Law judge a man
without first hearing from him and knowing what he does?**" That
is, is it according to the spirit of the Mosaic Law to give a verdict
before the trial? They sit there presuming to uphold the sanctity of

the Law—how does their condemnation of one absent square with that? Christ's claims are dividing Israel into two camps, and Nicodemus (St. John stresses) is aligning himself with the right side.

The rest of the Sanhedrin then present are dismissive of Nicodemus' plea. They do not deign to discuss his point about condemning Jesus without first giving Him a hearing. For them, the thought that Jesus is a true prophet is too absurd to be seriously considered, and Nicodemus's support of Jesus is only explicable by his being a Galilean partisan. Is he **also from Galilee?** What else could explain his ridiculous support for Jesus? Jesus the Galilean— a prophet! The very idea is ludicrous. Let Nicodemus **examine** the Scriptures for himself and **see that no prophet arises from Galilee.** That is, none of the great prophets who left their scriptural words behind (such as Isaiah and Jeremiah) came **from Galilee.** That, they feel, says volumes about that northern hinterland. It is the home of the uncouth and the impious—no prophets could be expected to **arise** from there!

In reporting this exchange within the Sanhedrin, St. John again offers his silent commentary. He does not need to state the obvious. The opponents of Jesus were motivated by bias and hatred and had no real concern to uphold the Law or to represent the people of Israel, as they claimed. John's audience could see at a glance how unjust was their condemnation of Jesus.

§III.7.iii.   *Insertion:* **The Woman Taken in Adultery (7:53—8:11)**

The story of the woman grasped in the act of adultery is certainly a true historical reminiscence (it has all the touches of an eyewitness account), but it is not an original part of John's Gospel. Both the external manuscript tradition and the style preclude it. It is not found in any of the ancient manuscripts nor the early Fathers. Some manuscripts include it, but contain asterisks to set it off as different from the rest of the text. Others place it at the end of John's Gospel, or at the end of Luke's Gospel. All of this argues against it being included by John in this place, after 7:52.

Internally, it reads like one of the many encounters Christ had
with the scribes and Pharisees during the last week of His earthly
life (narrated in Luke 20:1–40 and parallels). In fact, some manuscripts include this section after Luke 21:38 to indicate that it belongs to this last week of His life. It looks as if the situation of
catching the unfortunate woman was deliberately set up—for how
else could they catch her in the very act? And if it were not deliberately set up, presumably with the agreement of the adulterous man
involved, why let the man get away? The guilty woman was appre-
hended, but where was the guilty man? All of this points to a trap
artificially set for the specific purpose of trapping Jesus—just like
other similar traps set in His final week (e.g. Luke 20:22, 33).

I would suggest, therefore, that this represents a genuine reminiscence of what Christ did during that final week, preserved in
oral tradition and, in some manuscripts, attached to this place in
John's Gospel—doubtless because some early Christian scribe saw
it as an example of how Christ came not to judge the world, but to
save it (compare John 3:17 and especially 8:15, which immediately
follows this story). John did not record it himself, but it was an
historical event, and may be examined here.

🙟 🙟 🙟 🙟 🙟

8 53 And each one went to his house.

1　But Jesus went to the Mountain of Olives.

2　And at dawn He came again into the Temple,
and all the people were coming to Him; and
He sat down and taught them.

3　And the scribes and the Pharisees led a woman
caught in adultery, and having stood her in *the*
middle,

4　they say to Him, "Teacher, this woman has
been grasped in the *very* act of adultery.

5　"Now in the Law Moses commanded us to
stone such; what therefore do You *Yourself* say?"

6　And they were saying this, testing Him, that

> they might have *something* for accusing Him. But Jesus bent down, and with His finger drew in the earth.
>
> 7 But when they continued to ask Him, He straightened up and said to them, "Let the sinless one among you be the first to throw a stone at her."
>
> 8 And again He bent down and wrote in the earth.
>
> 9 And when they heard it, they went away, one by one, beginning with the older ones, and He was left behind alone, and the woman where she was, in *the* middle.
>
> 10 And straightening up, Jesus said to her, "Woman, where are they? Did no one condemn you?"
>
> 11 And she said, "No one, Lord." And Jesus said, "Neither do I *Myself* condemn you; go, and from now *on* sin no longer."

The story begins with **each one** of the Lord's hearers (during His final week?) going **to his house**, whereas the Lord **went to the Mountain of Olives**. When dawn came, Jesus came again into the Temple to resume His regular teaching (compare Luke 19:47 for the Lord's custom of teaching in the Temple during His final earthly week).

While the Lord taught, **the scribes and the Pharisees led a woman** whom they **grasped** and took hold of **in the *very* act of adultery**. As said above, this in itself argues for a setup—as does the absence of the guilty man, who must himself have been caught in the very act as well. Dragging her with them was not necessary, for she might have been detained until sentence was given and then dealt with. It seems as if they dragged her before Jesus to add poignancy to His dilemma and increase His difficulty. They wanted Him to look into her very eyes, in order to make it less likely that He would condemn her.

They brought her to Him and pretended to ask Him, as a distinguished rabbi, for a legal ruling on how to enforce the provisions of the Law. It was clear that she was guilty of adultery, for she had been grasped in the very act. And the Law was clear about what to do in such cases—**Moses commanded** them **to stone such** (compare Deut. 22:21–22). That was what Moses had commanded—but **what** did Jesus Himself **say**? (The pronoun **You** is emphatic—did He have a different view from Moses?) They had always accused Him of overthrowing the Law—let's see Him uphold it now! (The narrator goes on to state the obvious—that this was not a sincere question, but merely done **testing Him, that they might have** *something* **for accusing Him.**)

It was, they thought, an impossible set of alternatives for Him. If He agreed that she should be stoned, she would be lynched there and then, and responsibility for this act (which was technically illegal, for only the Romans had authority to put to death) could be laid at His feet. If He said that she ought not to be stoned, He would be contradicting God's Law, which said that adulterers *should* be stoned. They had Him now!

The Lord has nothing but contempt for such pretended zeal for God's Law, for it was but a cover for their utter disregard for His true will. He at first refused to dignify their request with an answer, but **bent down, and with His finger drew in the earth**. That is, He doodled on the ground, pointedly ignoring them. (There is no suggestion in the text that what He wrote had any significance. It seems as if He wrote simply to show that He was ignoring them.) But **they continued to ask Him**, and refused to be put off—or to let the woman go.

At length, He acceded to their request for a legal rabbinical ruling. He straightened up only long enough to give it. Did the Law say that adulterers must be stoned? Then let her be stoned. But **let the sinless one among** them **be the first to throw a stone at her.** Having given the requested ruling, He turned from them again, and **bent down** and **wrote** once more **in the earth**. Such men were not worthy of His attention.

It was a brilliant reply. He had given the ruling, but delivered it in such a way as to make it impossible for sinners like them to carry out. For **when they heard it, they went away, one by one, beginning with the older ones** (who had longer experience at struggling with their own sinful weakness). Finally **He was left alone**, along with **the woman**, who remained trembling **where she was** (or had been), **in *the* middle.**

When they had gone, He again straightened up to address her. He spoke to her formally and politely (**Woman** simply answers to our "Madam"; compare His use of this term when addressing His own mother in 2:4 and 19:26). He asked a question, the answer to which was all too obvious: "**Where are they? Did no one condemn you?**" That is, is this farce of a trial over? She could only breathe out the reply, "**No one, Lord.**" Well, responded Jesus, **neither** was *He* (the pronoun I is emphatic) going to **condemn** her. He had no such agenda. She was free to **go**, but must take care to **sin no longer.**

In conclusion, it is important to see our Lord's response for what it was. It was not a comment on the Law of Moses, nor on how it should be applied by the godly and pious. His task was not to refine applications of the Law, but to bring in God's grace. His response was meant as a rebuke to those who would entrap Him, who were *not* godly or pious, but who actually cared nothing for God's will. And it was meant as a demonstration of God's grace. Christ came to bring forgiveness to the penitent soul—to save the world, not to condemn it. When the woman was brought to Christ, she was in the process of stepping out of the realm of the Mosaic Law and into the realm of grace. If she would rightly respond to that grace, she would **sin no longer**, but embrace a life of righteousness. Thus does grace fulfill the true and inner goal of the Law, leading the soul to God and away from sin.

§III.7.iv. Continuation of Controversy: Jesus the Light of the World

ॐ ॐ ॐ ॐ ॐ

12 Again therefore Jesus spoke to them, saying, "I *Myself* am the Light of the world; he who

> **follows Me will never walk in the darkness, but will have the light of life."**

In the original of John's Gospel, 8:12 followed immediately after 7:52. That is, Christ cried out on the last and great day of the feast that He was the One who could supply divine water to the thirsty soul (7:37–38), and this utterance prompted a fresh spate of controversy—extending even to the Temple police who declined to arrest Him (7:45–46).

We have seen that Christ's word about offering spiritual water had as its background the water-pouring ceremonies in the Temple that occurred throughout the first seven days of the feast. Also prominent in that Feast of Booths were the great lamps that were lit in the Court of Women in the Temple every night during the festal week, but were not lit at the feast's close.

These lights form the background for Christ's next recorded utterance, "I *Myself* am the Light of the world." The lamps were not lit on that final day of the feast, but there still remained a light in the Temple—Jesus Himself, as He stood in that Court of Women where the lamps had been. Just as the great lamps had illumined the Temple and the surrounding part of the city, so Christ illumined the whole world. If one rejected Him, one was without the light of God and would stumble and fall. But the one **who follows Him** would **never walk in the darkness, but** would **have the light of life.** Without Jesus, those in the world would remain in the darkness.

Once again, we in the modern post-industrial world can have little sense of the horror the ancients had of the dark, since we have easy access to artificial light. It was otherwise in older times. In those days, once the sun set, men had to stay indoors huddled around a lamp, awaiting the coming of the light at dawn. Light was a deliverance, a joy to the heart, the precondition for all life. By claiming to be the Light of the world, Christ was claiming to be that universal joy and the bringer of life to all men. His followers and they alone would have that blessed light of life; discipleship to Him was the only way to escape the darkness of death.

ॐ ॐ ॐ ॐ ॐ

13 The Pharisees therefore said to Him, "You *Yourself* witness about Yourself; Your witness is not true."

14 Jesus answered and said to them, "Even if I *Myself* witness about Myself, My witness is true, for I know from where I came, and where I go, but you *yourselves* do not know from where I come, or where I go.

15 "You *yourselves* judge according to the flesh; I *Myself* do not judge anyone.

16 "But even if I *Myself* judge, My judgment is true; for I am not alone *in it* but I *Myself* and the Father who sent Me.

17 "Even in your Law it has been written that the witness of two men is true.

18 "I *Myself* am He who witnesses about Myself, and the Father who sent Me witnesses about Me."

19 Therefore they were saying to Him, "Where is Your Father?" Jesus answered, "You know neither Me, nor My Father; if you knew Me, you would know My Father also."

20 These words He spoke in the treasury, as He taught in the Temple, and no one took hold of Him, because His hour had not yet come.

This was another astonishingly bold claim. **The Pharisees** could not contain their hostility and cast about for some way to refute Him. They found a way, they thought, in His own words. He had said before that if He bore witness about Himself, His witness was therefore not true (5:31). He had meant, of course, that His witness about Himself was true because it was not a solitary witness, but was accompanied also by the witness of His Father. His union with the Father meant that His words were not His words alone, but the words of the Father.

His foes did not grasp this, and seized upon the outward and superficial meaning of His words. For them, the fact that He made *any* claims about Himself meant that this **witness** was **not true** and His testimony was invalid and worthless. He had no right, they thought, to witness about Himself.

The Pharisees were presuming to sit in judgment of Him and disqualify His witness as invalid because it was, they thought, unsupported. In reply, the Lord discounted their competence to sit in judgment of Him at all. He was from the heavenly realm, and knew **from where** He **came** and **where** He was to **go**, whereas they had no such knowledge (the pronouns **I** and **you** are emphatic in the Greek for greater contrast). As the Lord from heaven, He stood above all the uncertainties, ambiguities, and ignorance in this world, and knew all. They did not. They obviously were in no state to judge Him. They could only **judge according to the flesh**, with all the limitations and folly that attend worldly judgments. He was above such— and even so, He, unlike them (the pronoun **I** is again emphatic for contrast), did **not judge anyone**. They were quick to condemn Him; yet He did not come to condemn any. Instead, He came to save (3:17). He was utterly unlike them, with their failing judgments.

As the One sent by the heavenly Father, He could **witness about** Himself and His **witness** would be **true**. He could **judge**, and His **judgment** would be **true**, for He was **not alone** in such things. Rather, **the Father who sent** Him was with Him. **Even in** their own **Law** (for which they professed such a zeal), it was **written that the witness of two men** was **true** (compare Deut. 19:15). That is, it only took the concurrent testimony of two men to establish truth. Well, here was the testimony of Two—Christ Himself (the pronoun is emphatic) **and the Father who sent** Him. Both witnessed about Him that He was the Messiah and Light of the world.

Mention of His Father provoked the scornful challenge, "**Where is Your Father?**" He had claimed that the Father was with Him as a second witness. *They* didn't see any such Father!

The Lord's reply is significant: to see Him was to see the Father (compare 14:9), for He was the fullness of the Father and was one with Him. Obviously the Pharisees had no knowledge of *either* of the two Witnesses! They **knew neither** Jesus and who He was, **nor** knew His **Father**. If they had **known** Jesus, they would thereby **know** His **Father also**, for to know Jesus was to know the Father.

St. John adds another eyewitness touch, saying that **He spoke the words** of this exchange **in the treasury, as He taught in the Temple**. That is, He stood in full view in the Court of the Women, where the collection boxes stood by the walls (compare Luke 21:1f). Nonetheless, despite His teaching so boldly in such a public place, **no one took hold of Him, because His hour** to be arrested, killed, and glorified **had not yet come**. As one truly sent by God, He was under divine protection, and could only be taken as God willed.

ॐ ॐ ॐ ॐ ॐ

21 He said therefore again to them, "I *Myself* go away, and you will seek Me, and will die in your sin; where I *Myself* go, you are not able to come."

22 Therefore the Jews were saying, "Will He kill Himself, since He says, 'Where I *Myself* go, you *yourselves* are not able to come'?"

23 And He was saying to them, "You *yourselves* are from below, I *Myself* am from above; you *yourselves* are of this world, I *Myself* am not of this world.

24 "I said therefore to you that you will die in your sins; for unless you believe that I *Myself* am *He*, you will die in your sins."

The Pharisees' public verdict against Him (vv. 13, 19) made it necessary for the Lord to continue His warning to them. They were determined to arrest Him and triumph over Him, but would not be able to do so. As for Him (the **I** is emphatic), He would **go away** and return to the Father. They would **seek** Him then, but not find

Him. (The reference to **seeking** Him is to their futile determination to find His body after His death and burial. They would seek His dead body to disprove the claims of His Resurrection, but all in vain.) They would seek Him until their life's end and then **die in** their **sin**, for where He was to **go**, they were **not able to come**. He was to ascend in glory to the Father, and leave them behind in their self-chosen darkness, completely unable to follow Him on high. (**Sin** is here in the singular—compare to **sins** in the plural in v. 24—because here it refers to the single and definitive sin of rejecting Jesus.)

Following a previous pattern of blindness (2:19–20; 6:60–63; 7:34–35), **the Jews** misunderstand His words, taking them in a carnal manner. His talk of going where they could not follow—surely this did not mean that He was planning to **kill Himself**? (The Greek presupposes a negative answer.) That was the only way they could conceive of Him placing Himself out of their reach.

The Lord replies by again stressing His fundamental difference from them. (Emphatic pronouns for **I** and **you** are used throughout v. 23, to stress the contrast between Him and them.) They were **from below**, of the earth, merely human, bound by such human limitations as death. He, on the other hand, was **from above** and was more than merely human, being eternal with the Father. They were **of this world**, and thus unable to ascend to heaven; He was **not of this world**, but indeed able to return to the Father. If they continued to reject Him, they would **die in** their **sins**, with the full burden of their guilt. They thought that by denouncing Him, they were doing the will of God. On the contrary, says the Lord, their denunciation of Him will bring God's wrath. Their only hope of escaping this doom was to **believe** that He was who He claimed to be.

ॐ ॐ ॐ ॐ ॐ

25 Therefore they were saying to Him, "Who are You?" Jesus said to them, "That I speak to you at all!

26 "I have many things to speak and to judge

> about you, but He who sent Me is true, and the things which I *Myself* heard from Him, these I speak in the world."
>
> 27 They did not know that He had been speaking to them of the Father.
>
> 28 Jesus therefore said, "When you exalt the Son of Man, then you will know that I *Myself* am *He*, and I do nothing from Myself, but as the Father taught Me, these things I speak.
>
> 29 "And He who sent Me is with Me; He has not left Me alone, for I *Myself* always do the things that are pleasing to Him."
>
> 30 As He spoke these things, many believed in Him.

These further claims to hold such an exalted position provoked the Jews to incredulous scorn, and they retorted, "**Who are You?**" The pronoun **You** is emphatic in the Greek; the Jews were asking in scorn, "Who does He think *He* is?" "Who are You—a mere carpenter—to be claiming such things?"

The nature of our Lord's reply is not altogether clear in the Greek, and has been subject to varying translations. I would suggest that Jesus replies by rebuking such unbelief and by saying that it is a wonder that He **speaks** to them **at all**. Why should He continue to strive with them, faced with such deliberate stubbornness of heart? (This is also the view of St. John Chrysostom, who comments, "What He says is of this kind: 'You are not worthy to hear My words at all!'" —Homily 53 on John.)

Their constant refusal to accept Him means that, on the Last Day, He will **have many things to speak and to judge about** them, since they have been storing up judgment by their stubborn unbelief. For now, **He who sent** Him remains **true**, transcendent above their world of doubts. Jesus must continue to **speak in the world** those **things which** He **heard from Him**, and complete His mission.

St. John adds that His hearers continued in their unbelief and **did not know that He had been speaking to them of the Father.** By this it would seem John means that they did not believe that Jesus' words were the words that the Father had given Him to say, and that He had truly sent Him. Their problem was *not* that they could not understand that Jesus was claiming to have been sent by the Father. They understood well enough that Jesus was claiming this. Their problem was that they did not *believe* this claim; they did not believe that the One who sent Jesus was truly **the Father.**

The Lord therefore assured them that proof of His claim was coming. When they would **exalt the Son of Man, then** they would **know** He was who He claimed to be, and that He indeed **did nothing from** Himself, but only spoke **as the Father taught** Him. **He who sent** Him was always **with** Him; **He had not left** Him **alone,** for He (unlike them; the pronoun I is emphatic to contrast Jesus with His hearers) **always did the things that were pleasing to** God. Jesus' life was in total harmony with the will of the Father, and all that He did and said reflected that will. He was not the Law-breaker they took Him to be.

After He, the Son of Man, had been exalted and glorified, then they could know the truth of these claims. His Resurrection and glorification would reveal all. The word here translated *exalt* is the Greek word *upsoo*, sometimes translated "lift up." Here it probably represents the Aramaic word *zeqaph*, which is used to describe lifting up both in the sense of exalting and also in the sense of hanging—specifically crucifixion. Christ's use of the word here exhibits a certain (at that time undetected) irony—His exaltation and glorification would be accomplished through His being lifted up on the Cross.

As a result of Christ speaking **these things, many believed in Him.** That is, the crowd listening to this verbal exchange with the Jewish rulers began to side with Jesus.

ॐ ॐ ॐ ॐ ॐ

31 Jesus therefore was saying to the Jews who had believed Him, "If you *yourselves* remain in My Word, you are truly My disciples;

32 "and you will know the truth, and the truth
will free you."
33 They answered Him, "We are Abraham's seed,
and have never been enslaved to anyone; how
is it that You *Yourself* say, 'You will become
free'?"
34 Jesus answered them, "Amen, amen, I say to
you, everyone doing sin is a slave of sin.
35 "And the slave does not remain in the house
forever; the son remains forever.
36 "If therefore the Son frees you, you will be free
indeed.

Our Lord continued His teaching, speaking in the treasury
(8:20), in the Court of Women in the Temple. He had been challenged and denounced there by the Pharisees (8:13), and after the
previous exchange, was widely viewed by His hearers as having bested
them. His Pharisaical foes then probably went away, retreating for
now from the field of battle and leaving Him with those who had
been impressed by His performance. John refers to them as **the Jews
who had believed Him**. That is, though not committed to Him
from the heart as the Twelve were (compare 6:68), they had sided
with Him after His argument with the Pharisees and were prepared
to hear Him further.

Jesus therefore undertook to enlighten these (the pronoun **you**
is emphatic in Greek; Jesus deals with these who had sided with
Him and none others) and bring them to a place of true and saving
faith. For they needed not only to **believe** Him and side with Him
against the Pharisees, they also needed to **remain in** His **Word**. Only
then would they **truly** be His **disciples, know the truth**, and experience inner liberation and cleansing. The test was not simply the
willingness to align themselves with Him in public debate; it was
remaining in His **Word**, no matter what preconceptions that teaching shattered, no matter what persecution that loyalty to His teaching brought. To continue to place themselves under this tutelage
meant having all their previous ideas rearranged, and accepting many

hard words (compare 6:60). But only so could the new **truth** He brought to them **free** them from their sins.

His hearers instantly began to prove themselves unequal to this task. When they heard Him speak of being freed, their Jewish national pride was offended. They had been treated too much like slaves by the occupying Romans not to smart keenly under any suggestion that they were slaves! What did He mean by them being freed? Did He think they were cringing slaves, with no dignity or knowledge of God? Not likely! They were **Abraham's seed**, his true, legitimate, and direct offspring, and possessed a nobility of spirit like their father. (Indeed, a common Jewish proverb said, "All Israel are the children of kings.") They knew God, just as Abraham did! They had **never been enslaved to anyone!**—how is it that *He*, as if He were so much above them (the pronoun **You** is again emphatic), had the presumption to talk about them **becoming free?** They had always been of Abraham's royal line!

The Lord's answer is prefaced with His solemn **amen, amen, I say to you,** to assure them of the truth of what He says. For He had not been speaking of outer slavery, but of the inner slavery to the passions. Not just they, but **everyone doing sin** and living a life under its thrall (the present participle is used, indicating a continuing state of sin) was **a slave of sin.** Just as a slave had no power to break free from his master, but served him with every breath until his life's end, so it was with them serving sin.

As Jews, they looked to their Law for liberation from sin's power, but this was a vain hope. Study of the Law could not effect inner transformation. Only Christ could liberate the soul from the stranglehold of sin. For He was not in sin's power. He was indeed different from them and above them. He was as different from them as a true-born son in a household was different from the household slaves. **The slave** did **not remain in** that **house forever.** He could be sold at will and had no status. **The son,** set over the slaves, **remains** in the house **forever,** and could not be ejected at a whim. Jesus, **the Son** of God (like the son in the parable of v. 35), was able to liberate them. Just as the household's son could free his slaves, so Jesus could free them, and if He **freed** them by His word, they would **be free indeed.**

> 𝒮 𝒮 𝒮 𝒮 𝒮
>
> 37 "I know that you are Abraham's seed; but you seek to kill Me, because My word does not have room in you.
> 38 "I speak the things which I *Myself* have seen with the Father; therefore you *yourselves* also do the things which you heard from your father."

The Lord did not dispute that they were **Abraham's seed**. They were—which is why He was sent first to them (compare Jesus' declaration that His salvation was sent to Zacchaeus because he too was a son of Abraham; Luke 19:9–10). Nonetheless, they were not living up to that sacred heritage or acting like their forefather, for they were **seeking to kill** Him—and not because He had done anything worthy of death, but only **because** His **word** did **not have room** in them. They were simply unwilling to let His new teaching reconfigure all their old notions and shatter their old prejudices. *He* was **speaking the things which** He **had seen with** His **Father**, and they were **doing the things which** they **heard from** *their* **father** (once again, the two pronouns are emphatic, to indicate the contrast). Both were acting consistently in following their own fathers and being true to their own natures—and since they had different fathers, the collision and conflict were inevitable. How could they *not* **seek to kill** Him, when they had learned to do so from their father?

(We note in passing the subtle difference between Jesus seeing the Father, and His foes, as mere men, hearing their father the devil. As men, they could not pierce the veil to see spiritual realities; they could only hear the devil as he whispered into their hearts. But Jesus was the true Son of God, and was able to see God, as mere men were not; compare 6:46.)

> 𝒮 𝒮 𝒮 𝒮 𝒮
>
> 39 They answered and said to Him, "Abraham is our father." Jesus says to them, "If you are

> Abraham's children, do the works of Abraham.
> 40 "But now you seek to kill Me, a man who has
> told you the truth, which I heard from God;
> this Abraham did not do.
> 41 "You *yourselves* are doing the works of your fa-
> ther." They said to Him, "We *ourselves* were
> not born of fornication; we have one father,
> *even* God."

The Lord's hearers again insisted that **Abraham** was indeed their **father** and that He was wrong to imply that they had a different father than He did. This, however, the Lord would not allow. **If they were** indeed **Abraham's** spiritual **children**, then let them **do the works of Abraham** and welcome the truth. **But now** they were *not* imitating Abraham, but were **seeking to kill** Jesus, simply because He was **a man who told** them **the truth, which** He **heard from God.** They were so far from Abraham's spirit that the very mention of the truth provoked them to kill the one who told it to them—**this Abraham did not do!** It was apparent that they were **doing the works of** their **father**—the devil. *He* was their true father and their teacher, not Abraham.

They continued to insist on their spiritual succession from Abraham. They were **not born of fornication**, but were true Jews. They could indeed trace their lineage back to the great patriarch and friend of God, and therefore, like Abraham, could claim to have only **God** as their **one father.**

(The emphatic pronoun **we** in v. 41b may indicate that they were contrasting themselves to Jesus, saying that *they* were not born of fornication—implying that Jesus *was* born of fornication. If this slur was indeed intended, it would be an indirect witness to His Virgin Birth, for it would show that there was known to be something irregular about His paternity.)

჻ ჻ ჻ ჻ ჻

> 42 Jesus said to them, "If God were your father,
> you would love Me, for I *Myself* proceeded forth

and came from God, for I have not come from Myself, but that One sent Me.

43 "Why do you not understand my speaking? Because you are not able to hear My word.

44 "You *yourselves* are of your father the devil, and you want to do the desires of your father. That one was a man-killer from the beginning, and did not stand in the truth, because truth is not in him. Whenever he speaks the lie, he speaks from his own *nature*, for he is a liar and the father of it.

45 "But because I *Myself* speak the truth, you do not believe Me.

46 "Who among you convicts Me of sin? If I speak truth, why do you *yourselves* not believe Me?

47 "He who is of God hears the words of God; because of this you *yourselves* do not hear, because you are not of God."

The Lord responded to their claim that **God** was their **father**, just as He was the father of Abraham. If that were truly so, then they **would love** Jesus, for He **proceeded forth and came from God.** If they had God as their Father and loved Him, they would also love His Son, for how could one love a father and yet hate the son born in his image? One's love for a man always spilled over into love for his son too. This was true in human life, and much more true in the case of God the Father and His Son. And Jesus was truly such a Son of the Father—He did **not come** from Himself or on His own initiative. Rather, **that One**, God Himself, had **sent** Him.

Since He was speaking the very words given Him by God to say, **why** did they **not understand** His **speaking** and His message? The reason they could not recognize the truth of His **word** was that they were **not able to hear** it. They could not bear to hear the sound of God's truth, for it convicted them and forced them to change their proud ways.

In this, they were just like their **father the devil**. He could not

bear truth either. **That one was a man-killer from the beginning.**
In the Garden of Eden, he was intent on killing Adam and Eve, and
bringing death to them and their race (Gen. 3:1f)—just as Jesus'
opponents were intent on killing Him. His foes' murderous intent
showed that they were children of the devil, the original murderer.

The devil also hated truth from the beginning. He did **not stand
in the truth** in the Garden, but deceived Adam and Eve with his
lies—how could he do anything else, when **truth was not in
him? Whenever he speaks the lie, he speaks from his own** *nature*,
for he is not only **a liar**, but **the father of it**—all lies find their
source in him.

This was the true father of Jesus' hearers that day. No wonder
they could not bear to hear truth from Him, but wanted to kill
Him! Since the devil was their true father, they naturally **wanted to
do the desires** of their father. It was not that they did not believe
Him *even though* He spoke the truth. Since the devil was their father, they did **not believe** Him *because* He **spoke the truth.**

Did they claim that they rejected Him because He was a sinner?
Then **who among** them could **convict** Him **of sin** and prove that
He was indeed a sinner? Had not His miracles proven the truth of
His words? (Compare Mark 2:10–12.) They might *want* to accuse
Him of sin and say that He broke the Sabbath by counseling a man
to carry his pallet on that day (5:10), but His miracle of healing
vindicated His teaching that such carrying was not a sin. Try as they
might, they could not prove their case.

So, **if** He did nothing but **speak truth, why** did they **not believe**
Him? Anyone who was **of God** would obviously **hear the words of
God** with delight. It was therefore only **because of this** they did **not
hear** Him with delight and accept His word—that they were **not of
God**, but of the devil.

༄ ༄ ༄ ༄ ༄

48 The Jews answered and said to Him, "Do we
ourselves not well say that You *Yourself* are a
Samaritan and have a demon?"

> 49 Jesus answered, "I *Myself* do not have a demon,
> but I honor My Father, and you *yourselves* dis-
> honor Me.
> 50 "But I *Myself* do not seek My glory; there is
> One who seeks and judges.
> 51 "Amen, amen, I say to you, if anyone keeps
> My word, he will not ever see death."

Such denunciations from our Lord pushed them over the edge. It seemed clear to them that He was denying the chosenness of the Jewish people. It was a common saying that "all Israel had a share in the world to come," and here He was saying that, though they were Jewish, they were nonetheless children of the devil. This seemed to them to be not only heretical, but demonic and crazy too. They asked Him scornfully if they weren't right and did not **well say** that *He* was the one in error—that He was **a Samaritan** and **had a demon**?

The term *Samaritan* seems here to be used as a term of abuse, a kind of theological swear word. The Samaritans were heretics who were under (the Jews thought) the curse of God, and Jesus was no better. He had a demon (as the Pharisees had long said; compare Mark 3:22), which explained such crazy talk.

Christ responds to this blasphemy with calm and serenity. He does not revile in return, but simply tells them that *He* does **not have a demon**, nor does He teach things that dishonor the Father (such as counseling one to break His Sabbath Law). On the contrary, He **honors the Father**—and *they* are **dishonoring** Him—which means, by extension, that they dishonor the Father also. He was not concerned to vindicate Himself in the face of such blasphemy. He did **not seek** His own **glory**—there was **One** who was **seeking** it and who would **judge** them for their blasphemy. He was content to leave it all in His hands. Nonetheless, His claims were true. He solemnly assures them (with His characteristic **Amen, amen, I say to you**), **if anyone** would **keep** His **word** and continue steadfastly as His disciple, such a one would **not ever see death**.

ॐ ॐ ॐ ॐ ॐ

52 The Jews said to Him, "Now we know that You have a demon. Abraham died, and the prophets, and You *Yourself* say, 'If anyone keeps My word, he will not ever taste death.'

53 "Are You *Yourself* greater than our father Abraham, who died? And the prophets died; who do You make Yourself out *to be*?"

Such a claim was even more staggering than what He had said to this point. For them, this last utterance proved that Jesus was crazy, and that He **had a demon**. Anyone could see that! **Abraham died, and the prophets** died too. And yet *He* said (the pronoun **You** is emphatic, meaning "*You*, of all people!") that one need only **keep His word** to be spared a fate that overtook such great men! Did He think that He was **greater** than their **father Abraham, who died**? And greater than **the prophets** who **died**? For not only was He claiming now to be greater than Abraham and the prophets, but He was even claiming to be so great that He could *make His followers greater* than Abraham and the prophets! Such presumption and megalomania boggled the mind! **Who** did He **make** Himself **out** *to be*?

ॐ ॐ ॐ ॐ ॐ

54 Jesus answered, "If I *Myself* glorify Myself, My glory is nothing; My Father is the One who glorifies Me, of whom you *yourselves* say, 'He is our God';

55 "and you have not known Him, but I *Myself* know Him, and if I say that I do not know Him, I will be a liar like you, but I do know Him, and keep His word.

56 "Your father Abraham exulted to see My day; he saw *it* and rejoiced."

III. CHRIST'S MINISTRY TO ISRAEL

The Lord's foes were becoming ever shriller and more exasperated in their responses. We can almost hear their voices rising in volume. But Christ continues to calmly teach the truth and advance His claims.

Did they think He was saying this to **glorify** Himself, as if He were on some insane ego trip? If He were the only one concerned with His glory (the pronoun **I** is emphatic, meaning "if I and I alone glorify Myself"), then such claims would indeed be futile and His **glory** would amount to **nothing**. But as it was, He was not alone in such things, but His **Father** was **the One who** was concerned to **glorify** Him—the very One of whom *they* kept on **saying**, "**He is our God**." If God were truly the One they worshipped and honored, they would glorify Jesus too (compare v. 50). Their refusal to glorify Jesus meant that they had **not known** God at all. Jesus is the One who **knew Him**, and if Jesus agreed with them that His claims to give life were false and said that He did **not know** God after all, He would **be a liar like** them. But as it was, He **did know** God, **and kept His word**.

Did they stumble at His claim to be greater than Abraham? But He *was* greater than Abraham. Indeed, their **father Abraham exulted to see** Jesus' coming **day** of triumph; **he saw *it* and rejoiced!** (It was a common belief among the Jews that as a prophet—compare Ps. 105:15—Abraham was able to see the future Kingdom of God.) Jesus' hearers hated Him and delighted at the thought of His defeat, but **Abraham** (who they boasted was their spiritual **father**) was overjoyed when he saw Jesus' triumph in prophetic vision. That not only showed that Jesus was greater than Abraham; it showed how little His hearers were Abraham's spiritual children.

ॐ ॐ ॐ ॐ ॐ

57 The Jews therefore said to Him, "You do not yet have fifty years, and You have seen Abraham?"
58 Jesus said to them, "Amen, amen, I say to you, before Abraham came to be, I *Myself* am."

> **59 Therefore they took up stones to cast at Him, but Jesus was hidden and went out of the Temple.**

The Lord's words about Abraham seeing His day pushed their exasperation with Him to its furthest bound. They discounted Jesus as the Bringer of the Kingdom, and consequently, the possibility that Abraham could see Him prophetically. Jesus' only possible relationship to Abraham must therefore be physical. And that was impossible! Jesus did **not yet have fifty years** of maturity, and *He has seen Abraham?* What nonsense was this? (The number fifty is chosen probably as a round figure, indicating full maturity; it was the age when, for example, a Levite finished his career of service; Num. 4:3.)

Christ had one last claim for them, and like the others, it was prefaced with a solemn **Amen, amen, I say to you.** They could be sure of this. Not only was He greater and older than Abraham. **Before Abraham** even **came to be,** He Himself eternally existed.

The Greek for Jesus' claim "**I am**" is *ego eimi.* In other contexts, the words *ego eimi* could mean no more than "I am the one"— compare its use by Christ in 4:26; 8:24; and by the blind man in 9:9. In this context, however, it clearly means more, since Christ's hearers responded by trying to stone Him for alleged blasphemy.

It is, in fact, a reference to the Divine Name of God, which He revealed to Moses at the burning bush in Exodus 3. At that time, Yahweh was asked by Moses what His Name was, and He responded, "I am that I am"—in the Greek Septuagint, *ego eimi o on* (Ex. 3:14)— shortened later in that verse to "I Am"—Greek *o on.* By declaring to the Jews "I am," Christ was claiming nothing less than that He was the One who revealed Himself to Moses at the burning bush, that He was one with the Father, the eternal **I Am.** No wonder the Jews **took up stones to cast at Him** for what they thought to be the highest blasphemy. His hour, however, was not yet, and so He **was hidden** by the providence of God and evaded them. He finally **went out of the Temple** safe and sound after His foes had dispersed.

The controversy after those festal days had reached its climax,

with the Jews ready to lynch Him, hearing and rejecting His highest claims.

We may add a final word about the Greek words indicating the
Lord's divinity. The words denoting the Name of Yahweh in Exodus 3:14 in the Greek were, as we have seen, *o on*—literally "the
Being" or "He who is." The letters are *o*, the Greek letter *omicron*,
meaning "the," followed by *on*, that is, the Greek letters *omega nu*,
meaning "being," a participle of the word *eimi*, "to be." It is these
three Greek letters which adorn the head of Christ in our Orthodox
icons, looking like "*o wv*." These letters in the icons refer to the
Divine Name in Exodus 3:14, as rendered in the Greek Septuagint
version.

℘ EXCURSUS

ON JOHN'S CHARACTERISTIC VOCABULARY AND PURPOSE

St. John has a fondness for certain words and for reporting
the Lord's words in a certain way, and these are consistent
with the special didactic purpose of his Gospel.

John is especially concerned in his Gospel to present
Jesus as a focus of controversy—that John might resolve the
controversy in Jesus' favor. The language of controversy therefore abounds in his Gospel. This is even more apparent when
one compares John's vocabulary and the frequency with
which he uses certain words to the vocabulary and word-
frequency of other New Testament writers. (The word counts
in this excursus are taken from Leon Morris's commentary
on John.)

Thus John uses words that put Jesus front and center,
placing Him and His adversaries (as it were) before our eyes.
He uses the Greek word *orao* ("to see") 31 times, as compared to the next most frequent usage of the word, 16 times
in the Book of Acts.

Furthermore, emphatic personal pronouns abound
(rendered rather clumsily as "I myself," "you yourself," "you

yourselves"). John especially likes the personal words *ego* ("I myself") and *kago* ("and I myself"): *ego* is used 465 times in John's Gospel (compared with 215 times in Luke) and *kago* is used 30 times in John's Gospel (compared with the next most frequent usage of 10 times in 1 Corinthians). The effect of such frequent use is to sharpen the argumentative quality of the dialogue being narrated by heightening the contrast between the adversaries in the debate.

Indeed, John delights in the whole language of dialogue and argument: he uses the word *erotao* ("to ask a question") 27 times (compared to 4 times in Matthew, 3 in Mark, and 15 in Luke). He uses the word *apokrinomai* ("to answer") 78 times (compared to 55 in Matthew, 30 in Mark, and 46 in Luke). Continuing in the vigorously argued language of debate, he uses the word *oun* ("therefore") 194 times (compared to its next most frequent usage in Acts, 62 times).

All of this argument serves to advance the person of Jesus as the true Judge, and the verb *krino* ("to judge") is also a favorite of John's. He uses it 19 times in his Gospel, compared to 16 times in Matthew, 6 in Luke, and none at all in Mark.

The presence or absence of a certain word in itself is not that significant, and may reflect no more than John's stylistic preferences. Nonetheless, the *cumulative effect* of such word frequency is to make John's Gospel very much a controversial document. The language of thrust and counter-thrust, of question and answer, of sustained argument makes it clear that John is not simply telling a story—he is arguing a case.

§III.7.v. Sixth Sign: Healing of the Man Born Blind

ॐ ॐ ॐ ॐ ॐ

9 1 And passing by, He saw a man blind from birth.
2 And His disciples asked Him, saying, "Rabbi,

> who sinned, this one or his parents, that he was born blind?"
>
> 3 Jesus answered, "Neither this one sinned, nor his parents, but *it was* that the works of God might be manifested in him.
>
> 4 "It is necessary for us to work the works of Him who sent Me while it is day; night comes, when no one is able to work.
>
> 5 "Whenever I am in the world, I am the light of the world."
>
> 6 Having said these things, He spat on the ground and made clay from the spit, and anointed his eyes with the clay
>
> 7 and said to him, "Go, wash in the pool of Siloam" (which is translated, Sent). He went therefore and washed and came *back* seeing.

It would seem that this sign is connected with the preceding incident, in that it occurred after Jesus went out of the Temple (8:59) at the conclusion of the Feast of Booths. It was as He was leaving the sacred precincts and **passing by** (possibly as evening approached?) that **He saw a man blind from birth**—evidently one whose plight and history were well known. Blindness was very common in the ancient world and could be caused by many things, but here was something unusually tragic—a man who had never seen in his life. It was a sufficiently rare occurrence that it wrung the hearts of His disciples, and they asked what could have happened to cause such a tragedy.

It was axiomatic to the Jews that all suffering was caused by sin, and they felt that there must have been some great sin indeed to have caused such a catastrophe. The question was, whose sin? So it was that they asked the Lord to unravel that mystery and tell them, **"Who sinned—this one or his parents, that he was born blind?"** Did the man sin before God in the womb, or did his parents commit some secret sin for which they were being punished through their child's affliction?

The Lord moved the whole discussion onto higher ground, from a judicial examination of causes to discerning an opportunity for healing. It is a move from Jewish territory to Christian. For it is characteristic of Judaism to investigate and assign blame; it is characteristic of Christianity to reach out to transform. The Law could do the former very well; it was powerless to effect the latter. The Law of Moses could condemn a man; it could not heal him—for that, one needed the grace and truth that came through Jesus Christ (1:17).

So it was that Jesus dismissed the whole investigation into causes and blame. Not all suffering was the direct result of sin, and in this case, **neither this one sinned** in the womb, **nor his parents** before he was born. The disciples must not look for causes, as judges, but for opportunities that **the works of God**—those of healing, forgiveness, and newness of life—**might be manifested in him**. This was the work that God delighted to do: He was the One who opened the eyes of the blind, who raised up those who were bowed down (Ps. 146:8, part of the Second Antiphon of the Divine Liturgy). As Christ came to manifest the Name and love of the Father to the world (17:6), so it was **necessary** for Him, together with His disciples, to **work the works** of the Father who **sent** Him at every opportunity. No doubt many would blame Him again for healing on the Sabbath (see v. 14), but time was running out for doing such works. These opportunities must be seized, for His foes were even then scheming to put Him to death.

Just as a laborer had to work hard to make the most of the daylight hours because when night came **no one** was **able to work**, so it was with Christ. He also had to work **while it** was **day**; because for Him also the **night** was **coming** when He would be killed, and all His opportunities for work would be gone. (If this miracle was indeed done as evening approached, this would be an added and vivid illustration of the truth of this.) But until that time of His death, **whenever** and for as long as He was **in the world**, He was **the light of the world**. Just as men in the world were able to enjoy physical light because the sun remained in the sky, so they were able to find spiritual light as long as He remained alive and working.

Having said these things, He worked to prove them. Just as His multiplication of the loaves proved Him to be the Bread of Life (ch. 6), so His giving light and vision to the blind man would prove Jesus to be the Light of the world. And just as He would later, in the Church, use material things as instruments of His power (the water of baptism for bestowing new life, the oil of anointing to bestow healing), so here also Jesus uses material things as conductors of His power. In the ancient world, saliva was commonly known to possess healing properties. It was thus an appropriate medium for His healing, and it was so used by Christ more than once (compare Mark 7:33).

But Christ here did not merely use His saliva; He mixed it with the earth to create clay, and this clay was used as the healing medium. Why clay? The Fathers saw in this an echo of the original creation of man from the earth in Genesis 2:7—as God first made man from the red clay of the earth, so Christ God also makes new eyes for the blind man out of the clay. As St. Irenaeus said, "Therefore the Lord made clay, pointing out the original fashioning of man, manifesting the hand of God to those who can understand by what hand man was formed from the dust. For what the Artificer, the Word, had omitted to form in the womb [viz., the blind man's eyes], He then supplied in public" (*Against Heresies*, 5, 15, 2). Jesus used clay to fashion new eyes (by healing the old ones) to show His unity with His Creator Father.

There was more. Having **anointed his eyes with the clay**, He told the blind man, **"Go, wash in the pool of Siloam,"** which was perhaps 1300 feet to the south in the Tyropoenon Valley. The pool of Siloam was fed by a spring in the Kidron Valley next to it. It is the same as "the King's Pool" in Nehemiah 2:14, built long ago by King Hezekiah to bring water into the city (2 Kin. 20:20). It was called "Siloam" from the Hebrew word for *sent*, because the waters were "sent" by a conduit to the pool. The blind man obeyed. **He went** to the pool **and washed** the clay from his eyes and **came** *back* to his family and friends **seeing**. Washing obediently in the pool of Siloam had brought him healing and light. He could see!

John makes a point of telling us that the word **Siloam** is **translated** as **Sent**, and his concern is not simply historical. Rather, John means to reveal why Christ chose washing as a means of healing and why washing in that particular pool. The washing recalled the washing of baptism with which a man became Jesus' disciple, and by stipulating that the man had to wash in the pool of the Sent, Christ revealed Himself as the One who had been sent by the Father (v. 4). After washing in Christ's pool, the man could see light from the world. All the details of the healing combine to show how Christ is Himself the Light of the world and it is only as one becomes His disciple that one has the light of life. This was, in fact, exactly what Christ had said to the crowds that very afternoon (8:12).

> ॐ ॐ ॐ ॐ ॐ
>
> 8   The acquaintances therefore and the ones who formerly observed him as a beggar were saying, "Is not this the one who used to sit and beg?"
>
> 9   Others were saying, "This one is he"; others were saying, "No, but he is like him." That one kept saying, "I *myself* am *he*."
>
> 10 Therefore they were saying to him, "How then were your eyes opened?"
>
> 11 He answered, "That one, the man called Jesus, made clay and anointed my eyes, and said to me, 'Go to Siloam and wash'; I went therefore and washed, and I saw again."
>
> 12 And they said to him, "Where is that one?" He says, "I do not know."

The healing was complete and instantaneous—so much so that his **acquaintances and the ones who formerly observed him as a beggar** did not immediately recognize him when he returned excitedly from the pool. Not only could he see, but his whole demeanor was changed. Instead of fearful insecurity, there was new and growing confidence; instead of secret despair, radiant hope. Some, seeing this change, asked, **"Is not this the one who used to sit and** beg?"—for he seemed so different. Some said that it was indeed he; others denied it, though they admitted that it looked like him. The blind man put an end to all these wondering whispered questions by stating, "I *myself* am *he*."

If he was the one, however, how could he explain the change? **How then** were his **eyes opened?** The man answered, **That one** (the pronoun is emphatic), **the man called Jesus, made clay, and anointed** his **eyes and said** to him, **"Go to Siloam and wash."** That was all. He **went therefore** as he was told, **and washed, and saw again.** There was no sorcery (some said that Jesus worked His miracles by the power of the devil; see Mark 3:22), and no long prayer. Jesus simply spoke with sovereign authority, and the deed was done. His hearers, naturally enough, wanted to know **where that one** was who healed him. They wanted to learn more details from Jesus Himself, but the man did **not know** where He was.

❧ EXCURSUS

ON THE HEALING OF THE BLIND MAN AND HOLY BAPTISM

St. John records the healing of the blind man with an eye to Christian baptism, even as he recorded the multiplication of the loaves with an eye to the Church's Eucharist. The blind man is, for John, an image of the Christian convert.

This is apparent first of all from the fact that the blind man is required to wash in order to obtain healing. Christians who washed in the waters of baptism in order to obtain their own salvation and healing could hardly fail to read such significance into the act; indeed, this significance seems to have been intended by Christ Himself. The Christians too washed in the baptismal pool (or river) of the Sent One in order to find their own illumination, and John knew that his narrative would resonate in this way for his intended Christian audience.

Also, the fact that the miracle was the bestowal of sight to the blind—and to one who had been *born* blind—argues for such baptismal resonance. For all men are born spiritually blind, not being able to see the glory of God, and salvation is often portrayed in terms of illumination. Indeed, "illumination" was an early synonym for baptism (see Heb. 6:4), and St. Justin (c. AD 150) refers to baptism in this way, saying "This [baptismal] washing is called 'illumination'" (*First Apology*, ch. 61). The Church continues this practice, praying (in the Presanctified Liturgy) for those who are about to be baptized as "those who are preparing for holy illumination."

Even some of the vocabulary of St. John contains echoes of baptism. In most manuscripts, Christ is said to "anoint" the man's eyes (Gr. *epichrio*, a compound of the verb *chrio*, to anoint), which corresponds to the anointings that seem to have been a part of the early baptismal rite (compare also 2 Cor. 1:21–22; 1 John 2:20).

Further, the blind man's experience contains additional echoes of the baptismal experience. His final worshipping of Christ and his confession, "I believe, Lord" (v. 38), both find their parallel and fulfillment in the worship of the newly baptized. Even the blind man's post-washing experience of persecution from the Jews (v. 34) finds its parallel in the persecution of the Christian. For after baptism, the former compatriots of the Christians reviled the new converts also—especially when those converts were converts from Judaism. The newly baptized were *also* "cast out of the synagogue" (see John 16:2; Matt. 10:17).

Finally, baptism is the work of the whole Church (even though it is Christ Himself, working within His Body, who illumines the new convert). This corporate and ecclesial aspect of baptism may be reflected in the plural with which Jesus speaks in v. 4. Even though it was He and He alone who opened the man's eyes (the apostles perhaps taking the blind man down to the pool), Jesus nonetheless still speaks in the plural, saying, "It is necessary *for us* to work the works" of the Father. This plural may suggest the disciples' share, not just in this miracle (which share was fairly minimal), but also in the Church's work of illumination, of which this miracle was an image.

§III.7.vi. Controversy over Healing of the Blind Man— Jesus the Door and the Good Shepherd of the Sheep

ॐ ॐ ॐ ॐ ॐ

13 They led to the Pharisees him who was once blind.

14 Now it was a Sabbath on the day when Jesus made the clay and opened his eyes.

15 Again, therefore, the Pharisees also were asking him how he saw again. And he said to them, "He put clay on my eyes, and I washed, and I see."

16 Therefore some of the Pharisees were saying, "This man is not from God, for He does not keep the Sabbath." But others were saying, "How is a man *who is* a sinner able to do such signs?" And there was a division among them.

17 They say therefore to the blind one again, "What do you *yourself* say about Him, since He opened your eyes?" And he said, "He is a prophet."

As with the Lord's other miracles, this one too aroused a storm of controversy—for once more Jesus had healed on **a Sabbath**. Jesus was well known to the blind man's acquaintances as a figure of controversy. As they could not resolve the issues raised by their friend's healing, **they led him** (evidently the next day) **to the Pharisees**, as to the recognized religious leaders. The Pharisees, they thought, would be able to unravel this! It seems that this gathering of Pharisees was no informal exchange of opinions, but rather a kind of synagogue court. This was an official inquiry.

The Pharisees accordingly asked what happened to the man and **how** it was that **he saw again**. He simply related to them the facts as he knew them—that Jesus **put clay on** his **eyes**, and he **washed** and found that he could **see**.

The Pharisees then retire from the man they have been interrogating and confer in a kind of huddle. **Some of the Pharisees** are undeterred in their purpose. Their minds are made up, and they do not want to be confused by the facts! They say that **this man** (Jesus—they can scarcely bring themselves to say His Name) is **not from God**, for He does **not keep the Sabbath**. By healing like that on a Sabbath, He has offended their Sabbath interpretation, and therefore He cannot be a genuine prophet; he must be a sinner and a deceiver. **Others** in the huddle differ. **How is a man *who is* a sinner able to do such signs** as these? For God would not answer the prayer of one who defied Him. Thus **there was a division among** the Pharisees.

Since they have reached an impasse, **they say to the blind one again** (the historic present is used, giving the reader a ringside seat in the inquiry), **"What do you *yourself* say about Him, since He opened your eyes?"** The **you** is emphatic; they are asking for his own opinion of his healer. This is unusual in this kind of official inquiry. But they are not asking him for a final verdict; that is for them to give. Rather, they are asking him for what we would today call "vibes"—does Jesus inspire in him a kind of creepy feeling, as would be the case if He were demonic or a sorcerer? For those who asserted that He was a sinner also felt that He did His miracles through the power of the devil (Mark 3:22). The man replies that, in his mind, Jesus is indeed of God, and is a true **prophet**.

ॐ ॐ ॐ ॐ ॐ

18 The Jews therefore did not believe it of him, that he had been blind and had seen again, until they called the parents of the one who had seen again,

19 and asked them, saying, "Is this your son, who
   you *yourselves* say was born blind? How then
   does he now see?"

20 His parents answered them and said, "We know
   that this one is our son, and that he was born
   blind;

21 "but how he now sees, we do not know, or who
   opened his eyes, we *ourselves* do not know.
   Ask him; he is of age, he will speak about
   himself."

22 His parents said these things because they were
   afraid of the Jews; for the Jews had already
   agreed that if anyone should confess Him *to be*
   Christ, he would be *put* out of the synagogue.

23 For this *cause* his parents said, "He is of age;
   ask him."

The matter was inconclusive, and they seemed to have an impossible scenario before them. If He broke the Sabbath (according
to their interpretation of breaking the Sabbath), He *could not be* of
God—but if He healed the man, He *must* be of God. There was
only one possibility that fit the facts as they saw them (that is, the
fact of Jesus being a sinner and the man now seeing)—namely, that
the man himself was never blind in the first place. They would prove
this by cross-examining the man's parents. They would confirm for
themselves that it was all a mistake!

They therefore **called the parents of the one who had seen again**
(John refers to the man this way to stress the reality of the miracle)
and **asked them, "Is this your son, who you *yourselves* say was
born blind? How then does he now see?"** The **you** is again emphatic: *you* are the ones who claim he was born blind—if that is so,
how do you explain the fact that he now can see? Implicit in their
question is the assumption that Jesus did not work a miracle.

The parents were terrified by the power of this official inquiry,
for there was already an unstated but well-known policy that **if anyone should confess Jesus *to be* Christ, he would be *put* out of the**

synagogue. Common folk knew that the Jews who were seeking Jesus' life would take such action too against any who were vocal as His supporters (compare 7:13).

This expulsion from the synagogue was indeed something to be feared. There were three levels of censure in the synagogue: a simple rebuke (in Hebrew *neziphah*), in which the one so rebuked was punished for seven days; a thrusting out (in Hebrew *niddui*), which lasted thirty days; and the most extreme level, a final ban (Hebrew *herem*), which was of lasting duration. The one so banned was treated by the community as if he were dead. He was not allowed to study the Law with others, and others might have no social contact with him, not even to give directions for travel. The parents of the man born blind were poor themselves (which is why the man was reduced to begging), and such a ban would have had disastrous effects on their lives. No wonder they were reluctant to say anything more than they had to! They admitted that he was indeed their **son** and that he was indeed **born blind**. But beyond that they refused even to speculate. Their repeated chorus was, "**We do not know**." All they would say was, "**He is of age; ask him**."

> ॐ ॐ ॐ ॐ ॐ
>
> 24 Therefore a second time they called the man who was blind, and said to him, "Give glory to God; we *ourselves* know that this man is a sinner."
> 25 That one therefore answered, "Whether He is a sinner, I do not know; one thing I know, that though I was blind, now I see."
> 26 They said therefore to him, "What did He do to you? How did He open your eyes?"
> 27 He answered them, "I told you already and you did not hear; why do you want to hear again? Do you *yourselves* also want to become His disciples?"

The unofficial court **a second time called the man who was blind** (John once again stresses the fact of his blindness) and tries to talk him into changing his story and admitting that he was never blind at all. They admonish him to tell the truth—out with it!—and give glory to God. Let him just admit he was never blind and that Jesus never cured him. *They* **knew** the truth (the pronoun is emphatic)—Jesus could not have cured him, because He was **a sinner**. Just admit it! (The admonition to give glory to God does not mean, "Give the glory to God for the cure, not to Jesus." They are denying that a cure ever took place and that *anyone* need be given glory for it. Rather, the admonition is a formula calling the person to total truthfulness—compare its usage in Josh. 7:19.)

The man now begins to assert himself a little. He is not cowed by their intimidation (as his poor parents are). He insists on telling the truth. He admits that he may **not know** whether or not Jesus is **a sinner**. That is a theological interpretation. What he can state as a fact—the **one thing** he *does* **know**—is that **though** he once **was blind, now** he can **see**.

His powerful foes refuse to accept it. From a judicial inquiry called to hear evidence and give a just verdict, it is turning into a kangaroo court, determined to convict no matter what the evidence—and the man knows it. He knows the inquiry is not worthy of his respect, and he does not give it to them (even as future persecuted disciples of Jesus are encouraged to confess the truth and not be cowed by such unjust courts). So it is that when they ask him to state again what he experienced (doubtless hoping to find some evidence of sorcerous words secretly uttered), he answers them ironically, and deliberately baits them. He has **told** them **already** and given all his evidence, apparently (he says) in vain. **Why** do they **want to hear** it **again? Do** *they* (of all people—the pronoun is emphatic) **also want to become His disciples?** It was a courageous and nervy thing to do—to antagonize such powerful men. One can almost see him smile with feigned innocence and naiveté.

৩৭ ৩৭ ৩৭ ৩৭ ৩৭

ॐ ॐ ॐ ॐ ॐ

28 And they abused him and said, "You *yourself* are a disciple of that one, but we *ourselves* are disciples of Moses!

29 "We *ourselves* know that God has spoken to Moses, but as for this man, we do not know where He is from."

The response is immediate and explosive: they abuse him as a disciple of a heretic. They say, **You**—unlike us (the pronouns **you** and **we** are both emphatic)—**are a disciple of that one** (they refuse to even utter His Name), **but we are disciples of Moses!** That is, we are simply following what God said He wanted, whereas you are determined to go on a different course, heedless of God. They **know that God has spoken to Moses** and that it is right to keep the Sabbath. **But as for this man** (again the dismissive refusal even to name Him), they do **not know where He is from**—He has yet to prove His divine credentials. How foolish the healed man is to follow such an unproven innovator!

ॐ ॐ ॐ ॐ ॐ

30 The man answered and said to them, "For in this is the marvel, that you *yourselves* do not know where He is from, and *yet* He opened my eyes!

31 "We know that God does not hear sinners, but if anyone is godly-pious and does His will, this one He hears.

32 "Since the age *began*, it has never been heard that anyone opened the eyes of one born blind.

33 "If this one were not from God, He would not be able to do anything."

34 They answered and said to him, "You *yourself* were born entirely in sins, and are you *yourself* teaching us?" And they cast him outside.

The healed man responds to their abuse with even greater boldness and audacity, knowing he now has nothing to lose. They are debating a marvel and a miracle, but the real **marvel** consists **in this**: that *they*—educated religious leaders no less! (the pronoun **you** is emphatic)—do **not know where** Jesus **is from** and cannot figure out whether or not He is of God, even though **He opened** his **eyes**! Their inability to figure it out is the real marvel! For anyone can see that Jesus is of God. Everyone **knows that God does not hear sinners**, that He does not answer the prayers of those who sin defiantly. Their sacrifices and prayers to be blessed go unanswered (compare Ps. 50:16–23). **But if anyone is godly-pious** (Gr. *theosebes*, devout, eager to do what pleases God) **and does His will, this** is the **one** whom **He hears**. The truth is easy to determine and undeniable: **if this one** who healed him **were not from God, He would not be able to do anything**—much less do a miracle that has **never been heard** of **since the age** *began.* Obviously Jesus is of God!

This is the last straw. They are incensed at such defiance—and from one they consider to be part of the worthless and untaught rabble (compare 7:49). They denounce him as being **born entirely in sins**—that is, under the curse of God (as his being born blind proves, as far as they are concerned)—and there he is, presuming to be **teaching** *them?* The accursed sinner, teaching the enlightened teachers? Their sentence of ban and of being put out from the synagogue is left unnarrated. We are left to imagine their wrath. John simply states that **they cast him outside.** That is, they threw him out of the place where they met, as an expression of his ban from the synagogue and from pious Jewish social life.

ॐ ॐ ॐ ॐ ॐ

35 Jesus heard that they had cast him outside, and finding him, He said, "Do you *yourself* believe in the Son of Man?"

36 That one answered and said, "And who is He, Lord, that I may believe in Him?"

37 Jesus said to him, "You have both seen Him

> and that One is the one speaking with you."
>
> 38 And he said, "I believe, Lord." And he worshipped Him.
>
> 39 And Jesus said, "For judgment I *Myself* came into this world, that those who do not see may see, and that the ones who see may become blind."

But though expelled by Jewish authority and placed (as the Jews thought) under the curse of God, the man was not left alone. For the synagogue might have pretended to speak for God, but Christ was the One who truly spoke for Him. The man therefore had nothing to fear from the Jews' curse if Christ would give him His blessing. If Jesus opened the door into life, no council of men could shut it (compare Rev. 3:7–9), whatever their pretended authority.

So it was that after this, **Jesus heard** that the Jews had expelled the man for his courageous defense of Him and took steps to befriend him. **Finding him,** Jesus said, "**Do you**, unlike the others who are afraid (the pronoun **you** is emphatic, stressing his difference from the others), **believe in the Son of Man?**" That is, are you prepared to become a disciple of Jesus, the One who healed you? (Everyone knew that the messianic title Son of Man denoted Jesus, for it was His favorite self-designation.) The man had defended Jesus boldly at the inquiry—did he now want to become His disciple, or had the threats and expulsion cowed him?

The man is not cowed; He asks this anonymous stranger (whom he took to be Jesus' messenger) who Jesus is, that he **may believe in Him** and formally become His disciple. (He addresses Him respectfully as **Lord**—Gr. *kurios*, that is, "sir"; compare a similar use of *kurios* in 4:11.) That is, he asks to be shown where Jesus is, that he might give Him his allegiance. **Who is He?** Which of the people milling about in the city is Jesus? It was the obvious question for a formerly blind man to ask, since he could not recognize Jesus by sight. Let this nameless messenger point Him out and bring him to Him!

Jesus answers him with a kind of tender joy and delight in the man's own newfound happiness, identifying Himself as the Son of Man whom the man wished to meet. Jesus identifies Himself not only as **the one speaking with** him but also as the one whom he has **seen**. The eyes which Jesus opened now behold their Healer.

The man's reaction is immediate. He confesses Jesus, saying, **"I believe, Lord,"** and falls down prostrate before Him, and **worships Him**. The confession of Jesus as **Lord** (Gr. *kurios*) now must be invested with a fuller meaning than it had formerly when the man called Jesus *kurios* in v. 36. Formerly he respected his unknown friend as if He were but Jesus' messenger, calling Him "sir," but now he declares his allegiance to Jesus as to his Master and Teacher, calling Him "Lord."

He seals his allegiance by a formal act of reverence, falling down at His feet. The word translated *worshipped* is the Greek *proskuneo*. Its basic meaning of prostrating in homage is the dominant meaning here; the man is not offering Jesus the worship due to God, but the extreme veneration given to men—and to God's Messiah. (Compare also Jacob prostrating before Esau in Gen. 33:3.) But though the new disciple does not intend divine adoration in this act of worship, St. John's Christian readers know that such adoration is indeed due to Jesus. For them, the man did better than he knew, and his bowing down in homage was an image of their adoration of their divine Lord.

Jesus accepts the man's offer of discipleship, declaring that He **came into this world** to create just such division. Christ was a source of controversy among men, dividing them into those who sided with Him (like this newest disciple) and those who banded against Him (like the Pharisees). This represented the **judgment** of God, God's verdict upon the hearts of men. Those who had good hearts and were open to the truth (like this man) were enabled by Christ to **see** again, and were rewarded for their openness by being given spiritual illumination. Those who had hard hearts and who closed themselves to the truth (like the Pharisees) were judged by God by being robbed of whatever sense they had, becoming spiritually **blind**. The separation of men into these two groups represented the divine judgment upon Israel

ঞ্ঝ ঞ্ঝ ঞ্ঝ ঞ্ঝ ঞ্ঝ

40 Those of the Pharisees who were with Him heard these things, and said to Him, "Are we *ourselves* blind also?"

41 Jesus said to them, "If you were blind, you would not have sin; but now that you say, 'We see,' your sin remains.

10 1 "Amen, amen, I say to you, the one who does not enter in through the door into the fold of the sheep, but goes up some other way, that one is a thief and a robber.

2 "But the one who enters in through the door is a shepherd of the sheep.

3 "To this one the doorkeeper opens and the sheep hear his voice, and he calls his own sheep by name and leads them out.

4 "When he brings out all his own, he goes before them, and the sheep follow him because they know his voice.

5 "And a stranger they will never follow, but will flee from him, because they do not know the voice of strangers."

The Pharisees are present when Jesus finds the man; they **heard these things** and are not slow to get the point. They derisively ask Jesus if He thinks they are to be counted among the **blind** and undiscerning. Their question implies that they think such an idea is patently ridiculous.

Jesus' reply is unexpected—and a further attack on their pride. They expect Him to say, "Yes, you are blind." But He does not. Rather, He says that **if** they *were* **blind** and unable to see His works, they **would not have sin**. The problem is not that they are blind, but that they can see! Inability to see the truth of His works would give them an immunity from sin and guilt. But they *are* able to see what He has done. They have no excuse not to recognize Him as Messiah—their failure to do so is not the result of a genuine *inability* to see truth, but of a stubborn *refusal* to do so. It represents not a failure of the eyes and the head, but a hardening of the heart. Because they say they can already **see** and refuse to seek more light, their **sin** and guilt **remain**.

Jesus continues His reply (the beginning of a new chapter here is not original in the Greek) with another solemn assurance: they are not the leaders of God's people they claim to be, nor do they speak for God. They claim to possess authority as God's true leaders and shepherds, and are terrifying the crowd with their threats of banning them from the synagogue. But they have no such authority to speak for God at all.

To prove this, Jesus gives the figure of the sheep and the door. One can tell who the *true* **shepherd of the sheep** is—he is the one who **enters in** to the enclosure or fold where the sheep are kept **through the** proper **door. The one who does not enter in through** that **door**, but instead **goes up some other way** (such as climbing over the wall), **that one** is not the shepherd, but rather **a thief and a robber**. The true shepherd does not need to use such roundabout tactics. **To this one the doorkeeper opens**, because he recognizes him to be the true shepherd. Moreover, so do the sheep. **He calls his own sheep by name and leads them out** of the sheep-pen. After he **brings out all his own, he goes before them, and the sheep follow him**—but only **because they know his voice**. If he were not the true shepherd, the sheep would **never follow** him like that, but would **flee from him**, not recognizing his **voice**. Thus, the identity of the true shepherd can be known by the fact that he uses the door and by the fact that the sheep follow him.

ॐ ॐ ॐ ॐ ॐ

6   This figure Jesus spoke to them, but those *men* did not know what things they were which He was saying to them.

7   Jesus therefore said to them again, "Amen,

> amen, I say to you, I *Myself* am the Door of
> the sheep.
>
> 8 "All who came before Me are thieves and rob-
>   bers, but the sheep did not hear them.
>
> 9 "I *Myself* am the Door; if anyone enters in
>   through Me, he will be saved and will go in
>   and will go out and will find pasture.
>
> 10 "The thief does not come except to thieve and
>   slaughter and destroy; I *Myself* came that they
>   may have life and may have *it* abundantly.

Those *men* who were listening **did not know** or understand the **things** the Lord was striving to teach by this **figure**. Jesus' point, of course, was that He Himself was **the Door of the sheep**, and that by refusing to acknowledge Him, the Pharisees were proving they were not God's true leaders, just as one who refuses to use the door of the sheepfold proves that he is not the true shepherd. Also, the fact that men such as this blind man followed Jesus proved that Jesus was the true shepherd, for the blind man could recognize his own Messiah, just as sheep can recognize their own shepherd.

Because they did not understand this parable, **Jesus therefore** spoke **again**, explaining the figure to them (again with His oath **Amen, amen, I say to you**). He explained that He was the One who was the Door of the sheep (the pronoun **I** is emphatic), and the key to everything. **All** religious leaders **who came before** Him claiming to be such a key or to be the true interpreter of God's will and Law were nothing of the kind, but in fact were **thieves and robbers**. That was why the people of God, **the sheep**, did **not hear** or hearken to them.

Jesus has in mind here the Pharisees who tyrannized the common people with their interpretations of the Law (compare Mark 12:40), claiming they themselves were the door to knowing God's will. Just as the thief and robber came to the sheepfold in the night, before the shepherd arrived, in order to **thieve** and steal the sheep, to **slaughter** and **destroy** them, so it was with these men. They were not sent by God to care for the sheep. And the people knew instinctively that they were imposters and did not speak for God.

Christ continues with His figure that He alone is the Door, and the key to salvation. Just as the sheep would use the door into the sheepfold, so the true people of God would recognize Him, and would find all they needed in Him alone. It was the same with sheep: in the evening the sheep would **enter in through** the door to find safety in the sheepfold and, once in there, would **be saved** from wolves and other predators. In the morning, they would **go out** through that door and would **find pasture**, and so **have life**, and that **abundantly**. By using the door, they would have all they needed.

It was the same with Him. By following Him and recognizing Him as their true Leader, the people of God could have salvation and abundant life in the age to come.

ॐ ॐ ॐ ॐ ॐ

11 "I *Myself* am the good shepherd; the good shepherd lays down His life for the sheep.
12 "He who is a paid *servant* and is not a shepherd, whose own the sheep are not, observes the wolf coming and leaves the sheep and flees, and the wolf snatches them and scatters them.
13 "He flees because he is a paid *servant* and it is not a care to him about the sheep.
14 "I *Myself* am the good shepherd, and I know My own and My own know Me,
15 "just as the Father knows Me and I *Myself* know the Father; and I lay down My life for the sheep.

Jesus continues with His shepherd imagery. He is Himself **the good shepherd**—that is, not just morally upright (Gr. *agathos*) but the one whose beauty and goodness are obvious (Gr. *kalos*, used in Luke 21:5 to describe the beautiful stones of the Temple).

The image of the good shepherd is drawn from Ezekiel 34, especially vv. 11–16. In that chapter, Yahweh describes Himself as the good shepherd, the One who will search for His scattered flock and gather them together. In those far-off days, Israel His flock had been abused and left to be scattered by false shepherds (Israel's secular leaders), who cared only for themselves. In the Babylonian Exile, Israel was left defenseless, as sheep were left defenseless in the wilderness. But the Kingdom of God would come, and God would regather them and feed them with good pasture (v. 14); He would seek the lost and bind up the broken (v. 16).

Jesus applies this image to His own ministry of teaching and healing, for He is the fullness of the Father, and God gathers His people through Him. And the goodness of the shepherd can be seen in this—in His willingness to sacrifice His life for His flock and **lay down His life for the sheep.**

In this He differs from all the other religious leaders, like the Pharisees. They do not care for God's people. They are like mere **paid** *servants* (Gr. *misthotos*), men who work only because they receive a wage (Gr. *misthos*). Such a one **is not** a true **shepherd,** nor does he have a shepherd's heart. The sheep are **not** his **own;** he only works to look after someone else's animals. When he **observes the wolf coming** and feels a threat to his own safety, he instantly thinks only of himself. He **leaves the sheep and flees,** so that **the wolf snatches** the abandoned flock and **scatters** them. He will under no circumstances risk his own life, because it is just a job for him. By doing this, he reveals that he is just **a paid** *servant,* and **it is not a care to him** at all **about the** poor **sheep.**

By His love for the flock, Jesus reveals Himself as their true and **good shepherd.** There is a mutual relationship of love between Himself and His flock. Just as **the Father knows** and loves Him, and He Himself **knows** and loves **the Father,** so this same mutual bond unites Him and His followers. He **knows** them and His **own know** Him, just as the shepherd knows each one of his flock individually. This love for His flock is so strong that He will even lay down His very **life** and soul (Gr. *psuche*) for His sheep. Jesus' hearers no doubt assumed that He was simply speaking metaphorically, using death as an illustration for the extreme measure of His love. They could not then know what John's readers would know and read into Christ's words —that He would indeed lay down His life for them on the Cross.

(Though they refer to Christ, it is impossible not to apply these words also to the Church's pastors and clergy, to those also called to be shepherds and leaders under Christ, the Arch-shepherd. What is required of priests and bishops is primarily this—that they also love their flocks enough to die for them. Only then can they hope to prove themselves on the last day to be true shepherds, and not mere hirelings and paid servants.)

ॐ   ॐ   ॐ   ॐ   ॐ

16   "And I have other sheep which are not of this fold; it is necessary for Me to bring those ones also, and they will hear My voice and they will become one flock *under* one shepherd.

17   "Because of this the Father loves Me, because I *Myself* lay down My life that I receive it again.

18   "No one takes it away from Me, but I *Myself* lay it down from Myself. I have authority to lay it down, and I have authority to receive it again. This commandment I received from My Father."

Having spoken of laying down His life in death (v. 15), the Lord then alludes to the inclusion of the Gentiles. This follows naturally, because His death is not simply to give life to Israel, but to give life to the whole world (compare the universalism of 3:14–16). The Gentile as well as the Jew belongs to God, in that all people who are open to the light belong to Him as His children (11:52). Everyone who is of the truth, wherever they are in the world, **hears** the **voice** of Jesus calling them home (18:37); everyone who does the truth comes to the light (3:21). Thus among the Gentiles also are souls who belong to Jesus, ready to respond to Him. Jesus **has** these **other sheep** as well, even though they are **not of this fold** of Israel. **It is necessary** for Him, in obedience to the Father's will, **to bring those ones also** to join His Jewish sheep. Thus all will be joined together to **become one** single **flock**, *under* one shepherd.

Jews may think that the Gentiles will occupy an inferior place in the messianic age, serving perhaps as hewers of wood and drawers of water for the Jews. But it is not to be. Rather, all such ethnic divisions are to be transcended in Christ, as the sheep will all mingle and mix together in one single flock.

This truth can be seen in the very words John uses for *flock* and *shepherd*. The word for *flock* is *he poimen* (with the stress on the first syllable), and the word for *shepherd*, *ho poimen* (with the stress on the second syllable). By this play on words, it is shown that there must be only one *flock* (*poimen*) for both Jews and Gentiles, for there is only one *shepherd* (*poimen*).

Jesus continues to speak of His voluntary death, saying that such obedience is the reason **the Father loves** Him. That is, His willingness to submit to the Father's will no matter what the cost, even if it means laying down His life, is the reason He has such favor with God. In speaking of the Father **loving** Him, Jesus is not referring to love in the abstract or to His relationship with the Father in general. Rather, He refers to the love of the Father for Him as it will be manifested in His Resurrection and ascended glory. Because of Jesus' relentless determination to do the will of the Father even though it means He must **lay down** His **life**, God gave Him the **authority to receive it again**. Christ **received**, as a manifestation of the Father's love, the **commandment** to rise again and sit with Him at His right hand.

That is why Jesus here stresses that **no one takes away** His life from Him, but rather that He is the one (the pronoun **I** is emphatic) who **lays it down** of Himself, voluntarily. It is this voluntary aspect of His death that makes it meritorious before the Father; this is why the Father loves Him. It is as St. Paul will later write—it was *because* Jesus humbled Himself even to the death of the Cross that God therefore highly exalted Him (Phil. 2:6–9). The Jews may think they are the ones who are in control, and that Jesus' arrest and execution are testimony to their cleverness and strength. This is an illusion. Jesus is never the victim of circumstances, nor at the mercy of His foes. He only dies because He voluntarily chooses to give up His life. Jesus remains forever the One in control.

ॐ ॐ ॐ ॐ ॐ

19 A division again occurred among the Jews because of these words.
20 And many from them were saying, "He has a
   demon and is raving! Why do you hear Him?"
21 Others were saying, "These are not the words
   of one demon-possessed. Is a demon able to
   open the eyes of the blind?"

After this argument with the Pharisees over the healing of the blind man (9:35—10:18), **a division again occurred among the Jews because of these words**, as the bystanders begin to argue among themselves. There are **many** from the Jews who cannot abide such claims. To them, these words confirm what Jesus' foes said about Him having **a demon** (compare 8:48). (Their response is even more emphatic in the Greek, where the word *demon* stands at the head of the sentence for emphasis: "A demon He has!") It seems to this group that Jesus **is raving**, talking like one insane (Gr. *mainomai*; compare our English "mania"). **Why** should any sensible person **hear Him** at all? How can they continue to listen to this stuff?

The other group cannot write Him off so easily. **These** words that Jesus has spoken **are not the words of one demon-possessed**; they resonate within the hearers and have the ring of truth. Besides, they ask, **is a demon able to open the eyes of the blind?** How can the foes of Jesus explain that?

John leaves the debate (as it were) in full swing—for the debate was, in his day, still going on. Jesus' words and works still divided men into two groups—the persecuting world and the persecuted Church—and will divide them until the world's end. It only remains for his hearers to choose which of the two groups they will join.

§III.7.vii. More Controversy on the Feast of the Dedication

༄ ༄ ༄ ༄ ༄

22 There occurred then the Dedication among the ones in Jerusalem;

23 it was winter, and Jesus was walking in the Temple, in the portico of Solomon.

24 The Jews therefore encircled Him and were saying to Him, "Until when will You hold our souls *in suspense?* If You *Yourself* are the Christ, tell us openly."

25 Jesus answered them, "I told you, and you do not believe; the works that I *Myself* do in My Father's Name, these witness about Me.

26 "But you *yourselves* do not believe, because you are not from My sheep.

27 "My sheep hear My voice, and I *Myself* know them, and they follow Me;

28 "and I *Myself* give eternal life to them, and they will never ever perish; and no one will snatch them from My hand.

29 "My Father, who has given them to Me, is greater than all; and no one is able to snatch them from the Father's hand.

30 "I *Myself* and the Father are one."

The scene switches to the time two months later, that of the feast of the **Dedication** of the Temple under the Maccabees (or Hanukkah). Though this feast was not one of the three for which the Law insisted upon pilgrimage to Jerusalem (those three being Passover, Weeks, and Booths; Ex. 23:14–16), Jesus was again **among the ones in Jerusalem** and **was walking in the Temple, in the** covered-over **portico of Solomon.** This was because **it was winter,** and it was warmer inside the portico.

It was because He was walking inside that **the Jews** were able to **encircle Him** and trap Him. They had a question for Him, since

He had been **holding** their **souls** *in suspense*: if it was He that was **the Christ** (the personal pronoun **You** is emphatic), let Him **tell** them **openly**! Their whole lives had been spent in waiting for the Messiah to come and liberate them from Rome. Should they look to Him to provide this liberation?

It was impossible for Jesus to provide a simple yes or no answer to such a question. He could not answer this question for them any more than He could answer it for Pilate (18:33–34), for the answer all depended on what the inquirer meant by Messiah. If he meant a military deliverer, the answer was no. If he meant the one sent by God to liberate men from their sins by the word of truth, the answer was yes.

So it is that Jesus does not answer directly, but simply says that He has already in fact answered their question—even though they did **not believe** Him when He **told** them. He does not tell them in words; rather **the works** that He continually **does in** His **Father's Name, these witness** about Him, and tell all about what kind of Messiah He is. But they **do not believe** because they are not inwardly receptive; they are **not from** His **sheep** and so refuse to allow Him to rearrange their basic presuppositions about the nature of the Messiah.

They are, in fact, among those who are upholding the ban placed on His disciples in Jerusalem (such as the blind man; compare 9:22, 35). Israel is divided into those who are sympathetic to Jesus and those who oppose Him as a deceiver. It is only the former, His followers and **sheep**, who can **hear** His **voice** and understand what His works mean; it is they who can hear Him telling them that He is the Christ. His relationship is with them, not with the crowd.

He is the One who **knows** and recognizes these sheep (the pronoun I is emphatic), whatever the authorities may say. The rulers of the Jews may disown these, but He takes them in. As they continue to **follow** Him, He is the one who will **give eternal life to them** so that **they will never ever perish**. The ban from the synagogue cannot ban them from God. **No one**, whatever his pretended authority, will be able to **snatch them** away out of His **hand**. His authority is infinitely greater than that of the synagogue and Sanhedrin. These poor men are safe. His **Father has given them** to Him as His gift, and the Father is **greater than all** earthly authority. **No one**, not even the great Sanhedrin in Jerusalem, **is able to snatch them** and take them **from the Father's hand**. The rulers of the Jews have no authority to overturn the judgments of the Father.

In fact, Jesus says, to be in His hand is the same as being in the Father's hand, for He Himself and **the Father are one** (Gr. *en*, in the neuter—one thing, not one person). That is, to follow Jesus is to follow the Father, for He is the fullness of the Father's nature (compare 1:18), and Jesus' words are a full and genuine revelation of the Father's will. If Jesus says these men are safe, they are safe, and no court on earth can overturn this!

---

෨ ෨ ෨ ෨ ෨

31 Again the Jews bore stones that they might stone Him.

32 Jesus answered them, "I showed you many good works from the Father; for which of them do you stone Me?"

33 The Jews answered Him, "For a good work we do not stone You, but for blasphemy; and because You, being a man, make Yourself God."

34 Jesus answered them, "Has it not been written in your Law, 'I *Myself* said, you are gods'?

35 "If he called those ones 'gods' to whom the Word of God came (and the Scripture is not able to be destroyed),

36 "do you *yourselves* say of Him whom the Father sanctified and sent into the world, 'He blasphemes,' because I said, 'I am the Son of God'?

This pairing of Himself with the Father is too much for them, for they recognize it as a claim to equality with God. Though He is plainly a mere **man** (as they think), nonetheless He **makes Himself out to be God**—this is **blasphemy**, pure and simple. They therefore **bore stones that they might stone Him**. (The word rendered *bore* is the Gr. *bastazo*, elsewhere translated "carry" and used in Gal. 6:2 to denote the carrying of a burden. These are not small stones, but sizable rocks!)

Jesus does not panic nor run. He simply asks them (with superlative irony) to specify the good work for which they are punishing Him. He has done so many **good works from the Father**, and so many miracles (such as those mentioned in 5:9; 9:14)—would they care to tell Him before they kill Him which miracle and good deed they have a particular objection to? His foes give the obvious answer (through gritted teeth?)—that it is not for any **good work** that they are stoning Him, but for **blasphemy**.

Jesus answers by referring to the Scriptures. They object to Him claiming a divine authority, but even in their own **Law** certain people were given divine authority. Concerning those whom God sent to rule His people, it has **been written "I said, 'you are gods'"** (Ps. 82:6). That is, as judges, some were called to share God's authority and to have the power over life and death, acquitting some so that they lived and condemning others to death. If these were **called 'gods'** even though they were mere men, those to whom the divine **Word of God came**, and if these could share God's authority, how much more could Jesus, **whom the Father sanctified and sent into the world**, claim to be **the Son of God** and to share the divine authority? **The Scripture is not able to be destroyed**, and thus can only speak eternal truth—as they freely acknowledge. This very Scripture designates mere men to be gods, and they have no problem with that. How can they blame Jesus and say that **He blasphemes** because He claims to be the Son of God? Their objection assumes that men cannot share God's authority in any way, yet Jesus shows that even on a human level this is not so. How much more can He, as the pre-existent Son, charged by the Father to do His will, share His authority!

༄ ༄ ༄ ༄ ༄

ॐ ॐ ॐ ॐ ॐ

37 "If I do not do the works of My Father, do not believe Me;

38 "but if I do *them*, even if you do not believe Me, believe the works, that you may *come to* know and *continue to* know that the Father *is* in Me, and I *Myself am* in the Father."

39 Therefore they were seeking again to take hold of Him, and He went out from their hand.

He continues to challenge His adversaries. **If** He does **not do the works** of His **Father** and fill Judea with miracles, they are indeed justified in their unbelief and should **not believe** Him. His claims are indeed extraordinary. But He *does* do the works of His Father, and it is these works that effectively make His claim and prove His case, witnessing to who He is (v. 25). They therefore have no excuse for their unbelief. Even if they can **not believe** Him for the sake of His words alone and for their ring of truth, yet they can **believe** the witness borne by **the works**. By listening to what His works have to say, they **may** *come to* know and *continue to* know of His eternal union with the Father and that He and the Father are one. (The words rendered *come to know* and *continue to know* are both the Gr. verb *ginosko*, the first in the aorist tense and the second in the present tense. That is, by hearing the witness of His works, they can be enlightened and continue in that light. His works are capable of turning them into His true disciples, if only they will listen.)

His adversaries, however, refused the light and turned from the knowledge He offered. They **were seeking again to take hold of Him** and hand Him over to the authorities, but once again He **went out from their hand** and eluded arrest. His hour had not yet come.

§III.8 Into Perea

§III.8.i. Resettling in Bethany-beyond-Jordan

ॐ ॐ ॐ ॐ ॐ

40 And He went away again beyond the Jordan
to the place where John was at first baptizing,
and He remained there.

41 And many came to Him and were saying, "John
indeed did no sign, but everything which John
said about this man was true."

42 And many believed in Him there.

After this, Jesus **went away again beyond the Jordan to the place where John was at first baptizing.** This refers to the area to the east of the Jordan River, in Perea. In 1:28, it is described as "Bethany beyond the Jordan," doubtless to differentiate the site from the Bethany which was near Jerusalem in Judea. Jesus went back to this place in the Transjordan because it was safer than Judea. He **remained there,** according to our estimate, about two months. (This assumes His departure from Jerusalem at the end of December and His return to Jerusalem shortly before the Passover in April, leaving enough time for a further brief sojourn in Ephraim after the raising of Lazarus; see 11:54.)

While He was in the Transjordan, He continued to attract disciples from John's movement. People from this area would remember John the Baptizer vividly (the place is described as **the place where John was at first baptizing**) and would reverence John as a prophet (compare Matt. 21:26). **Many** of these came to side with Jesus and **believed in Him,** being led to this loyalty by their prior loyalty to John. John had pointed to Jesus as the Lamb of God, the fulfillment of their messianic hopes (1:29–34). It was true that John **did no sign** and performed no miracle, but seeing Jesus had renewed their belief in John as a prophet nonetheless. For **everything** which **John said about** Jesus was being proven **true**, so that John's words were proving themselves to be prophetic. Seeing Jesus convinced them that He was the fulfillment of John's prophecies—that He was indeed, as the Baptizer had said, the Son of God.

§III.8.ii. Seventh Sign: Raising of Lazarus

> ৯৯ ৯৯ ৯৯ ৯৯ ৯৯
>
> **11** 1   Now a certain man was ailing, Lazarus of Bethany, from the village of Mary and her sister Martha.
>
> 2   And it was the Mary who anointed the Lord with perfume and wiped His feet with her hair whose brother Lazarus was ailing.
>
> 3   The sisters therefore sent to Him, saying, "Lord, behold, he whom You love is ailing."
>
> 4   But when Jesus heard it, He said, "This illness is not unto death, but for the glory of God, that the Son of God may be glorified through it."

Though no note of time is given, the following sign seems to have taken place in early to mid-March, which would leave some time for Christ to remain in Ephraim after the miracle (see 11:54) and still enter Jerusalem shortly before the Passover in early April.

This sign is the seventh one narrated by John and is presented as being the crown of all His miracles. It is introduced by reference to **a certain man Lazarus** who was **ailing**. Lazarus is described as being **from the village of Mary and her sister Martha**, and these last two are mentioned as if they were well known to the Church. Mary was especially well known, and is mentioned first (even though she would seem to be the younger sister; compare Luke 10:38–42). St. John expects his readers to be familiar with the story of the prepaschal anointing at Bethany (compare Matt. 26:6–13; Mark 14:3–9), and he identifies **Mary** as the (otherwise anonymous) woman in that anointing story, the one **who** anointed the Lord with perfume and wiped His feet with her hair.

Lazarus' illness grew worse, and **the sisters** felt that they had no choice but to call for Jesus. They **therefore sent to Him** with a message to come at once. No doubt the actual message was long and detailed, but John focuses on the core of it and the part the sisters felt would exert the most "pull" on Jesus: **he whom You love is ailing.** The word used here for *love* is the Greek *phileo*, cognate with the word for friend, *philos*. The sisters were appealing to the sacred bonds of friendship as they urged Him to come, despite the danger of entering Judea again. His dear friend was in need of Him—how could He not respond?

The Lord indeed responded—as He does to all who cry out to Him in need. He replied to the messenger, **"This illness is not unto death, but for the glory of God, that the Son of God may be glorified through it."** It was just the reply they hoped to receive, and they interpreted it as meaning that Jesus would come to heal him.

ॐ ॐ ॐ ॐ ॐ

5 Now Jesus loved Martha, and her sister, and Lazarus.

6 Therefore when He heard that he was ailing, He remained then two days in the place where He was.

7 Then after this He says to the disciples, "Let us go into Judea again."

8 The disciples say to Him, "Rabbi, the Jews were now seeking to stone You, and are You going there again?"

9 Jesus answered, "Are there not twelve hours in the day? If anyone walks in the day, he does not stumble, because he sees the light of this world.

10 "But if anyone walks in the night, he stumbles, because the light is not in him."

But the Lord's next actions seemingly did not suit that reply. For when He **heard** their message, **He remained then two days in the place where He was** and did not hurry back. (John assures us that the delay was not caused by any indifference to the family; on the contrary, **Jesus loved Martha, and her sister, and Lazarus.**) Yet, having received news of Lazarus's situation, He made no move to visit him in Judea.

The **therefore** of v. 6 is at first sight puzzling—and is only resolved when the whole story of Lazarus's final raising has been told. Jesus loved the family—and therefore He remained where He was and did not go to them. One might expect John to say that "Jesus loved the family and therefore went at once." But Jesus' love was not to be manifested in a simple healing of the sick man—in fact, Lazarus had died shortly after the messengers left to find Jesus, though the messengers could not have known that. Rather, His love would be manifested in an astounding demonstration of the glory of God. Jesus remained where He was and waited so that the dead man could be seen by all as quite dead. His intention was not simply to restore Lazarus to life, but for Lazarus to manifest the power of God over decay and corruption, so that he could be a promise of the final resurrection.

The messengers could not have known that Lazarus had died, and we may think they did hurry back. Perhaps they concluded from Jesus' words that Lazarus's plight was not as extreme as they feared, and that he would still be alive when Jesus returned later after His (as they thought) inexplicable delay.

Then after this delay, **He says to** His **disciples, "Let us go into Judea again."** The disciples were alarmed at this, as they were doubtless alarmed at the sisters' plea for Jesus to come to them in Judea. Perhaps they assumed from Jesus' words in v. 4 that Lazarus would not die, but would be saved from death by Jesus' prayer—which He would offer to God where He was, in Perea, far enough away from danger in Judea. And here Jesus was, seemingly changing His mind, and planning to go into Judea again after all!

They responded respectfully, addressing Him as **"Rabbi,"** yet still sought strenuously to dissuade Him from this plan. Had He forgotten so soon that **the Jews were** just **now seeking to stone Him?** Why jump back into the lion's mouth?

Jesus assured them of their safety with a parable. It was the same as a man who **walks in the day.** There are a whole **twelve hours in the day,** and as long as he walks during those daylight hours, he is safe and **does not stumble, because he sees the light of this world,** the sun shining in the sky. It is only if one **walks in the night,** without the sun shining above and with **the light not in him,** that he **stumbles** and trips in the dark. So it is with them. As long as Jesus, the light of this world, is still with them (8:12; 9:5), they are safe—even in the closing hours of the day.

ॐ ॐ ॐ ॐ ॐ

11 These things He said, and after that He says to them, "Our friend Lazarus has fallen asleep; but I go that I may awaken him."

12 The disciples therefore said to Him, "Lord, if he has fallen asleep, he will be saved."

13 Now Jesus had spoken about his death, but they supposed that He was speaking of the slumber of sleep.

14 Then Jesus therefore said to them openly, "Lazarus died—

15 "and I rejoice for your sakes that I was not there, so that you may believe. But let us go to him."

16 Thomas therefore, the one called the Twin, said to his co-disciples, "Let us also go, that we *ourselves* may die with Him."

After saying **these things** to reassure them, Christ summons them to follow Him to Judea. "**Our friend Lazarus has fallen asleep,**" He says, and now He must go to **awaken him.** (We note in passing how Jesus associates the disciples with Him in His friendship with Lazarus, for He says not "*My* friend Lazarus," but rather "*our* friend Lazarus"; in the communion of saints, each friend of Christ is also friend to all His other friends, so that all Christians are brothers and family.)

The disciples misunderstand Christ's meaning and do not catch the metaphor. **They suppose** that Jesus is **speaking of the** literal **slumber of sleep**, and saying perhaps (through His supernatural knowledge?) that Lazarus's fever has broken, and now he is sleeping peacefully. If that is the case, he will **be saved** and will recover. So there is no need for them to make the journey to Judea after all.

Jesus, of course, was speaking about Lazarus's death, and so He **said to them openly** and plainly, "**Lazarus died.**" And He adds that He **rejoices for** their **sakes** that He was **not there** to heal him, so that the disciples **may believe** in Him and have a further proof that He is the Messiah. But enough of words, the Lord says; **let us go to him.**

The disciples still cannot foresee the coming miracle: their minds are too filled with fear of the Jews and what they think will be certain death if they return to Judea. Their Lord has said that Lazarus has died, and now He is determined to go to him. They assume that Jesus means that He is prepared to visit Lazarus's grave even if He is stoned and dies in the attempt. One can almost see them hanging back, their faces filled with doubt and dread. **Thomas**, however (known to the Church at large as **the Twin**, just as Simon was known to the Church at large as Cephas), takes the lead and rallies **his co-disciples**, appealing to them as fellow-members of the same group. "**Let us also go**," he urges them, "**that we may die with Him.**" He loves the Lord and cannot stand to see Him go into such danger alone. If He is going to His death, His own disciples (the **we** is emphatic in the Greek) will stand with Him to the end!

ॐ ॐ ॐ ॐ ॐ

17 So when Jesus came, He found that he had already been in the tomb four days.
18 Now Bethany was near Jerusalem, about fifteen stadia away;
19 and many of the Jews had come to Martha and Mary, that they might console them about their brother.

20 Martha therefore, when she heard that Jesus was coming, went to meet Him, but Mary sat in the house.

21 Martha therefore said to Jesus, "Lord, if You had been here, my brother would not have died.

22 "Even now I know that whatever You ask God, God will give You."

23 Jesus says to her, "Your brother will rise again."

24 Martha says to Him, "I know that he will rise again in the resurrection on the last day."

25 Jesus said to her, "I *Myself* am the resurrection and the life; he who believes in Me will live even if he dies,

26 "and everyone who lives and believes in Me will never ever die. Do you believe this?"

27 She says to Him, "Yes, Lord, I *myself* have believed that You *Yourself* are the Christ, the Son of God, the One who comes into the world."

After a day's journey, Jesus and His disciples come to Bethany and find that Lazarus has **already been in the tomb four days**, having died shortly after his sisters sent the messengers. (John adds a geographical note, saying that **Bethany was near Jerusalem**, only **fifteen stadia away**—that is, about two miles. He does this to show how it was that **many of the Jews** could come from nearby Jerusalem to **console** the sisters **about their brother**; Bethany was a kind of suburb of Jerusalem, and so many people from the Holy City could be present to comfort the grieving.)

Friends of the family must have seen Jesus approaching and told **Martha**, as the older sister and the mistress of the house. When she **heard that Jesus was coming** to them, she **went to meet Him**, leaving her sister **Mary** none the wiser as she **sat in the house** immersed in misery. All of Martha's thought has been on Jesus since Lazarus took a turn for the worse, and resentment for His absence has been eating at her since Lazarus's death. Now that He is approaching at last (and too late), she cannot contain herself nor wait for Him to arrive. She flies from the house to meet Him on the road.

She has but one thing to say, that which fills and overflows her heart: **"Lord, if You had been here, my brother would not have died."** It is more a heartbroken sigh of sadness and loss than an open rebuke, but the implied note of blame cannot be missed. What she wants to blurt out, like a cry of pain, is the question, "Where *were* You?" But this question is all she can manage without going utterly to pieces. And in the midst of her pain, she wants to salvage whatever she can for her brother; so she says to Jesus, **"Even now I know that whatever You ask God, God will give You."** That is, she wants Jesus to intercede for Lazarus that he be given a place in Paradise.

The Lord does not stop to answer the implied rebuke, nor explain His absence at all, even as He *never* in this age gives us the explanations we think we need. Rather, He remains focused on the task He has from the Father. And so He simply tells her, **"Your brother will rise again."** Martha still assumes that death is final, and that Jesus is offering her the standard comfort of assuring her that her brother **will rise again in the resurrection on the last day**. She will see him then, no doubt, and then all will be well in the sweet by-and-by of the age to come.

But Jesus is not talking about the age to come or the final resurrection. For He is *Himself* the presence of the age to come; He is *Himself* the power of the final resurrection made incarnate and active here and now. So He directs her focus away from the future and redirects it to the power standing before her face. He tells her that *He* is the **resurrection** and **life** of the age to come (the **I** is emphatic), the One even now able to raise the dead. He has claimed to be **the Christ**, the messianic **Son of God, the One who comes into the world** to liberate it from death. It is for these claims that the Jews were but lately seeking to stone Him. As the Son of God, He is able to bestow life as He wills; **he who believes** in Him **will live** eternally in the age to come **even if he dies**, and **everyone who lives** and **believes** in Him as His obedient disciple will **never ever die**. His word can save from eternal death and bestow life with God (compare 8:52). Does she **believe this?**

By asking if she believes this claim, He is not merely asking for her views; He is demanding her discipleship. Will she side with Him against the world and trust Him to do as He sees fit? Martha meets the challenge. She has always **believed** that He is the Christ (the pronouns **I** and **You** are emphatic). She is prepared to stand publicly with Him now.

> ৩৯ ৩৯ ৩৯ ৩৯ ৩৯
>
> 28 And when she had said this, she went away and called Mary her sister, saying covertly, "The Teacher is here and is calling for you."
> 29 And when that one heard *it*, she arose quickly and came to Him.
> 30 Now Jesus had not yet come into the village, but was still in the place where Martha met Him.
> 31 When the Jews therefore who were with her in the house and consoling her saw that Mary rose up quickly and went out, they followed her, supposing that she was going to the tomb to weep there.
> 32 Therefore, when Mary came where Jesus was, she saw Him and fell at His feet, saying to Him, "Lord, my brother, if You had been here, would not have died."

Both of them knew that Mary must be involved in this, since Mary also had long been His follower (see Luke 10:42). So it was that Martha **went away and called Mary her sister**. She called her **covertly**, whispering to her as Mary still sat in the house. That message was the one they had both been praying and hoping to hear prior to Lazarus's death: "**The Teacher is here**." That is, Jesus had finally arrived, and wanted to see her.

When that one (the pronoun is emphatic, Greek *ekeine*) **heard** this message, she arose quickly and bolted from the house, running down the road, for **Jesus had not yet come into the village**. Rather, He waited **in the place** outside it **where Martha met Him**.

Mary did not come alone. She did not ask **the Jews who were with her in the house** to accompany her; that was the reason Martha gave Mary the news covertly, for she had wanted them to have a more private time with Jesus. Nonetheless, these comforters (including the professional mourners) **saw** her **rise up quickly** and **they followed her, supposing that she was going to the tomb to weep there**. As professional mourners, it was their job to accompany her and provide that service.

But Mary did not go to the tomb; she left the village and met Jesus on the road. Mary was of a more emotional temperament than her practical sister (this is apparent from the account of them in Luke 10:38–42), and when she **saw Him**, she immediately **fell at His feet** in a heap of outpoured grief and emotion.

She could hardly get her words out. She seems to gasp them out between sobs. The message is the same as her sister's, but in the Greek the word order is different: "**Lord, my brother, if You had been here, would not have died.**" In the Greek, Mary says, *Kurie, ei es ode ouk an mou apethanen o adelphos*; in the Greek, Martha says *Kurie, ei es ode ouk an apethanen o adelphos mou*. The words are the same, but the order is different, and this difference in order seems to be John's way of reflecting Mary's disordered and gasping speech.

ॐ ॐ ॐ ॐ ॐ

33 When Jesus therefore saw her weeping, and the Jews who came with her weeping, He was indignant in spirit and was shaken in Himself,

34 and said, "Where have you put him?" They say to Him, "Lord, come and see."

35 Jesus shed *tears*.

Mary then dissolved into **weeping**, as did **the Jews who came with her**. The Lord saw His dear friends (perhaps known since childhood) prostrate with grief. As He looked, He saw not just what death had done to them, but what it had done to all the human race. Man, bearing the image and beauty of God, was meant to stand radiant and eternal, bound heart to heart with unbreakable bonds as one shining family, triumphant in the love of God. And here death had worked its woe and torn down all the work of God. All that was left on earth of that shining and radiant vision was a scattered collection of weeping women, wailing to break the heart, clawing the dust, rending their robes in grief, powerless to stop the worms from eating the flesh of their family.

So it was that Jesus **was indignant in spirit and was shaken** with anger **in Himself**, furious at the ancient serpent for wreaking this havoc (Gen. 3:1f). The word rendered here *indignant* is the Greek *embrimaomai*. It is sometimes translated "deeply moved," but this translation gives the idea that He was moved with grief. The Greek word, however, savors not of grief, but of anger. It is used for the snorting of horses in secular literature; in Mark 1:43 and Matthew 9:30 it is translated "sternly warn," and in Mark 14:5 it is translated "scold." In all of its uses, the word conveys the idea of indignation. Christ, therefore, was not here moved with grief over His friend; He was moved with anger at the Enemy, and indignation that all the Father's world could be so ruined.

He asked the sisters, **"Where have you put him?"** and they led Him back to the tomb, saying, **"Lord, come and see."** (It is interesting that this **come and see** parallels the earlier invitation to "come and see" in 1:46; in the earlier encounter, the disciples' path led to life, whereas here the path leads to death. Perhaps John means to subtly show us the world from the Lord's perspective, and that all He discovers here is death.) When the Lord arrived at the tomb, He indeed encountered death. And looking on that blocked-up cave, He beheld not just the buried corpse of His friend, but the corpse of the whole world.

So it was that **Jesus shed** *tears*. The word used is different from the one used in v. 33 to describe Mary's loud weeping. There it was *klaio*; here it is *dakruo* (cognate with *dakruon*, "a tear"; compare its use in Luke 7:38). Mary and the mourners wept with loud wailing. Here John says that tears ran down Jesus' cheeks. Unlike Mary's weeping, this was no emotional outburst, but a mourning over the ruin of all God's work—over His beloved Lazarus, and all like him.

ॐ ॐ ॐ ॐ ॐ

36 And so the Jews were saying, "See how He loved him!"

37 But some of them said, "Was this one, who opened the eyes of the blind, not able to make *it* so that even this one should not die?"

38 Jesus therefore, again being indignant within Himself, comes to the tomb. Now it was a cave, and a stone was lying upon it.

39 Jesus says, "Lift the stone *away*." Martha, the sister of the one who died, says to Him, "Lord, already he smells, for it is *the* fourth day."

40 Jesus says to her, "Did I not say to you, if you believe, you will see the glory of God?"

41 Therefore they lifted the stone *away*.

The bystanders were impressed at such love, but some of them misunderstood it, misinterpreting His tears as an expression of His powerlessness in the face of death and decay. **This one who opened the eyes of the blind**—that was such a miracle! To think that He is **not able to make** *it* **so that even this one** whom He loves so much **should not die!**

Jesus was **again indignant within Himself** over the victory of death, and He **comes to the tomb**, determined to rob the Enemy of his victory and to manifest the triumph of God. Lazarus was buried in a **cave**, with **a stone lying upon it**. With complete confidence and serene sovereignty, Jesus orders them to **lift the stone** *away* from the mouth of the tomb, so that Lazarus can come forth.

Martha (called here **the sister of the one who died**, to stress the fact of Lazarus's death) instinctively recoils from such an order. That stone was all that kept sealed within the tomb all the appalling stench of death. She protests, "**Lord, already he smells, for it is** *the* **fourth**

day since he died." Jesus once again does not explain. He simply reminds her of her previous promise to obey (v. 27). Did He not say to her just now that if she would **believe** she would **see the glory of God**? The stench must be endured if she is to see that glory.

It was to be a miracle of unparalleled proportions, eclipsing anything He had done before. The times He had previously raised someone from death, it was immediately after that person had died (e.g. Luke 7:11f; 8:49f), but this was to take place after decay had already set in. It was to be a reversal of the very power and process of decomposition itself, the undoing of death. Flesh which had already decayed was to be restored to health and vitality, and all the body, which was collapsing in upon itself, was to return to its previous state of health before the onset of illness. It was to be, in fact, a picture and image of the final resurrection of the flesh.

At a signal from Martha, **they lifted the stone** from the mouth of the cave.

ॐ ॐ ॐ ॐ ॐ

41 And Jesus lifted His eyes up and said, "Father, I thank You that You heard Me.

42 "And I *Myself* knew that You always hear Me, but because of the crowd standing around I said it, that they may believe that You *Yourself* sent Me."

43 And having said these things, He yelled with a great voice, "Lazarus, come outside!"

44 The one who had died came out, bound hand and foot with bandages, and his face was bound around with a neckerchief. Jesus says to them, "Loose him and leave him to go."

They lifted the stone; Jesus now **lifts His eyes** in response (the same Greek verb *airo* is used for both). In the prayer John records, it is significant that there is no request to God to raise Lazarus. Jesus will raise him by His own power, as a manifestation of His own sovereign authority.

In His prayer to the **Father**, Jesus simply **thanks** Him that He **heard** Him—a reference to Jesus' previous prayer to the Father regarding Lazarus some days back, when Jesus first heard of his death. He thanks the Father for having heard that prayer—even as He **knew** that God **always hears** Him. There was never any suggestion that God would *not* hear Jesus' prayer, for Jesus always does only what the Father tells Him. In fact, the only reason for thanking God for having heard His prayer is **because of the crowd standing around**. It is important that they realize that He does this miracle through the power of God, **that they may believe** that God is the One (the pronoun **You** is emphatic) who **sent** Jesus. Jesus is not working some demonic sorcery. Here is the glory of God.

Having said these things and having confirmed the divine origin of the miracle, Jesus **yelled with a great voice, "Lazarus, come outside!"** And then, in answer to these few words (three in the Greek), **the one who had died** obediently **came out**. He shuffled out immediately, as ordered, without taking time to remove his burial wrappings, still **bound hand and foot** with the **bandages** and the usual **neckerchief** that was still **bound around his face** (the word rendered *neckerchief* is the Greek *soudarion*, the word used in Luke 19:20 and Acts 19:12).

The crowd, we may imagine, gasped and drew back in amazement. Jesus simply ordered them to "**loose him and leave him** be **to go**."

A word may be added about the possible way in which Lazarus was wrapped, because the Orthodox iconography depicting him and his raising would seem to be more poetic than historical. It appears (though these details are disputed) that Lazarus, like other Jews of his time, was wrapped for burial in the following way. A neckerchief was folded upon itself so as to form a long piece of cloth. This was wrapped around the head in order to keep the jaw from dropping open and then tied in a knot at the top of the head to hold it in place. A large sheet was then laid over the body so as to cover the front of the corpse from the feet to the head and then down the back to the feet again. This long sheet was tied together by another bandage about the feet (or ankles). The hands and arms were perhaps tied together by another bandage or strip of linen wrapped around the chest and securing the arms in front of the body. It appears that these bandages and this neckerchief were the burial wrappings referred to by St. John.

❧ EXCURSUS

ON THE SEVEN SIGNS OF CHRIST

The term for "miracle" preferred by St. John in his Gospel is "sign" (Gr. *semeion*). That is, Christ's works were not simply wonders (Gr. *teras*) or acts of power (Gr. *dunamis*, the usual word for miracle), but works which "signified" something (Gr. *semaino;* compare its use in 12:33; 21:19). Just as signs by the roadside indicate and point the way to an unseen destination, so the miracles of Christ indicate and point the way to previously hidden truth about the Kingdom of God.

Out of the multitude of miracles he could have chosen to relate, St. John chose seven, this being the number of perfection. (In his Apocalypse or Book of Revelation, the number seven recurs again and again.) But these were not just any seven signs. They were chosen to reveal seven truths about the nature of the Kingdom of God that Christ was bringing.

First Sign: Water Changed into Wine (2:1f). This sign reveals how the glory of the Kingdom is seen only by His disciples, by those with faith. Just as the majority of the guests did not know where the new wine had come from and did not appreciate this as a manifestation of Christ's glory (but only as a glass of good wine), so it is with the Kingdom. It requires faith to see where the signs are pointing. The faithful disciple will see this and appreciate it as a manifestation of Christ's glory; the faithless Pharisee (for example) will see it only as a violation of the Law or even as the work of the devil (5:16; 9:16).

Also, this Sign reveals how the water of Judaism is transformed into the richer wine of the Kingdom. As wine differs from water, so the Kingdom of God differs from Israel's previous experience of the Law. The Kingdom is not simply a more glorious *extension* of the Law, not simply an era when the Law is more perfectly kept. It is a state in which the Law is *transcended.*

Second Sign: The Healing of the Royal Servant's Son (4:46f). This sign reveals how salvation in the Kingdom comes through trusting in Jesus' word alone. The father of the sick boy was required to trust Jesus' word that his boy was healed, and return home to him without any further proof. In the same way, in the Church, salvation comes simply by faithfully committing oneself to Christ. One will be saved in the age to come if one has humble trust in Christ (Gr. *pistis*, also translated as "faith").

Third Sign: The Healing of the Paralytic by the Pool (5:1f). This sign also reveals that salvation in the Kingdom of God comes simply by trusting Christ's word, and not by reliance on the Law. The paralytic at first relied on the pool for salvation; however, salvation came not through the pool but through the word of Jesus. The paralytic was saved only when he ceased looking to the pool for salvation and transferred his hope to Jesus (who healed in defiance of Pharisaical Sabbath rules). In the same way, salvation comes not from reliance on the Law (with its Sabbath rules), but only when one transfers one's ultimate loyalty from the Jewish Law to Jesus Christ.

Fourth Sign: The Multiplication of the Loaves (6:1f). This sign reveals that salvation comes through the death of Jesus, and from appropriating that death by eating Jesus' Body and Blood in the Church's Eucharist. Thus, acceptance of the Kingdom of God requires a complete reversal of old Jewish attitudes (such as the horror of eating blood), and an openness to new truths.

Fifth Sign: The Walking on the Sea (6:16f). This sign reveals how the Kingdom of God transcends all the categories of this age, with its politics and military might. The Jews wanted a military and political king (6:15), but the Kingdom Jesus offered was a supernatural one, rooted in the realities of the age to come and not the realities of this age. This was imaged by His transcending the natural and physical realities of this age by walking on the sea.

Sixth Sign: The Healing of the Blind Man (9:1f). This sign reveals that salvation comes only to those who trust and obey Christ (and not to all Jews simply by virtue of their being Jewish). The man was illumined when he went and washed as he had been told. Similarly, salvation comes to us only as we also obey Christ's word, becoming His disciples and washing in the waters of baptism. Personal discipleship to Jesus is required for salvation.

Seventh Sign: The Raising of Lazarus (11:1f). This last sign reveals that Christ's Kingdom consists of resurrection and life, not of politics (which aims at preserving one's place and nation; see 11:48). Salvation comes only as one trusts Christ to bestow new life (11:25–26) and confesses Him openly as the Son of God and the One who comes into the world, Israel's Messiah.

§III.8.iii. Resettling in Ephraim

ॐ ॐ ॐ ॐ ॐ

45 Many therefore of the Jews who had come to Mary and observed the things He did believed in Him.

46 But some of them went away to the Pharisees and told them the things Jesus did.

47 Therefore the chief priests and the Pharisees assembled a council and were saying, "What are we doing? For this man is doing many signs.

48 "If we leave Him thus, everyone will believe in

> Him, and the Romans will come and take both
> our place and our nation."
>
> 49 But a certain one of them, Caiaphas, being high
> priest that year, said to them, "You *yourselves*
> do not know anything at all,
>
> 50 "nor do you reckon that it is advantageous for
> you that one man should die for the people,
> and that the whole nation should not perish."
>
> 51 Now this he did not say from himself, but
> being high priest that year, he prophesied
> that Jesus was about to die for the nation,
>
> 52 and not for the nation only, but that He might
> also assemble into one the children of God who
> are scattered out.

This miracle, like all the rest of our Lord's words and works, had the effect of dividing Israel. **Many of the Jews who had come to Mary** when she ran to meet Jesus outside the village (v. 31) and who accompanied them to Lazarus' tomb and **observed the things He did** there, **believed in Him**. That is, they aligned themselves with Jesus as His supporters, and not with His detractors.

Others found themselves on the opposite side of this divide. These **went away to the Pharisees and told them the things Jesus did** at the tomb of Lazarus, of this latest setback (as they took it to be) for their cause.

Jesus' foes responded quickly and **assembled a council**. This was not a formal meeting of the supreme Council (Gr. *Sanhedrin*), but an informal meeting behind closed doors of **the chief priests and the Pharisees** who opposed Christ. They evaluated **what** they were **doing**, and how effective their opposition to Christ was. They had sent out the word that if anyone confessed Jesus to be Messiah, he was to be banned from the synagogue (9:22), but this was evidently ineffective. That is what *they* were doing; what **this man** was **doing** was **many signs**, multiplying miracle after miracle, and their bans and threats could not keep up. If they continued to **leave Him thus**, and continued their present strategy, then soon **everyone** would

believe in Him! At this rate, they reasoned, there would soon be a mighty swell of support for Him and the populace would rise up to declare Him messianic King. Then **the Romans** would **come** in response. They would kill Him and His followers and, worse yet, **take** away both their **place** (the Temple) and their **nation** (their national independence). The inevitable Roman reprisals against the messianic uprising they expected Jesus to spark would be disastrous.

At this point, **a certain one of them, Caiaphas, being high priest that** fateful **year**, stands up to bring matters to a head. He begins by denouncing their dithering, and calls for a decisive and energetic response. They (fools that they are; the pronoun **you** is emphatic, stressing their difference from him) **do not know anything at all!** They cannot **reckon** up what it all means, nor work out what to do. Surely the answer is obvious! They are fiddling about with bans from the synagogue, fretting about His popularity and trying to put Him in a bad light. Can they not see that such half-measures are useless? Jesus must die; it is as simple as that. Surely they can see that it is **advantageous** for them that **one man should die** if it means that **the people** and **the whole nation should not perish!** It is Jesus or the nation, Him or them. If He lives, they will die. If He dies, they will live. There is nothing for it but to take Jesus out of the way.

John has his own editorial comment about the words of Caiaphas. Humanly speaking, his counsel was responsible for the death of Jesus. But John realizes that it was God's will that Jesus die, for His death indeed meant life for the world. So he says that Caiaphas did **not say** those words **from himself**, nor was he carrying out only his own agenda. Rather, God was using him, even though he did not know it. Since he was **high priest that year** (indeed, he was high priest AD 18–36), God used him as His instrument for fulfilling His will. Just as God used the prophets of old (with their knowledge), he also used this rebellious high priest (without his knowledge), so that **he prophesied** and spoke the truth. Caiaphas meant his words about Jesus dying so that the nation should live as a piece of cynical political expediency—but his words were truer than he knew. For Jesus' death would indeed give life to Israel! Indeed, St. John adds, the truth was even bigger. For Jesus' death would give life not to **the nation** of Israel only, but to the whole world. Jesus was to **assemble into one** people and one Church all **the children of God who were scattered out** through the entire world, Gentiles as well as Jews.

---

৯৭ ৯৭ ৯৭ ৯৭ ৯৭

53 From that day therefore they deliberated *how* to kill Him.

54 Jesus therefore no longer walked openly among the Jews, but went away from there to the country near the wilderness into a city called Ephraim, and there He remained with the disciples.

55 Now the Passover of the Jews was near, and many went up to Jerusalem from the country before the Passover, that they might purify themselves.

56 Therefore they were seeking Jesus and saying to one another, as they stood in the Temple, "What does it seem to you—that He will not come to the feast?"

57 Now the chief priests and the Pharisees had given commandments that if anyone knew where He was, he should report it, that they might take hold of Him.

Caiaphas' words carried the day, and all agreed. **From that day, they deliberated *how* to kill Him**, looking constantly for their opportunity. Previously they had striven to isolate Jesus from the affection of the people. Now they were intent on killing Him.

Jesus was aware of this, and **therefore no longer walked openly among the Jews**. Instead, He went away to the safety of **a city called Ephraim**, out in **the country near the wilderness**, about thirteen miles from Jerusalem. He **remained there with** His **disciples**, safely awaiting the coming Passover.

As that Passover drew near, **many went up to Jerusalem** in order **that they might purify themselves.** That is, they went up in plenty of time to perform the rites required to cleanse themselves of any ceremonial defilement, which sometimes could take up to a week (2 Chr. 30:17; Lev. 13:6). John mentions this to explain the immense number of people who were in Jerusalem prior to the Passover.

All these were **seeking Jesus,** looking to spot the famous (or infamous) rabbi. **As they stood in the Temple** (the place where He would be sure to come, if He came for the feast at all), they asked themselves how likely it was that He would dare to show up and **come to the** approaching **feast.** Given the fever pitch of the opposition, all considered this very unlikely—for **the chief priests and the Pharisees had given commandments** and orders **that if anyone knew where He was, he should report it** to them. The word was out, and they were determined to **take hold of Him** if He dared to show His face!

§III.9. Final Visit to Jerusalem

§III.9.i. Anointing at Bethany

ॐ ॐ ॐ ॐ ॐ

12 1 Jesus, therefore, six days before the Passover, came into Bethany where Lazarus was, whom Jesus had raised from the dead.

2 Therefore they made Him a supper there, and Martha served, but Lazarus was one of the ones reclining with Him.

3 Mary therefore took a pound of precious perfume of pistic nard and anointed the feet of Jesus, and wiped His feet with her hair, and the house was filled with the odor of the perfume.

4 But Judas Iscariot, one of His disciples, who was about to deliver Him up, says,

> 5   "Why was this perfume not sold *for* three hundred denarii, and given to *the* poor?"
>
> 6   Now he said this, not because it was a care to him about the poor, but because he was a thief, and having the case, he used to bear *away* what was cast *into it.*
>
> 7   Jesus therefore said, "Leave her; that she may keep it for the day of My burial.
>
> 8   "For the poor you always have with you, but Me you do not always have."

The scene switches to a time **six days before the Passover.** Jesus **came into Bethany**, on the outskirts of Jerusalem. Bethany is here described as the place **where Lazarus was, whom Jesus had raised from the dead**, because the whole of Bethany was abuzz with the news that Jesus was there. The locals of the town (the **they** of v. 2 probably has **Bethany** as its antecedent) **made** Jesus **a supper there** to honor the celebrity. **Martha served** the meal as the older of the two sisters, with **Lazarus reclining** at table with Jesus and His disciples. (In fact, Lazarus and his family were probably the ones who gave the banquet in thanksgiving for Christ's miracle.) The supper was held at the house of one of the locals, Simon the leper, perhaps because Simon's home was larger than Lazarus's and better able to accommodate the crowd (Mark 14:3).

On such a festive occasion, the usual practice was to anoint the head of the guests with a bit of oil upon their arrival, and this was no doubt done here. For Mary, however, that was not enough. More given to emotion than her pragmatic sister, she wanted to augment the usual anointing with a lavish anointing of her own. She took **a pound of precious perfume of pistic nard and anointed** the Lord with it, pouring it first over His head in the usual manner (Mark 14:3), and then, overcome with gratitude and having so much yet remaining in the broken alabaster flask (which could not be stoppered up), poured the rest of the flask onto His **feet**.

It was an astonishingly generous and flamboyant gesture. The perfume was pistic nard (that is, nard, an aromatic oil made from the pistachio nut), and a pound of it (Gr. *litra*, being about twelve ounces) was worth more than **three hundred denarii**—more than three hundred days' wages for the common laborer. The alabaster flask containing this perfume was probably a family heirloom.

There was more to come. The remaining contents which she poured onto His feet proved to be too much for a single anointing (was it too sticky on the feet?). In a gesture which would have shocked her contemporaries, she removed her veil, let down her hair, and **wiped His feet with her hair.** Respectable women never went unveiled, even in their own homes. This was a gesture of extreme lowliness, the unstoppable outflow of the heart's love. **The house** where they sat **was filled with the odor of the perfume,** calling all the more attention to such reckless abandon.

The disciples of Jesus certainly gave this act their undivided attention (Matt. 26:8), especially **Judas Iscariot.** John characterizes him as **one of His disciples** (who should have stuck with Him to the end), who nonetheless **was about to deliver Him up** to His foes. He was exasperated by this open love shown to the one for whom he had secret hostility, and he gave vent to his anger, expressing what all of the disciples were thinking anyway. He scolded Mary, demanding to know **why this perfume** was not **sold** *for* **three hundred denarii and given to** *the* **poor.** St. John, having identified Judas as the voice of rebuke (the Synoptic Gospels leave the speaker unidentified), stresses that Judas was not really concerned about the poor. Rather it was because **he was a thief.** As the treasurer, he was the one who held **the case,** the box used to hold their funds, and he **used to bear** *away* and remove **what was cast** *into it,* pilfering secretly. (Perhaps this habit grew as his disillusionment with Christ grew, and he was using such petty indulgences to console himself.)

Jesus immediately defended Mary's act, publicly rebuking his disciple in favor of the woman. "**Leave her,**" He retorted, "**that she may keep it for the day of My burial.**" The word rendered *keep* is the Greek *tereo.* It is sometimes rendered "observe" when used in reference to keeping a law (it is used in 9:16 for keeping the Sabbath). What the Lord is saying here is that Mary is to be permitted

219

this anointing as her way of observing (in advance) His burial rites. Just as a dead body was washed and anointed in preparation for burial, so Mary's anointing was to be considered part of this funerary ritual. If they were so concerned to help the poor, there was plenty of time to do that. **The poor** they would **always have** at hand; Him they would **not always have**.

The remark must have perplexed all who heard it. Why speak about His burial so many years (as they thought) in advance? And why do it in advance at all? Surely His corpse would be anointed when the time came. They could not know how imminent His death was, nor that the haste with which He was to be buried would make the normal rites difficult to perform.

> ॐ ॐ ॐ ॐ ॐ
>
> 9 Therefore the great crowd of the Jews learned that He was there, and they came, not because of Jesus only, but that they might also see Lazarus, whom He raised from the dead.
> 10 But the chief priests deliberated *how* to kill Lazarus also,
> 11 because on account of him many of the Jews were going away and believing in Jesus.

This supper was a great local event, and a **great crowd of the Jews** from the surrounding area came to Bethany also, **that they might also see Lazarus** as well as Jesus. News of the raising of Lazarus was spreading like wildfire. The **chief priests**, who had deliberated how to kill Jesus (11:53), now **deliberated *how* to kill Lazarus also**, because through his witness many were **going away** from their visit with Lazarus and **believing in Jesus**. They must find a way to shut him up. The plot to kill Jesus was widening, and now included Lazarus as well. In this way Lazarus is here an image of the Church. Jesus' foes were persecuting both Him and all those whose lives He touched (compare 15:20; 16:2).

§III.9.ii. Triumphal Entry

ॐ ॐ ॐ ॐ ॐ

12 On the next day the great crowd who had come to the feast, having heard that Jesus was coming to Jerusalem,

13 took branches of the palm trees and went out to a meeting with Him, yelling, "Hosanna! Blessed *is* He who comes in *the* Name of *the* Lord, even the King of Israel!"

14 And Jesus, finding a *little* donkey, sat upon it, just as it is written,

15 "Do not be afraid, daughter of Zion, behold your King is coming, sitting on a donkey's colt!"

16 These things His disciples did not know at the first, but when Jesus was glorified, then they remembered that these things about Him had been written and that these things they did to Him.

17 Therefore the crowd who was with Him when He called Lazarus from the tomb and raised him from the dead were witnessing *to Him.*

18 For this *reason* also the crowd met Him, because they heard that He had done this sign.

19 The Pharisees therefore said to one another, "You observe that you are not profiting anything; look, the world has gone after Him."

The next day after the banquet in Bethany, **the great crowd** of pilgrims **who had come to the** Passover **feast** from all over Palestine **heard that Jesus was coming to Jerusalem** after all, despite the danger (compare their previous skepticism; 11:56). They **took branches of the palm trees** to wave in tumultuous greeting and **went out to a meeting with Him** with nationalist fervor (compare those waving palm branches in 1 Macc. 13:51).

The word translated *meeting* is the Greek *upantesis*, meaning "encounter," and it savors of the official welcome given to a newly arrived dignitary. **The crowd who was with** Jesus **when He called Lazarus from the tomb were witnessing** about Him, sharing the story with everyone in Jerusalem. It was **for this** *reason* that the festal **crowd** in Jerusalem **met Him** with such a welcome, **because they heard that He had done this sign.** They now considered His claims to be true, and that He was indeed the Messiah, the King of Israel. They welcomed their Liberator, **yelling** the old acclamation of the Psalmist (Ps. 118:26), "**Hosanna!** (meaning at that time simply, "hurray!"). **Blessed** *is* **He who comes in** *the* **Name of** *the* **Lord!**"

For the people, this was a spontaneous outpouring of joy at the thought of their imminent liberation from Rome. In this, they were mistaken. But they were not mistaken in recognizing Jesus as the Liberator, even if they could not see that He came to free them, not from the passing power of Rome, but from the more terrible shackles of sin (8:31–36).

As usual, St. John looks deeper to find the true significance of the act. When Jesus entered Jerusalem, it was not on foot (as might have been expected, since He went everywhere on foot), but only after **finding a** *little* **donkey** as arranged (see Mark 11:1–7). He **sat upon** this little animal as a proclamation of His kingship and of the type of king He was. Warriors could be expected to enter a city on a warhorse; Jesus entered on a little donkey, in peace. The apostles had gone to great lengths that day to find that donkey.

St. John sees this detail as a further confirmation of Jesus' messiahship, for in the Scripture it was written, "**Do not be afraid, daughter of Zion, behold your King is coming, sitting on a donkey's colt!**" (Is. 40:9; Zech. 9:9). That **His disciples did not know** the significance of **these things** they did **at the first** also confirmed this. For they were not then acting in conscious imitation of the Scriptures, but were fulfilling them by their actions without knowing it. It was only later, when **Jesus** had been **glorified**, that they **remembered** the Scriptures that prophesied their actions and how the **things they did to Him** fulfilled what had **been written.**

For their part, **the Pharisees** were discouraged by this outpouring of enthusiasm and acclaim. They **said to one another** that anyone could **observe** what was painfully apparent—they were **not profiting anything** from all their elaborate efforts. The Holy City was in happy tumult; the whole **world has gone after Him**, enrolling as His disciples.

By narrating their pessimism, John means to reveal how powerfully Jesus' sign of raising Lazarus affected the people, and how much the glory of God had been manifested (compare 11:40). Jesus had prophesied that the Son of God would be glorified (11:4), and He was right.

It is possible too that John narrates this with a subtle touch of irony. He knew that soon events would show only too clearly how little the world had truly gone after Him (compare 19:15–16). Indeed, the world did not recognize Him at all, but could only hate Him, because He spoke the truth (1:10; 7:7).

§III.9.iii. Conclusion of Ministry to Israel

> ℘ ℘ ℘ ℘ ℘
>
> 20 Now there were some Greeks among the ones going up to worship at the feast.
> 21 These therefore came to Philip, who was from Bethsaida of Galilee, and asked him, saying, "Lord, we want to see Jesus."
> 22 Philip comes and tells Andrew; Andrew and Philip come and tell Jesus.
> 23 And Jesus answers them, saying, "The hour has come for the Son of Man to be glorified.

The Lord's ministry to Israel comes to its climax and conclusion with the coming of the Gentiles. **Some Greeks** were **among the ones going up to worship at the feast** of the Passover. (It seems from v. 36, which speaks of the Lord's final departure from public sight, as if the events of vv. 20–50 happened at the conclusion of the week the Lord spent teaching in the Temple after His triumphal entry.)

These Greeks were almost certainly not simply Gentiles but "God-fearers," Gentiles who had ceased to worship pagan gods and had attached themselves to the God of Israel. They attended the synagogue services, kept the food laws, read the Torah, and considered themselves in some sense members of the extended Jewish community. They were a feature of synagogue worship (and in fact were the special focus of St. Paul when he would later come preaching in the synagogues). Nonetheless, they had not yet taken the definitive step of being circumcised and therefore technically were not Jews, but Greeks.

These **came to Philip** with their request for an audience with Jesus. (It is possible they picked Philip because he was **from Bethsaida of Galilee**, a place where there was much Gentile-Jewish mixing, and they thought his understanding of Greek would be better than the others'. Indeed, they may even have come from Bethsaida themselves, or from the Greek cities of the Decapolis.) But for whatever reason they selected him, they made known their request in a few words: "**Lord** (or "sir"), **we want to see Jesus.**" Jesus' fame was now stretching across the boundary between Jew and Gentile and reaching into the Gentile world. They had heard so much from others about this famous teacher, and wanted to be taught by Him themselves.

Philip is somewhat perplexed about this request from Gentiles to be instructed (the concept of a Gentile disciple was at that time a contradiction in terms to them), so **Philip comes and tells Andrew. Andrew** takes **Philip** and they both **come and tell Jesus.**

This is a dramatic and significant event, and St. John narrates it in the historic present to show that. The coming of the Gentiles to Jesus signals that His time in Israel is almost through. Though He came first to His own people (1:11), He did not belong exclusively to them, but to the whole world. The coming of these Gentile God-fearers, with their implicit desire to be instructed, was the confirmation of this. It was the sign that **the hour** had **come for the Son of Man to be glorified**, to finish His time in the flesh among Israel and be offered to all the nations.

❧ EXCURSUS

ON THE USE OF THE WORD "LORD" (OR *KURIOS*)

The Greek word *kurios* (consistently translated here as "lord") is a word with a breadth of meaning. It is used as a term of respect, but the nature of this respect can vary greatly according to its context.

Firstly, it can denote simply respect, and mean no more than "sir" (its meaning in the above passage, in 12:21, and also in 4:49; 5:7; 6:34; and 9:36).

Secondly, it can also be used in the stronger sense of the respect and personal loyalty the disciple gives to his teacher, "guru," or master; it is this stronger use of the term the disciples of Jesus intend when they refer to Him as their "Lord" (compare 6:68).

Thirdly, it can be used in the somewhat stronger sense of the respect that the slave gives to his earthly master and owner, for the master has absolute authority over the slave, and the slave owes his master absolute obedience and loyalty. (It is in this sense that St. Paul refers to the masters of slaves as "lords" in Eph. 6:5, 9 and in Col. 3:22; 4:1.)

Finally, it can be used of the absolute respect, worship, and adoration owed to Almighty God, the God of Israel. In the time of Jesus (and for many years before that), God was never referred to by His ancient tribal Name of Yahweh. By the time of Jesus, this Name was considered too sacred to openly pronounce in day-to-day speech; it seemed to bring the transcendent God of Israel down to the level of the gods of the Gentiles. Such gods might have personal names (such as Asclepios or Mithras), but He, the God of Israel, did not. He was above such things. As He properly had no image (but was above the particularities of visible appearance), so He properly had no Name either, in that names denoted one thing among many. He was not one thing among many, one god among many gods. He needed no name, for He was above all names. Accordingly, the Jews simply referred to Him as "Lord"—*Adonai* in Hebrew, and *Kurios* in Greek. When the Jews read their Law and encountered the divine Name, the Name of Yahweh, they read it as *Adonai*. When they translated their Law into Greek (the so-called Septuagint version), they rendered the divine Name as *Kurios*, "Lord."

It was this elasticity of meaning (preserved in the translation of *kurios* in 12:21 as "lord") that the Christians were later to find so helpful in dealing with the Scriptures in a Greek context. The Gentiles and God-fearers of the Jewish Diaspora read the Law in the Greek Septuagint version. There they found the Jewish God referred to as "Lord." Jesus Himself had always been referred to by His disciples as "Lord" (usually with the second sense referred to above, as their Teacher). It was but a natural and easy step to apply these Old Testament references to God as "Lord" to Jesus. Thus, for example, Joel 2:32 speaks of calling on the Name of the Lord (Gr. *Kurios*; Heb. *Yahweh*) to be saved. St. Paul, in Romans 10:13, applies this text to calling on the Name of the Lord Jesus in baptism.

From the perspective of the Church, all this was quite legitimate, for Jesus was indeed true God, one with the Father, the great I AM who revealed Himself to Moses at the burning bush. As Thomas would declare after the Resurrection (20:28), Jesus was not only *Kurios* and Teacher (in the second sense mentioned above)—He was also God, and "Lord" in the final and absolute sense. In Christian usage, the term "Lord," *kurios*, could have a wide and spiritually fruitful range of meaning.

ॐ ॐ ॐ ॐ ॐ

24 "Amen, amen, I say to you, unless the grain of
wheat falls into the earth and dies, it remains

> alone; but if it dies, it bears much fruit.
>
> 25 "He who loves his life loses it; and he who hates his life in this world will keep it for eternal life.
>
> 26 "If anyone serves Me, let him follow Me, and where I *Myself* am, there will My servant be also; if anyone serves Me, the Father will honor him.

We are not told if (or when) the Lord saw these Greeks who wanted an audience, or what He said to them if He did. But before dealing with them, He continues to address His disciples, instructing them regarding what this request for an audience means to them, and what is ahead.

It means, in short, that it is soon time for Him to die. But His death is the only way He can give life to the world. It is the same with **the grain of wheat** used for making bread: If it **falls into the earth and dies**, it **bears much fruit** and produces a whole stalk of grain, which can be made into bread. If it refuses to die, it **remains alone**, a single grain, useless for bread-making, unable to give life to the hungry. So with Him also. He also must **die** and **fall into the earth**, buried away from the children of men. Only so can He become the Bread of Life that gives life to the world (6:33).

Christ would lead the way for His disciples and Church coming after Him. He refuses to **love** and save His **life**, His soul, His earthly existence (Gr. *psuche*). Rather, He will **hate** it, reject it, and not shrink from the Cross. In so doing, He sets the pattern for His disciples to imitate, and blazes the way for them to follow after. If they too will be prepared to **hate** their **life** and soul (Gr. *psuche*) in this world, and confess Him even though they be martyred for it, they will **keep** their soul **for eternal life**. If they would **serve** Him truly, they must **follow** Him, even down the road to death and martyrdom. Where He was, **there** His **servants** must **be** found **also**. It was the job of servants to stay with their master, and never to desert him. Jesus' disciples must apply this and be true servants now. They must join Him in suffering. If they would do this, and not shrink from this solidarity of suffering, **the Father** would **honor** them with eternal life and glory.

ॐ ॐ ॐ ॐ ॐ

27 "Now My soul has been shaken; and what will I say, 'Father, save Me from this hour'? But because of this I came to this hour.

28 "Father, glorify Your Name." There came therefore a voice from heaven, "I have both glorified *it* and will glorify *it* again."

29 The crowd, therefore, who stood and heard it were saying that it had thundered; others were saying, "An angel has spoken to Him."

30 Jesus answered and said, "This voice has not come because of Me, but because of you.

The path to such suffering was not easy. Jesus admits that **now** His **soul has been shaken**, and that He is tempted to shrink from such fearful separation from the Father. Here it is not simply a matter of Jesus' fearing the physical suffering of crucifixion. That was indeed appalling enough, though it would be over in a few hours. More fearful was the nameless and (to us) unimaginable darkness of abandonment, of shouldering the sins of the world and letting all the wrathful waves break over Him (Ps. 42:7; 88:7), of being forsaken by the Most High (Mark 15:34). Here is a mystery we cannot fathom, from which we must draw back in fear and leave it cloaked in reverent silence.

Jesus is unbowed by this prospect. He refuses to **say, "Father, save Me from this hour."** Rather, it was **because of this** need to save the world that He **came to this hour**. All that He had done—His incarnation from the Virgin, His life, His miracles, His perseverance to that present moment—had been done to reach that fearful hour. Rather, His prayer to the **Father** was that He **glorify** His **Name**—give Him the strength to come to the Cross. Jesus' suffering on the Cross is never considered in John's Gospel as the sacrifice that merits a future glorification in heaven. Rather, the Cross *is that glorification*, present on earth even now. The future glory in heaven is seen as the heavenly outworking of that glorification already accomplished. When Jesus therefore prays here for the Father to **glorify** His (the Father's) **Name** through Him, He is praying that He might be empowered by God to mount the Cross.

At that moment, **there came a voice from heaven.** Jesus (and His disciples?) heard the noise as actual words, as the Father's instantaneous reply to the prayer of His Son. The Father assured the Son that just as He had **glorified** Jesus in the past (such as at the raising of Lazarus; compare 11:4), so He would **glorify** Him **again** in the future, empowering Him to fulfill His mission.

Here is the Johannine acknowledgment of the truth narrated by the Synoptic Gospels in their telling of Jesus' prayer in the Garden of Gethsemane. John will not relate that scene. He assumes his readers' familiarity with it, and is concerned at that place rather to relate Christ's sovereign composure and authority in all circumstances. When John comes to the Garden scene, He shows his readers not how Christ trembled there (though he would not deny that), but rather how Christ was selflessly concerned for the salvation of His flock (17:6f), and how He boldly went forward to surrender Himself and thus save His disciples from arrest (18:4f). He stresses that Christ's offering was voluntary (compare 10:18). John, however, does not deny Christ's humanity, nor that He was shaken as He approached that dread hour of sacrifice. He therefore narrates that reality here, after His entry into Jerusalem, on the day that Christ took His troubled heart and offered it to the Father, and the Father thundered back His approval.

The crowd that **stood** by **and heard it** could hear the noise, but could not discern a voice. (It was the same later with Paul at his conversion: Jesus spoke to him on the road to Damascus, and the persecutor heard Jesus' voice. Those with him, however, heard only the noise and could not understand the voice; Acts 22:9.) The crowd around Jesus said that it had thundered, no more. Others thought that it came too immediately in reply to be normal thunder. For them, it was clear that **an angel had spoken to Him.**

Jesus simply says that the voice they heard did **not come** because of Him. He had no need of open confirmation of the Father's voice. He always heard the voice of the Father. It came solely, He says, **because of you**, to confirm for them Jesus' identity as the Messiah. It is significant that the divine Voice came in such a way that those open to the truth could hear in it confirmation of Jesus as Christ (since the thunder occurred immediately), but not in such a way as to *compel* that belief. If they were determined to remain in the darkness, they could conclude simply **that it thundered**. Faith remained a possibility, but was not compelled. The Father thus respected the free will of the people. The decision to come to the light remained with them.

ॐ ॐ ॐ ॐ ॐ

31 "Now is the judgment of this world; now the ruler of this world will be cast outside.
32 "And I *Myself*, if I be exalted from the earth, will draw all to Myself."
33 But He was saying this to signify the kind of death He was about to die.

The Lord continues to speak about the meaning of the coming Cross. **Now** was the time for Him to die, and this meant **the judgment of this world**. That is, the Cross would not be the victory of the world and of the forces arrayed against Him, but their condemnation by God and their defeat. Christ would be tried and found guilty of sin by the Sanhedrin of Israel. But it was not Christ who would be thus condemned, but those who found Him guilty. The world would refuse to know Him or recognize His authority (1:10), and by rejecting Him, it condemned itself.

More than this, the Cross was the defeat and expulsion of Satan, **the ruler of this world**, the force that stood behind it in his rejection of God. He would find himself altogether banished, and his power overturned (not simply "cast out," Gr. *ekballo*, but **cast**

outside, Gr. *ekballo exo*.) The image here is of one being ejected from a position of power. After the Cross, Satan would still be active, to be sure. (In fact, Rev. 12:12 portrays him as working with greater fury in his persecution of the saints after his expulsion from heaven.) But the Cross still spells the end of his reign. Formerly, he was free to rule as god in the world, unchallenged by men (compare 2 Cor. 4:4, which refers to him as "the god of this world"). But now his might has been broken, and mortal men can overcome him in the Name of Jesus. The Church's power of exorcism (expressed at every baptism) manifests Christ's victory over Satan, and Satan's defeat by the Cross.

As for Jesus, when He (the pronoun **I** is emphatic to show how He rises as the devil falls) is **exalted from the earth**, He **will draw all** to Himself—even such as the Greeks and Gentiles who were beginning to seek Him. The word rendered *exalted* is the Greek *upsoo*. As mentioned above, it probably represents the Aramaic word *zeqaph*, which describes lifting up both in the sense of "exalting" and also in the sense of "hanging" or "crucifying." By saying this, St. John adds, Jesus spoke to **signify the kind of death He was about to die**. One might have expected Jesus to die by stoning, at the hands of a mob, for this had been attempted before (8:59; 10:31). But the Lord knew that He would die by crucifixion, by being lifted up from the earth on a cross. By mentioning this, John shows that Jesus' foreknowledge of His death was not simply skilled guesswork. Many people in Jerusalem knew that plots were being laid against His life and might have guessed He would be killed (compare 11:56–57). But Jesus knew the details of His death because He was the Son of God and knew all things (16:30).

By using this word "exalt/lift up" with such a double meaning, the Lord is again declaring that His exaltation will be accomplished through His death. But while in His previous uses of the word (3:14; 8:28) this double meaning was not understood by His hearers, now His audience realizes that He is speaking also of His death. Here His meaning is clearer, for here He speaks not just of being exalted or lifted up, but also of being exalted or lifted up from the earth.

The physical image of being hoisted up above the earth makes the idea of crucifixion more obvious. (It is possible too that the Lord added some words, not recorded by St. John here, about that lifting up on the wood being prefigured by Moses lifting up the wooden pole in the wilderness, as in 3:14.)

ॐ ॐ ॐ ॐ ॐ

34 The crowd therefore answered Him, "We *ourselves* have heard from the Law that the Christ remains forever; and how can You *Yourself* say, 'It is necessary for the Son of Man to be exalted'? Who is this Son of Man?"

The crowd perhaps thought that Jesus' image of crucifixion was simply a vivid metaphor for death, and not a prediction of an actual reality to take place in a few days. Nonetheless they are clear that Jesus is speaking about death, and about a removal from the earth. This seems ludicrous to them. They had **heard from the Law**, the prophetic Scriptures, **that the Christ remains forever.** (By the Law, the Jews meant *all* the Scriptures; compare 10:34, where a citation from the Psalms is said to be written in "the Law.") The Messiah is a figure of victory, of triumph over the Gentile kingdoms, and after the last and cataclysmic battle which would bring in the Kingdom of God, He would remain to rule over Israel.

How can *Jesus* say that it was **necessary for the Son of Man**, the Christ, **to be exalted** and lifted from the earth and to die? (The **we**, referring to the crowd, and the **You** referring to Jesus, are both emphatic in the Greek, stressing the opposition between them.) They could not see how Jesus' words could possibly be true. They seemed to fly in the face of all their expectations. **Who** was **this Son of Man** that Jesus was talking about? (They knew, of course, that Jesus was referring to Himself when He spoke of the Son of Man. But the force of their question was "Who is *this* Son of Man, this new kind of Messiah who is supposed to die?") Jesus' words about Messiah dying overturned all their notions about Messiah and the Kingdom of God.

> ❧ ❧ ❧ ❧ ❧
>
> 35 Jesus therefore said to them, "For a little time yet the light is among you. Walk as you have the light, that darkness may not grasp you; he who walks in the darkness does not know where he is going.
> 36 "While you have the light, believe in the light, that you may become sons of light."

Once again, Christ does not explain, for their questions came from hearts which were hard and unteachable, and until their hearts had been softened, there was no sense in replying to their questions directly. Jesus encourages them rather to **walk as** they **had the light** and to learn in the brief time remaining. Let them open their eyes, see what was before them, and come to Him! Let them not be like those who **walked in darkness** and did **not know where** they were **going**, but stumbled and fell, not able to see what was before their faces.

If these words were indeed uttered immediately before His departure from public sight towards the end of His final week, they constituted Jesus' final appeal to Israel. With infinite patience, even in these closing hours, He strives to bring them to saving faith. **For a little time yet**, He, **the light** of the world, would be **among** them. Once He had been taken away in death, the **darkness** would **grasp** and overtake them (Gr. *katalambano*; compare its use in Gen. 19:19, where it speaks of calamity overtaking one). The "sun of righteousness" was even then beginning to set (even as the sun was perhaps even then going down in the sky as He spoke), and time was running out. Let them **believe** in Him, **the light**, while there was time, that they **may become sons of light**. The Jews expected a final messianic battle of the sons of light against the sons of darkness. Here was the only way to be the **sons of light**, and for them to be saved on the Last Day.

꤯ ꤯ ꤯ ꤯ ꤯

36 These things Jesus spoke, and having gone away, He was hidden from them.

37 Though He had done so many signs before them, they did not believe in Him,

38 that the word of Isaiah the prophet might be fulfilled, which he spoke, "Lord, who believed what was heard from us? And to whom was *the* arm of the Lord revealed?"

39 For this reason they were not able to believe, for Isaiah said again,

40 "He has blinded their eyes, and He hardened their heart; that they might not see with their eyes and understand with their heart, and turn and I cure them."

41 These things Isaiah said, because he saw His glory and spoke about Him.

John adds that this was Jesus' final public appeal to Israel. After Jesus **spoke these things**, He departed from the midst of the Temple where He had been teaching, and **having gone away, He was hidden from them.** That is, by the providence of God, His foes did not find Him, though they searched the city diligently for Him. (His arrangements to observe the Passover within the city had been made with the utmost secrecy to avoid capture; compare Mark 14:12–16).

For John, the wonder was that **He had done so many signs before them**, and yet still **they did not believe in Him**. In the words of the hymn for Holy Friday Vespers, He had "filled Judea with miracles" and "raised the dead by His word alone"; how could they still harden their hearts and resist such a love? For John, the only solution to such a mystery was that Israel stood under the judgment of God. They had hardened their hearts so often that Christ came, not only to gather the softhearted, but also to judge the hardhearted and confirm them in their chosen hardness.

Isaiah the prophet had predicted such massive unbelief ages before: **"Lord, who believed what was heard from us? And to whom was *the* arm** and power **of the Lord revealed?"** (Is. 53:1). Christ had revealed the power of God abundantly with His many signs, but still most did not see it. The faithful were such a small remnant that they could scarcely be found. Indeed, the judgment of God was on the majority, confirming them in their self-chosen rebelliousness so that they were **not able to believe**. It was as **Isaiah** had predicted in Isaiah 6:10: God had **blinded their eyes and hardened their heart**. The massive popular rejection of Jesus by Israel's leaders did not mean He was not the Messiah of the Scriptures. It just meant that the Scriptures' dire prophecies of judgment on Israel were being fulfilled. Jesus fulfilled the messianic prophecies of Isaiah (and the other prophets).

In fact, John adds, it was because **Isaiah** the prophet **saw** the **glory** of Jesus in the Temple at the start of his ministry (recorded in Is. 6) that he **spoke about Him**. When Isaiah saw the Lord Yahweh high and exalted, with the glory of His Presence, the train of His robe, filling the Temple (Is. 6:1), it was the preincarnate Word that Isaiah was seeing. Isaiah spoke about Jesus, John says, because he first had an experience of His glory. Christ manifested His glory to Israel in His day (such as when He changed the water into wine; 2:11), just as He previously manifested it in the days of Isaiah. To be true to the words of the prophets, Israel must acknowledge Jesus as Messiah.

ॐ ॐ ॐ ॐ ॐ

42 Nevertheless, many even of the rulers believed in Him, but because of the Pharisees they were not confessing *Him*, lest they should be *put* out of the synagogue;

43 for they loved the glory of men rather than the glory of God.

Despite this massive apostasy in Israel, **many even of the rulers**, members of the Sanhedrin, **believed in Him** and were His followers. But they kept their faith secret and **were not** openly **confessing** *Him*, because of the opposition of **the Pharisees**. Through the Pharisees' influence, it was a policy that if anyone would confess Jesus to be Messiah, such a person would be *put* **out of the synagogue** and banned from pious Jewish social life (compare 9:22). St. John has little approval for such cowardice. The disciples of Jesus were called to follow Him, even to the place of suffering, if they would keep their souls to eternal life (vv. 25–26). The blind man had done that (9:34), and the rulers were called to do that as well. But they **loved the glory of men** and their high position rather than **the glory of God** which was shining forth in Jesus. Sympathy for Jesus was not enough. One must openly confess Him in defiance of the world to be saved.

ॐ ॐ ॐ ॐ ॐ

44 Yet Jesus cried out and said, "He who believes in Me does not believe in Me, but in the One who sent Me.

45 "And he who observes Me observes the One who sent Me.

46 "I *Myself* have come *as* light into the world, that everyone who believes in Me may not remain in the darkness.

47 "And if anyone hears My sayings, and does not keep them, I *Myself* do not judge him; for I did not come that I may judge the world, but that I may save the world.

48 "He who rejects Me, and does not receive My sayings, has one who judges him; the Word I spoke, that will judge him on the Last Day.

49 "For I *Myself* did not speak from Myself, but the Father who sent Me, He Himself has given

> Me commandment what to say and what to
> speak.
> 50 "And I know that His commandment is eter-
>   nal life. Therefore the things I *Myself* speak,
>   just as the Father has told Me, thus I speak."

These last words of Jesus are John's final summary of the Lord's public teaching, and do not represent His utterance on that occasion. John has already said that after His appeal for the crowd to believe in the light (vv. 35–36), He departed and was hidden, making no more public appearances in the Temple (v. 36). Accordingly, these final verses represent a compendium of the Lord's open teaching. The rulers were afraid to openly confess Him (v. 42), but Jesus Himself was not afraid to openly **cry out** and proclaim the truth.

The Lord's basic message to Israel is that it is not He Himself who is being accepted or rejected, but the Father. He has come as the fullness of the Father's person, with all the Father's authority and His words, carrying out all the Father's will. Thus, **he who believes** in Jesus does **not believe** in Jesus alone, **but in the One who sent** Him. He was different from all the other rabbis. In their case, one could accept a certain rabbi's interpretation of the Law or reject it, preferring instead some other rabbi's interpretation. Rejecting that rabbi's interpretation did not mean rejecting God. But it was otherwise with Jesus. He was not just another interpreter of the Law, not just another teacher. The one **who observes** Him **observes** also **the One who sent** Him. To see Jesus is to see the Father, and to reject Jesus means also to reject the Father.

The Lord thus came not just to add another interpretation of the Law to the many interpretations already given. He did not come to state an opinion, but to enlighten. He, unlike the others (the **I** of v. 46 is emphatic), **came** *as* **light into the world.** To reject Him means therefore to **remain in the darkness.**

His message did not originate with Him, and He did **not speak** from Himself, as if muddling out His own ideas. Rather, **the Father who sent** Him was the One who **gave** Him **commandment what to say and what to speak.** The basic message (**what to say**) and the very words of it (**what to speak**) come from the Father, **given** authoritatively to the Son for Him to deliver to Israel.

Thus, if anyone **rejects** Jesus and repudiates Him, **if anyone hears** His **sayings** (Gr. *remata*) and yet **does not keep** them, Jesus Himself **does not judge him**. That is, Jesus is not personally offended, nor does He condemn him from any bruised personal sense of ego. The Lord is full of love, and **came** that He **may save the world**, not **judge** and condemn it. Jesus' ego is not what matters; what matters is **the Word** (Gr. *logos*) which He **spoke**, which is the authoritative Word of the Father. Because it is the Father's Word, it **will judge** the man who rejected it **on the Last Day** and condemn him. The **commandment** the Father gave Jesus to deliver to men **is eternal life**, and so to reject Jesus' word is to reject that life.

This for St. John is the issue: to receive Jesus' Word and message as the Word of the Father, or to reject it. Sympathy for Jesus or admiration for His message is not sufficient. He does not present Himself simply as a teacher, but as the fullness of the Father. The Jews knew that they must submit to God to be saved. St. John shows that they must also submit as fully to Jesus.

❧ IV ☙

CHRIST'S MINISTRY TO HIS OWN
(13:1—17:26)

§IV. 1. Washing His Disciples' Feet

ॐ ॐ ॐ ॐ ॐ

13 1 Now before the feast of the Passover, Jesus knowing that His hour had come that He should move on from this world to the Father, having loved His own who were in the world, He loved them to *the* end.

The scene now switches from Christ's public ministry to Israel to His ministry to His own disciples. St. John focuses on Christ's words to them on the night in which He was betrayed. Christ **knew** long **before the feast of the Passover** that this would be His last evening with His own, and that after that feast **His hour** would **come** when He would **move on from this world to the Father.** He therefore did not fail in His love for **His own** disciples who would be left **in the world.** Just as He **loved them** and cared for them throughout His ministry to Israel, so now **He loved them to *the* end.** That is, He took care to prepare them for the events that would follow, omitting nothing they would need to know.

ॐ ॐ ॐ ॐ ॐ

2 And when supper was happening, the devil having already cast into the heart of Judas

> Iscariot, the *son* of Simon, to deliver Him up,
> 3 *Jesus*, knowing that the Father had given all things into His hands and that He had come from God and was going back to God,
> 4 arises from the supper, and puts *aside* His garments; and taking a towel, He girded Himself about.
> 5 Then He casts water into the washbasin, and began to wash the disciples' feet and to wipe them with the towel with which He was girded about.

St. John first relates how the Lord taught them one last crucial lesson. It was **when supper was happening**. The supper referred to was the Passover meal (compare Luke 22:7ff). The Lord had earnestly wanted to eat that meal with them, for it was to be His last (Luke 22:15–16). St. John passes over the details of that supper, with its institution of the Eucharist, just as He passes over the account of the Transfiguration. His purpose, unlike that of Matthew, Mark, and Luke, is not to tell the basic story of Christ's ministry, but to present a case for faith. John presupposes his readers are familiar with the basic facts of Christ's ministry, and he does not relate them again.

From a comparison of those Synoptic Gospels, we know that there was contention among the Twelve, and it seems that they argued over who was to have the best places at the supper table (see Luke 22:24–27). In our culture, we do not have such rigorous customs about rank at table, but it was otherwise in first-century Palestine. At the Passover meal, all reclined on couches which had been put against a low U-shaped table, and one leaned on one arm while eating with the other, in the Greco-Roman fashion. The head of the family would have the place where the two arms of the "U" joined together, with others arranged around the table according to rank, with the first person reclining to the left of the host, the second person on the host's right. Thus, one could tell a person's relative importance by the place he occupied at table.

All the Twelve (save Judas) expected the Kingdom of God to come soon with all its glory, and all of them coveted the most important positions in that Kingdom. (On the way up to Jerusalem several days before, John and James had strenuously lobbied for those positions—though without success; compare Mark 10:35–41.) This rancor continued right up to the very end, as they quarreled over who was more important than the other.

It was this quarrel which caused all to omit the customary foot-washing. Usually when one entered a friend's home, one was welcomed by having the dust of the road washed from one's feet. (In the days of sandals and no socks, this would have been a welcome ritual!) In the absence of servants, the youngest or humblest person present would perform this task. It would seem that, with the abiding rancor about who was to be first among them, none of the Twelve consented to perform this task, and so it seems that all sat down and reclined with their feet remaining unwashed.

Jesus knew the end was at hand. The Cross was already throwing its long shadow over that supper, and His foes were on the move. **The devil** had **already cast into the heart of Judas** the intention **to deliver Him up** to His enemies. His foes had been told, and probably as the apostles sat down to eat, arrangements were being made elsewhere in the City to gather the soldiers to arrest Him later in the Garden. Jesus knew all this, and did not panic. He knew **that the Father had given all things into His hands**, and that His triumph was assured; He knew that **He had come from God** at His Incarnation through the Virgin, and **was going back to God** at His Ascension. The future was not a mystery to Him, but all was to occur as He desired it. The time was running out, and He had one more lesson to teach His disciples, which they would need for the future.

We can follow the events as they happen. The supper begins with the first cup of wine, the so-called "cup of *Kiddush*" or sanctification, with which one customarily began a meal. Jesus as the head intones the blessing of God over the wine, and then all drink. A basin of water is then brought in and all prepare to rise from the table to wash their hands.

It is here that Christ surprises them. At this point He **arises from the supper, and puts** *aside* **His garments** so that He remains clad only in His loincloth, just as if He were a slave. (The historic present is used for vividness. One can almost see the strange puzzled looks on the faces of the Twelve.) And instead of washing His hands and passing the basin to them to do likewise, He wordlessly takes a long linen towel and girds Himself about with it. **Then He casts water into the washbasin, and began to wash the disciples' feet** as they continue to recline around the table, and then to **wipe them with the towel with which He was girded about.** (One reclined for meals without sandals, so such a washing could be easily done.) A more stunning rebuke of their pride (did they snipe at one another even after the blessing of the *Kiddush* cup?) could not be imagined. One can only picture the horror of each one as they see their Master take the lowest place—the place each of them in turn refused to take.

ॐ ॐ ॐ ॐ ॐ

6 Therefore He comes to Simon Peter. He says to Him, "Lord, do You *Yourself* wash my feet?"

7 Jesus answered and said to him, "What I *Myself* am doing you *yourself* do not know now, but you will know after these things."

8 Peter says to Him, "Never ever will You wash my feet!" Jesus answered him, "If I do not wash you, you have no part with Me."

9 Simon Peter says to Him, "Lord, not the feet only, but also the hands and the head!"

10 Jesus says to him, "He who has bathed does not need to wash, except for his feet, but is entirely clean; and you *yourselves* are clean, but not all."

11 For He knew the one who was to deliver Him up; for this reason He said, "Not all are clean."

We do not know how many disciples' feet the Lord washed before **He comes to Simon Peter.** The others doubtless remained struck speechless with faces burning as the Lord poured the water over their tired feet and lovingly dried them with the long towel. Peter, however, explodes in passionate protest: "**Lord, do You** *Yourself*—our Master and Rabbi (the **You** is emphatic)—stoop to **wash my feet?**" It is not a question; it is a refusal. The others might have allowed this, but not Peter. He loves Jesus, as he thinks, more than those others (compare Mark 14:29; John 21:15). Jesus quietly tries to calm Peter's anxiety, saying, "**What I** *Myself* **am doing you** *yourself* **do not know now, but you will know after these things.**" That is, He asks Peter to trust Him that this is for his own good.

Peter, however, is on a roll, and is not about to be calmed. He refuses to let Christ do what He said He must do. We can almost see him draw back His feet safely out of reach while he insists, "**Never ever will You wash my feet!**"

The Lord knows that this is not the voice of humility, but the voice of pride. Humility would let Christ have His way and humbly receive the rebuke and the lesson. Peter refuses the lesson—which only shows how badly he needs it. The Lord does not force the lesson. Peter may choose. But He informs Peter that **if** He does **not wash** him, then Peter will **have no part** with Him and will not be allowed to eat with Him. That is, humility is the indispensable condition of discipleship. The time is late—the traitor is already set to do his foul work, and the end is at hand. Peter, with the others, must learn now of the necessity of love. This is to be the mark of all His disciples, and the commandment which they must obey (13:34–35). If they refuse to love, they cannot be His own. The one that refuses to love remains in the grip of darkness and death (1 John 3:14).

Peter, as always, is a bit slow. He misses the inner significance of the Lord's words about the necessity of humility and love, and fastens only on the fact that Jesus makes outward washing the mark of His disciple. He still thinks that he is better than his fellow disciples. Certainly he professes to have more zeal than they. If washing is the mark of true discipleship, he says, then let the Lord not wash his **feet only, but also the hands and the head**! Let Jesus wash *all* his extremities, for he is more loyal to Him than these others!

Christ replies (we imagine with a wry smile) that that will not be necessary. Just as **he who has bathed** all over in water **does not need to wash** all over again or take another bath when returning home, but only needs to wash **his feet** and then is **entirely clean**, so it is with Peter and the others. They are clean through the Word He has spoken to them (15:3); they have been inwardly cleansed by their baptismal commitment to Him. Like the man who bathed and then returned home and needed only the washing of his feet, so they need only this one more lesson in humility. The world with its pomp has given them a coating of dust and grime, coating their souls with pride. This small lesson will wash it off, and then they will be entirely clean again.

But not all. In saying that they, His disciples (the **you** of v. 10 is emphatic in the Greek), are **clean**, the Lord adds an exception. For **not all** of the disciples are inwardly cleansed. Jesus **knew the one who was to deliver Him up** and betray Him. St. John wants his readers to be clear that the Lord's words about all the disciples being clean did not mean that He thought they were all loyal and that He was surprised by the betrayal. As the Son of God, Jesus knew all.

ॐ ॐ ॐ ॐ ॐ

12 Therefore when He had washed their feet, and taken His garments, and reclined again, He said to them, "Do you know what I have done to you?

13 "You *yourselves* call Me the Teacher and the Lord, and you say well, for I am.

14 "If I *Myself* therefore, the Lord and the Teacher, washed your feet, you *yourselves* also ought to wash one another's feet.

15 "For I gave you an example that you *yourselves* also ought to do as I *Myself* did to you.

16 "Amen, amen, I say to you, a slave is not greater

> than his lord, neither is he who is sent greater
> than he who sent him.
> 17 "If you know these things, blessed are you if
> you do them.

The Lord then moves to drive home His lesson. **When He had washed** all **their feet** (even Peter's, even Judas's) and had once again **taken His garments**, He **reclined again** at His place at the low table. All eyes are upon Him. Like a rabbi giving a lesson, He asks them a question: **"Do you know what I have done to you?"** They, as disciples, **call** Him **"the Teacher"** and **"the Lord,"** and they **say well**, for so He is. They acknowledge that they are lower than He. Just as the **slave** is **not greater than his lord** and owner, just as the messenger who **is sent** is not greater than the master **who sent him**, so they will freely admit that they can have no more dignity than Jesus their Lord and Teacher.

If He, as the **Lord** and **Teacher**, **washed** their **feet**, then they certainly **ought to wash** the **feet** of **one another**. They cannot refuse to do so any longer, taking their stand on the dignity they pretend to have. They can have no more dignity or rank than He has. And He is willing to abase Himself to serve them (compare Luke 22:27)! By doing this, He **gave** them **an example** to follow and copy. They must be willing to serve one another too, even if they imagine that it somehow involves their abasement. They might **know these things** in theory, for He has spoken of the necessity of humility before. But they will only be **blessed** by the Father if they will **do them**.

ॐ ॐ ॐ ॐ ॐ

> 18 "(I am not speaking about all of you. I *Myself*
> know whom I have chosen, but *it is* that the
> Scripture may be fulfilled, 'He who devours
> my bread has lifted up his heel against me.'
> 19 "From now on, I am telling you before it

> happens, that when it happens, you may be-
> lieve that I am *He*.)
> 20 "Amen, amen, I say to you, he who receives
> whomever I send receives Me, and he who re-
> ceives Me receives Him who sent Me."

Jesus had spoken of being blessed by the Father. But again His thought turned to Judas, for he was not to know any blessing. The Lord was not speaking about all of them. Judas's defection was no surprise to Him. *He* at least (the pronoun **I** is emphatic) **knew** the ones whom He **had chosen**, and which ones were loyal. This defection from within the inner ranks does not show that Christ had been blindsided by the traitor (as His enemies imagined). Rather it was the inevitable fulfillment of the prophecy of the **Scripture**. For it was written (in Ps. 41:9), "**He who devours my bread**"—who enjoys My hospitality, with its sacred bonds of duty and friend-ship—this very one has "**lifted up his heel against me**" to kick me when I am down. In the original context, David was talking about treachery against himself and against the House of David, but Christ, as the messianic Son of David, applies the fullness of the psalm's meaning to His own experience. David spoke of betrayal by his intimate friends, but this was only a type of the betrayal of Christ, the prelude to the time when He would be "raised up" and would be "set in God's Presence forever" (Ps. 41:10, 12).

Christ revealed this to His disciples in order to confirm their faith and strengthen them for the dark trial ahead. When the pre-dicted betrayal **happens**, they will remember and **believe** that He was who He claimed to be.

After this parenthesis, Jesus goes on to sum up the lesson. They must not shrink from serving one another, for each has a great dignity, and by serving one another, they are but recognizing that dignity, for it is the dignity of the Lord whose servants they are. In **receiving** and serving **whomever** He **sends**, they will be **re-ceiving** Him—and also the Father who **sent** Him. They must not refuse to serve one another, for it was the service of God the Father Himself.

§IV.2. Betrayal by Judas

After this lesson, in which Christ came to each of His own disciples in humility to wash their feet, St. John turns immediately to narrate Judas's betrayal. These two events are not juxtaposed simply to highlight the contrast between love and hate (as was the case for the juxtaposition in the Matthew 26:6–16 and Mark 14:3–11 narratives, where Judas's betrayal is juxtaposed with the anointing of Mary). Rather, John creates this juxtaposition to show more vividly the truth of 1:11, that Jesus "came to His own and His own did not receive Him." The incident of the foot-washing shows how Christ came literally to each of "His own" disciples—including Judas— bowing before them in humility, and yet was betrayed. The betrayal of Judas was thus a concentrated example by an individual of what was done by Israel as a whole, for Jesus came to His own people, humbling Himself by appearing in the flesh, and serving them in tireless humility. Like Judas, Israel repaid the service by renouncing and disowning Him.

ॐ ॐ ॐ ॐ ॐ

21 When Jesus had said this, He was shaken in spirit and witnessed and said, "Amen, amen, I say to you, one of you will deliver Me up."

John continues with his narrative of that last supper together. After **Jesus had said** His words about the necessity of love and mutual service, **He was shaken in spirit.** The word translated here *shaken* is the Greek *tarasso*, used also in 11:33 to describe Christ's agitation at the grave of Lazarus. There (where it was used with the verb *embrimaomai*) it described Him being shaken with anger and indignation at the ruin of mankind. Here, however, it describes Him being shaken with sadness at the thought of being betrayed by a friend. John mentions this to show Jesus' full humanity. In John's day, the Church was being plagued by heretics who denied Jesus' humanity, and said that He did not really come "in the flesh" or have a human existence like everyone else (2 John 7). In his Gospel, John is at pains to show the Lord's full humanity. Like us, He became tired and thirsty (4:6–7) and was truly subject to death (19:30, 34; 1 John 5:6).

John also says that Jesus **witnessed**. This is unusual in his Gospel, for the word "witness" (Gr. *martureo*) is usually used to describe the witness of *others*; Jesus Himself is rarely described as witnessing. Its use here is important; John means to stress Christ's foreknowledge that **one** of them was about to **deliver** Him **up** to His enemies. The Lord's foes considered that their successful plot to arrest our Lord by surprise proved that He was no prophet, nor the Son of God as He claimed. St. John shows here that Christ's foes did *not* surprise Him, but that He knew all in advance, and voluntarily allowed Himself to be taken.

> ৺ ৺ ৺ ৺ ৺
>
> 22 The disciples looked at one another, perplexed about whom He was speaking.
>
> 23 One of His disciples whom Jesus loved was reclining on Jesus' bosom.
>
> 24 Simon Peter therefore gestures to this one to inquire about whom it may be that He is speaking.
>
> 25 That one, therefore, leaning back thus on Jesus' breast, says to Him, "Lord, who is it?"
>
> 26 Jesus therefore answers, "It is that one for whom I *Myself* will dip the morsel and give *it* to him." Therefore, having dipped the morsel, He takes and gives *it* to Judas, the *son* of Simon Iscariot.

When He said this, **the disciples looked at one another, perplexed about whom He was speaking.** The Lord had said that one of them would betray Him—who could it be? Their perplexity shows how well Judas had hidden his disillusionment with Jesus and his plot to betray Him. None of the Twelve suspected him, but all were aghast at the thought that one of *them*—the inner circle—could do such a thing.

With the light of hindsight, we see that Jesus was speaking about a deliberate betrayal, one motivated by hostility and hate, and one that was imminent. But this is from hindsight. It was equally possible, to their mind, that He was speaking about an involuntary betrayal, and that one of them was to deliver Him up by being tricked into leading His foes to Him. And the betrayal need not be imminent. It could be that it was not to occur for some days or weeks. Had not the Lord much earlier on (compare 6:70) predicted that one of them would be a devil? The news, however, was distressing.

One of His disciples, from the inmost circle, one **whom Jesus loved** (St. John himself; compare 21:20, 24) **was reclining on Jesus' bosom**. That is, as each one reclined on his couch with his head near the low dining table, John lay closest to Him. For since each one at table leaned on his left arm to feed himself with his right, each would therefore be lying somewhat on his left side. John, in order to have his head on Jesus' bosom (and not on His back), would therefore have been reclining to Jesus' right.

Simon Peter (who probably was reclining next to John, on John's right—and thus not one of the highest places) could not stand not knowing who was to be traitor. He **therefore gestures** to John with a silent nod, indicating that he **inquire** of Jesus **about whom it may be that He is speaking**. Peter need not have said anything at all to his close friend; a silent but significant movement of the head in Jesus' direction would have been enough to relay all his meaning.

John immediately understands. Since he is **leaning back thus on Jesus' breast**, he can speak to Him without being overheard. Without turning to Him (and thereby alerting the others to his question), he whispers, **"Lord, who is it?"**

The Lord responds, **"It is that one for whom I *Myself* will dip the morsel and give *it* to him"**—that is, the one who receives it directly from Christ's hand. And so saying, He **dipped the morsel** and then **gives *it* to Judas, the *son* of Simon Iscariot**. Judas' full name is given, Judas, the son of Simon Iscariot, to avoid any possible confusion with the other Judas among the Twelve (compare 14:22). The whole scene is related in the historic present to convey a sense of dramatic vividness.

This presupposes that Judas was reclining next to Christ—in what was, in fact, the first place of honor. In distributing a morsel to others, Christ would have had to give to one who passed it on. But Judas could receive his own morsel directly from Christ, since he was reclining next to Him. The act of giving it to Judas would have excited no interest. What made it a sign for John was Christ's word to him that the one receiving the morsel from His hand was the traitor.

Which morsel was this? It is difficult to be certain. The impression given in Matthew 26:20–29 and Mark 14:17–26 is that the word to Judas *preceded* the institution of the Eucharist. Even in the present Johannine account (which does not mention the institution of the Eucharist), the impression is still that the word to Judas and his departure took place *before* Christ settled in to talk to the disciples *as disciples* (John 13:31f). It would seem, therefore, that Judas was not present for the institution of the Eucharist.

He was there, however, for the preliminary course that preceded the actual Passover meal. Every Passover meal began with this preliminary course, which included green herbs, bitter herbs (reminiscent of the hardship of Egypt), and a sauce made of fruit puree. After the blessing of the first cup of wine (the so-called *Kiddush* cup), the host then took some of the herbs, dipped them, and gave them to others. The story of the Exodus from Egypt was then recounted, Psalms 113–114 were sung, and the second cup of wine was drunk (the storytelling or *Haggadah* cup). The main meal then began with the blessing, breaking, and distribution of bread.

Since that blessing, breaking, and distribution of the bread formed part of the institution of the Eucharist (as most agree that it did), Judas *must have left before this initial blessing and breaking of the bread began.* If that was indeed the case, then the morsel for which Judas was present was the morsel dipped and given during this preliminary course. This is all the more appropriate since that morsel was an image of the hardship and tears of Egypt.

In giving the morsel to Judas, who was seated (we think) in the first place of honor, Christ was making one last appeal to him, reaching out to him in love.

> ৯৵ ৯৵ ৯৵ ৯৵ ৯৵
>
> 27 And after the morsel, Satan then entered into that one. Jesus therefore says to him, "What you do, do quickly."
> 28 Now no one of those reclining knew for what *purpose* He spoke to him.
> 29 For some were supposing, since Judas had the case, that Jesus was saying to him, "Buy the things we have need of for the feast," or that he should give something to the poor.
> 30 Therefore, after receiving the morsel, that one went out immediately; and it was night.

That proffered love was again and finally spurned. In hardening his heart against Christ, in receiving **the morsel** given in love and intending all the time to betray, Judas seals his fate. **Satan then entered into that one** along with the morsel. Seeing that Judas was still intent on his betrayal, **Jesus therefore says to him, "What you do, do quickly."**

At the time, **no one of those reclining** at table **knew for what** *purpose* Jesus **spoke to him.** As far as they were concerned, His words about immediate action must have had something to do with the Passover feast. Since **Judas** was the treasurer and **had the** money **case, some were supposing that Jesus was saying to him, "Buy the things we have need of for the feast"**—that is, go buy the *Hagigah*, the sacrifice required to be offered on the day after Passover (still accounted as part of the Passover sacrifices). On Passover night, such purchases were allowed, especially if the day after Passover was a Sabbath, when such purchases were not allowed (compare 19:31, which states that the day after the morrow was a Sabbath). Or they thought that Judas was being told to **give something to the poor.**

Such alms were usual on Passover night, and in fact, with the Temple opened at midnight for the festive sacrifices of the next day, many poor congregated there to receive such alms. (Such almsgiving at night, it should be noted, was only customary on Passover, not on any other night. Apart from Passover, almsgiving was a daylight task.)

Thus, though John (and Peter) recognize that Judas is to betray Christ, they do not imagine that the betrayal is imminent, or that he is leaving to betray Christ at that time. Having learned from Jesus that Judas is the designated "weak link," they doubtless resolve to watch him carefully in the future. They cannot know that the moment of deliberate betrayal is at hand.

But at hand it was. **After receiving the morsel**, Judas (referred to emphatically as **that one) went out immediately**. St. John adds a characteristic time note, saying **it was night**.

This reference to night is not simply, however, a temporal reference. That might have been assumed, given that Judas immediately left the supper table during the late evening meal. St. John means us to remember Christ's earlier words about walking in the darkness (12:35). There Jesus challenged Israel to walk as they had light and to beware of rejecting Him, lest the darkness grasp and overcome them. If they walked in the darkness, they would not know where they were going, and would stumble and fall.

Judas, St. John stresses, had indeed rejected this light. By going out into the night to betray his Lord, Iscariot showed that he was truly walking in the darkness. His fall was inevitable.

§IV.3. Final Discourse to Disciples

ॐ ॐ ॐ ॐ ॐ

31 When therefore he had gone out, Jesus says, "Now is the Son of Man glorified, and God is glorified in Him.

32 "If God is glorified in Him, God will also glorify Him in Himself, and will glorify Him immediately.

> 33 "*Little* children, I am with you yet a little while.
> You will seek Me, and as I said to the Jews, I
> now also say to you, 'Where I *Myself* am go-
> ing, you are not able to come.'
> 34 "A new commandment I give to you, that you
> love one another, as I have loved you, that you
> *yourselves* also love one another.
> 35 "By this all will know that you are My disciples,
> if you have love among one another."

After the traitor **had gone out**, Jesus is left alone with His true disciples, and He proceeds in love to give them the instructions they will need for the dark days to come.

Though it is impossible to be certain at what point in the meal these words were spoken, I suggest they were spoken at the conclusion of the meal. That meal began, as did all Jewish meals, with the blessing and breaking of bread. At this meal Christ told them to "take it and eat—for this is My Body" (Matt. 26:26). After that enigmatic word (as the disciples thought it), the meal continued. It was as the meal was finishing, I think, that Christ turned His attention to the approaching crisis and readied His disciples to meet it.

His first thought is to tell them that He must go away. The Lord begins with this note of assurance. Even **now** the process which will result in His being glorified on the Cross is under way (since Judas is on the way to gather Jesus' enemies). It is through that death that God will be glorified in all the earth and that His Kingdom will come. And because **God** will be **glorified in Him** and His death, **God** will in return **also glorify** Jesus **in Himself**, and will **glorify Him immediately**. Jesus' final vindication will not have to wait until the end of history and the Last Day. It will follow immediately, on the third day after His death.

The Lord then addresses them as *little* children (Gr. *teknion*, an affectionate diminutive). For there is no disguising or denying it: this all means that He will be **with** them **yet** only **a little while** longer. They may **seek** Him, but as He **said** before **to the Jews** (7:34), where He is **going**, they will **not** be **able to come**. He will be passing through the door from this life into the Kingdom, and they will not be able to follow Him through that passage yet. For a while, they must remain together behind.

It is during this time, this life, that they must wait. But the time is not to be filled with simple passive waiting, like time spent in a waiting room. Rather, it must be spent in active loving. As Jews, they know what it is to be given a commandment by God. A commandment is a gift from heaven, an opportunity to please God. And a commandment is an authoritative order, a revelation of the divine will: an order, not a suggestion. Jesus is **giving** to them **a new commandment**: that they **love one another** as He has loved them. The divine love He has shown them—that love and no other they must show to one another. As the Jews live by the Law's commandments, so His disciples must live by this commandment.

It is important to see that Jesus did not say, "*Another* commandment I give to you." He was not giving them an additional commandment, one to be observed along with all the other 613 commandments of the Jewish Law. The commandments of the Law were commandments for this age; Jesus' new commandment is characteristic of the new age, the age to come. It partakes of all the freshness, radiance, and life of that new age. The word for *new* is the Greek *kainos*, which means "fresh, brand-new." It is different from the word *neos*, also translated "new," which means "young." Jesus' commandment was new not just in the sense of never having been given before (*neos*), but in the sense of the new creation He was bringing into being (compare 2 Cor. 5:17). Here was a life that would never die. This life-giving love was so characteristic of Him personally that if they would **have** this **love among one another**, **all** the world would see and **know** that they were His **disciples**.

༄ ༄ ༄ ༄ ༄

36 Simon Peter says to Him, "Lord, where are you going?" Jesus answered, "Where I go, you are not able to follow Me now; but you will follow later."

> 37 Peter says to Him, "Lord, why am I not able to follow You now? I will lay down my life for You!"
>
> 38 Jesus answers, "Will you lay down your life for Me? Amen, amen, I say to you, a rooster will never sound, until you deny Me three times."

Simon Peter is still traumatized by the Lord's announcement of His final departure from them. He asks Him, **"Lord, where are you going?"**—not out of curiosity, but because he has no intention of being left behind. Jesus answers simply that Peter must trust Him. Peter is **not able to follow** Him **now**, but he **will follow later**. The time for death (and martyrdom!) will come soon enough.

Peter, however, does not understand that Jesus is talking about His death, any more than the Jews understood the reference (7:35). He demands to know **why** he is **not able to follow** Him **now**. He assumes that Jesus is preparing to leave them behind because He feels the journey will be too dangerous for them. Not so, Peter protests. He is up for any adventure, and will bear any danger. He **will** even **lay down** his **life** for his Lord!

The protestation is well meant, but Jesus knows His apostle better than he knows himself. Jesus knows how little that apparently iron determination will actually hold. Peter is thinking of physical danger, of the peril that would come in a fight. For that he is prepared (see 18:10). But he cannot foresee all circumstances, nor guess from how unlikely a source a crisis can suddenly spring forth. He will, in fact, **deny** His Master, not once, or twice, but a full **three times** before **a rooster** next **sounds**.

ॐ ॐ ॐ ॐ ॐ

14 1 "Let not your heart be shaken; you believe in God; believe also in Me.

2 "In My Father's house are many dwelling-places; if it were not *so*, would I have told you that I go to prepare a place for you?

> 3 "And if I go and prepare a place for you, I will come again and receive you to Myself, that where I *Myself* am, you *yourselves* may be also.
> 4 "And you know the way where I am going."

All the disciples are distressed at the news that their Lord is leaving them. At the height of danger, it seems to them, Jesus is going into hiding in some foreign land, abandoning them to lay low for a while, until this crisis blows over. They are aghast, agitated, filled with panic and apprehension at the thought of being left leaderless at such a critical juncture. Who will lead them? Who will protect them? Where will they go? Who will hold them together?

Responding to these fears, the Lord tells them **not to let** their **heart be shaken**. They need not be rattled so. As good Jews, they have all been taught to **believe in God** and trust in His power to save Israel. Let them **believe also** in Jesus, and trust *His* power to save them as well.

They are anguished at the thought of being separated from Him, but it is in order that they may always be together in the Kingdom that He is leaving them and passing to the Father. They need not fear. **In His Father's** heavenly **house** there are **many dwelling-places**, room for all of them. Each of them fears to be left behind, but none of them will be. There is a place and reward for them all. **If it were not so**, **would** He **have told** them in the first place (in 13:33) that He was going away?—for He is only going **to prepare a place** for them. If He is to **go and prepare a place** for them, He will **come again and receive** them to Himself—for what would be the point of Him going and preparing their place if they were not to come and enjoy the place prepared? Obviously He will return for them. The goal of His departure is only that they might be forever together in the Kingdom—that **where** He is, they **may be also**. And they all **know the way** to the Kingdom **where** He is **going**.

Despite the Lord's assurances, the disciples still have little comprehension of His meaning. By their subsequent responses (such as Thomas' question in v. 5), they show that they still think in terms of Christ leaving to go to another place on earth. Their understanding

of the Kingdom is still earthly, and they cannot see that He is referring to passing to the Father in heaven and sitting at His right hand,
far above all earthly rule.

The dwelling-places He is referring to are the places in heaven
and in the Kingdom of the age to come. He is going to prepare a
place for them by appearing in the presence of God as the Lamb
slain, as the abiding intercession for sinful men before the divine
throne (Rev. 5:6; Heb. 7:25). That is how He is to prepare their
places—by reigning as Messiah until all enemies have been put under His feet—including the final foe, death itself (1 Cor. 15:25–26).
Then, at the close of the age, He will come again to earth at His
glorious Second Coming and receive them to Himself, bestowing
on them all the Kingdom and reward which He has prepared for
them (Matt. 25:34). Then they will be with Him forever. And they
know the way home to that Kingdom.

> ৯৯ ৯৯ ৯৯ ৯৯ ৯৯
>
> 5 Thomas says to Him, "Lord, we do not know
>   where You are going; how are we able to know
>   the way?"
> 6 Jesus says to him, "I *Myself* am the way and
>   the truth and the life; no one comes to the Fa-
>   ther, but through Me.
> 7 "If you had known Me, you would have known
>   My Father also; from now on you know Him,
>   and have seen Him."

Like the others, Thomas still imagines Christ is leaving secretly
for another location on earth (probably in the Diaspora; compare
7:35). Christ is talking about knowing the way there so they can
rejoin Him later, but that makes no sense! **Thomas** protests that
they do **not know where** He is **going**. He has not yet told them His
secret destination—**how** are they **able to know the way** there to
rejoin Him later?

Jesus answers on the spiritual plane. They are asking about

finding the way to where He is going. He is going, not to some earthly destination, but to the Kingdom of heaven, and they all know the way to that destination! He Himself (the **I** is emphatic in the Greek) is **the way** to the Kingdom. Their discipleship to Him is the way to rejoining Him in the Kingdom of God. He is **the truth** of God manifested on the earth, **the life** of God given to men. Thus, if they continue as His obedient disciples, they will **come to the Father** through Him. Indeed, He is the only way to the Father, for men cannot willfully reject Him and still have access to God. The Pharisees might think that one can renounce Jesus and still stand before the Father in joy in the Kingdom, but they are utterly mistaken. One cannot reject Him and still come to the Father—for He *is* the Father, manifested in the flesh among men. To have **known** Him is therefore to have **known His Father also. From now on,** His disciples may be sure that they have both **known** the Father and **seen Him**.

ॐ ॐ ॐ ॐ ॐ

8   Philip says to Him, "Lord, show us the Father, and it will satisfy us."

9   Jesus says to him, "Have I been so long a time with you *all*, and you have not known Me, Philip? He who has seen Me has seen the Father; how do you *yourself* say, 'Show us the Father'?

10   "Do you not believe that I *Myself am* in the Father, and the Father is in Me? The sayings that I *Myself* say to you I do not speak from Myself, but the Father remaining in Me does His works.

11   "Believe Me that I *Myself am* in the Father, and the Father in Me, but if not, believe because of the works themselves.

Jesus' reference to their knowing and seeing the Father (v. 7) prompts Philip to think that Christ is promising them an imminent theophany of the Father. The Jews asked for some such manifestation from heaven (Mark 8:11)—is Jesus about to grant such an appearance of the Father now, perhaps some vision such as Isaiah or Ezekiel saw (Is. 6:1f; Ezek. 1:26f)? If He will **show** them **the Father** in this way, it will **satisfy** them and sustain them during their long separation from Him, while He is (as they think) hiding in some foreign land.

Their request to be shown the Father is somewhat disheartening to Jesus. Has He been **so long a time with** them all (the first **you** of v. 9 is plural), showing them all the miracles from the Father, and still Philip (this second **you** is singular) has **not known** Him? The one who **has seen** Jesus has also thereby **seen the Father**—how can an apostle, of all people (this last **you** of v. 9 is emphatic), say, "**Show us the Father**"? Obviously Jesus is **in the Father** and **the Father in** Him. The two are one (10:30), in that Jesus is the perfect expression of the Father's nature (John 1:18; Heb. 1:3). Thus, all **the sayings** that Jesus says to them are not His own ideas. He does **not speak** from Himself, but as the Messenger sent by **the Father**, who **remains** in Jesus and through Him **does His works**. Let all the disciples (the verb is plural) **believe** and trust Him for His own sake, that He is **in the Father** and **the Father in** Him, and that they are inseparably One. Or **if** they can **not** believe Him for His word alone, let them **believe because of the works** that He does **themselves**. Surely these miracles prove that the Father remains in Him and does His work through Him!

༃ ༃ ༃ ༃ ༃

12 "Amen, amen, I say to you, he who believes in Me, the works that I *Myself* do, that one will do, and greater than these will he do, because I *Myself* go to the Father.

13 "And whatever you ask in My Name, this will I do, that the Father may be glorified in the Son.

14 "If you ask Me anything in My Name, I *Myself* will do *it*.

They may well believe for the sake of His miracles—for they
will soon be doing such miracles themselves! He solemnly assures
them (with His characteristic **amen, amen, I say to you**), the one
who believes in Him, **that one will do** His **works** also. Moreover,
he will even do **greater than these** works, because Christ is **going to
the Father**.

It is because Christ is going to the Father that His disciples will
be able to do greater works. That is, Jesus is going to be glorified at
the right hand of God, receiving all authority in heaven and earth
(Matt. 28:18). As such, **whatever** they **ask** in His **Name** (that is, as
His representatives on earth and as those who have His authority),
this He will **do** for them, **that the Father may be glorified in the
Son**. They will ask Him for a miracle (such as a miracle of healing)
and He will do it through them (compare Acts 9:34, where Peter
heals a man and says, "Jesus Christ heals you"). It is as Jesus' disciples manifest power in His Name, and as they do miracles and
convert the nations, that the world will come to believe that Jesus is
indeed the true Messiah. Thus **the Father** will be **glorified in the
Son** as the Son is shown to be the Father's power on earth.

This conversion of the nations is the greater work of which Christ
speaks. During the days of His flesh, Jesus reached only those in
Palestine. The Scriptures, however, promised that through Jesus,
the Suffering Servant, all the world would come to God (see Is.
49:6–7). These greater works Jesus did through His Body, the Church
(compare Acts 13:46–47 and how Paul applies the passage in Is.
49:6 to the work of the Church). By Himself, during His ministry,
Christ reached only those in Israel. But His Church would eventu-
ally bring the whole world to God.

ॐ ॐ ॐ ॐ ॐ

15 "If you love Me, you will keep My commandments.
16 "And I *Myself* will ask the Father, and He will
give to you another Advocate, that He may be
with you forever,

> 17 "the Spirit of truth, whom the world is not able to receive, because it does not observe Him or know Him; you know Him because He remains with you and will be in you.

This life of doing miracles and bringing the world to God presupposes that the disciples will walk in obedience to Him. This they will do, **if** they truly **love** Him. The apostolic power to perform miracles is not disconnected from a life of **keeping** His **commandments**. Which commandments does He mean? We may think they are all summed up in His new commandment to love one another as He has loved them (13:34), but the plural form used here means He is thinking of more than one. He means the whole body of His teaching that He has given during His ministry, such as the necessity of reconciliation (Matt. 5:23f), of honesty of heart (Matt. 5:33f), of nonretaliation (Matt. 5:38f), of performing pious works for God's sake and not for public approval only (Matt. 6:1f), of forgiveness (Matt. 6:14–15). It is as His disciples walk in the way of these commandments, this way of love, that they will know His blessing and His Presence with them.

This Presence will culminate in knowing the power of the Spirit. If they walk in love, He, the one glorified at God's right hand (the **I** is emphatic), **will ask the Father,** and the Father will **give** to them **another Advocate** and Friend **that He may be with** them **forever,** even **the Spirit of truth.** Through the Church's sacramental Mysteries of Baptism and Chrismation, the Spirit is given to men by the intercession of Christ. He is the One who sits glorified at the Father's right hand and pours out the Spirit upon His Church (Acts 2:33).

This **Spirit** is the Spirit **of truth,** revealing all the truth of God (even as Christ embodies and *is* that truth), and therefore **the world is not able to receive** Him, for the world resists the truth, preferring instead to cling to lies. The world **does not observe** the Spirit or **know**; it does not see or experience the Spirit working savingly in its midst. The world remains a stranger to the power of the Spirit. By the term *world*, the Lord of course means the world as a system that stands aloof from God in all its pride (compare 7:7). This world *by definition* cannot but resist God's grace.

It is otherwise with the disciples of Jesus, those who have left the world (15:19). The Spirit **remains with** them still, and soon **will be in** them. Through Christ's ministry and miracles, the disciples have known the Spirit's power. Soon they will know Him more intimately yet. Up to that time, the Spirit has remained with them as an external companion. After Pentecost, He will be in them, dwelling in their inmost being, as an internal source of life (4:14; 7:37–39).

This Spirit is called by Jesus **another Advocate**. The word translated here *Advocate* is the Greek *Paracletos*, which means literally "one called alongside." The word has a legal feel to it, like one who is called to another's aid in a cause or a legal case. In 1 John 2:1, Jesus Christ is said to be "our *Paracletos* with the Father" when we sin, our Advocate and defense before God. The idea seems to be of a Friend, a support, someone to stand by us in a time of need and come alongside to our help and defense. This is why the Spirit is described here as *another* Advocate. Jesus, during the days of His ministry, was the Advocate, the Friend of His disciples, the One whom they leaned on for support and encouragement (for *paraclesis*). Now that He is going away, they will not have this support any more. But they will have the Spirit as their support. He will do the work of helping them which Jesus did when He walked among them.

༄ ༄ ༄ ༄ ༄

18 "I will not leave you *as* orphans; I will come to you.

19 "Yet a little *while* and the world will observe Me no more; but you *yourselves* will observe Me; because I *Myself* live, you *yourselves* will live also.

20 "In that day you *yourselves* will know that I *Myself am* in My Father, and you in Me, and I *Myself* in you.

> **21** "He who has My commandments and keeps them, that one is the one who loves Me, and he who loves Me will be loved by My Father, and I *Myself* will love him and will reveal Myself to him."

Despite Christ's assurance about receiving another Advocate and Friend, the disciples are still not at rest. They don't want *another* helper, they want *Him*! So it is that He also assures them that He will **not leave** them **orphans**, abandoned and helpless, but **will come** to them again. And they will not have to wait a long time to see Him again, but only **a little** *while*. **The world will observe** Him **no more**, but *they* **will observe** Him and be comforted by His Presence (the pronoun **you** is emphatic, stressing their difference from the world). The Lord is referring to the time of reunion after His death (when the world will observe Him no more) and after His Resurrection. Having risen from the grave, He will spend forty days with them, teaching them about the Kingdom of God (Acts 1:3). It is because He will **live** again that they will also **live**; His Resurrection will be the source of theirs also.

In that day, on the other side of the Resurrection, they will **know** with certainty of His divine authority (for His Resurrection will prove that authority) and that He is **in** His **Father**. Moreover, they will have experience of His union with them also. They will be in Him and He in them, as they share an inner union with Him, just as He shares a union with the Father. They are afraid of being forever separated from Him, but He assures them that He will be with them to ages of ages. Not only will He physically see them again after His Resurrection, but they will share the same intimate union with Him that He has with the Father.

This presupposes that they **have** His **commandments** and will **keep** them. This experience of inner union with Christ is not for merely nominal adherents and casual followers. He who would know this secret union with Christ must continue to treasure His teaching and fulfill it. Only then can he be His true disciple, one who truly **loves** Him. For if such a one **loves** Him, he will **be loved** by Christ's **Father** in return, and by Jesus Himself. To this one the Lord will **reveal** Himself through this secret union of the heart.

> ৵ ৵ ৵ ৵ ৵
>
> 22 Judas (not Iscariot) says to Him, "Lord, what then has happened that You are about to reveal Yourself to us and not to the world?"
> 23 Jesus answered and said to him, "If anyone loves Me, he will keep My Word, and My Father will love him, and We will come to him and make Our dwelling-place with him.
> 24 "He who does not love Me does not keep My words; and the Word which you hear is not Mine, but the Father's who sent Me.

The disciples still think in physical terms. The idea of Jesus **revealing** Himself to them and **not to the world** makes no sense to them. For them, the Messiah *by definition* will be revealed to the world—His worldly glory is what identifies Him as the Messiah. **Judas** (St. John is careful to clarify that this Judas is **not Iscariot**) asks **what has happened** that Christ can establish His Kingdom in Jerusalem in power and reveal His glory to His disciples, and the world not see it?

Jesus answers him that He is not speaking about a physical and political Kingdom, one established openly with governments and armies. This is a spiritual and inner Kingdom. Christ is to sit, not on some piece of real estate in Jerusalem, but by the throne of God in heaven, and His Presence on earth will be spiritual and invisible. His Presence will not come enforced by the might of an army, but only if **anyone loves** Him and will **keep** His **Word** and teaching. Then His **Father** and He will **love him** and will **come to him** and **make** Their **dwelling-place with him**. His Presence with His disciples is an inner union of the heart, not the visible result of some armed *coup d'état*. This revelation to the heart is based on love and obedience, and so of course the world (which does **not love** Him or **keep** His **words**) cannot know His Presence. In rejecting Jesus' words, they have rejected **the Father's Word** as well, for the Father **sent** Jesus to speak His message to the world. The Father therefore of course refuses to dwell in those who have rejected His message.

꧁ ꧁ ꧁ ꧁ ꧁

25 "These things I have spoken to you while remaining with you.

26 "But the Advocate, the Holy Spirit, whom the Father will send in My Name, He will teach you all things and remind you of all that I said to you.

27 "Peace I leave with you; My peace I give to you; not as the world gives do I *Myself* give to you. Let not your heart be shaken, nor let it be cowardly.

28 "You heard that I *Myself* said to you, 'I go away, and will come to you.' If you loved Me, you would have rejoiced, for I go to the Father, for the Father is greater than I.

29 "And now I have told you before it happens, that when it happens, you may believe.

30 "I will no longer speak much with you, for the ruler of the world is coming and he does not have anything in Me;

31 "but as the Father has given Me commandment, thus I do, that the world may know that I love the Father.

The Lord prepares to leave, and He concludes His conversation at the Passover supper table. **These things** He has **spoken** to them **while remaining** with them, but now it is time for Him to go. They need not fear because they do not understand it all now and may forget all that He has said. **The Advocate** He promised, **the Holy**

Spirit, whom the Father will send in His **Name,** He will **teach** them **all things** they need to know and **remind** them of **all that** He has **said** to them.

Still, however, the disciples are agitated. What dangers will they have to endure, and how can they face them without Him? So it is that the Lord **gives** to them His **peace.** And this is not peace such **as the world gives,** a peace which remains when things look hopeful and gives way to fear when things look bad. This is His own peace, a peace that is unshakable, invincible, dependent on God, not on circumstances. They need **not let** their **heart be shaken** by news of His departure, nor be **cowardly** when they survey the coming dangers.

They have **heard** Him **say** that He will **go away** and will later **come** to them. This filled them with panic, but if they **loved** Him as they claimed, they **would have rejoiced** when they heard this news, for He is not going into the Diaspora, but **to the Father.** They should not implore Him to stay, but rejoice that He is going! His departure is a cause for rejoicing, for **the Father is greater** than He and will glorify Him in the Kingdom. Christ tells His disciples about this departure **before it happens,** so that **when it happens,** they may not be blindsided by it and fall away, but **may** continue to **believe** in Him. His aim in telling them of His departure is not to disturb them, but to prepare them.

But the time for such preparation is drawing to its end. He **will no longer speak much** with them, for Satan, **the ruler of the world,** is **coming** and time is running out. (Even now, Judas is preparing to lead the arrest party.) But Satan **does not have anything** in Him, no claim on Him nor power over Him. The Enemy can inspire men to arrest and kill Jesus, but he cannot hold Him. Christ's final victory is assured. Christ will leave the Passover supper to be arrested by Satan's minions in the garden, but that is not because He feels Satan is too strong to be resisted. On the contrary, He is only surrendering because He will **do** just **as the Father has given** Him **commandment, that the world may know** that He **loves the Father.** The Jews consider Him to be a deceiver and a Law-breaker. His arrest, death, and Resurrection will prove them wrong.

❧ EXCURSUS

ON THE GREATNESS OF THE FATHER (14:28)

A final word may be added about the Father being greater than the Son (v. 28). Though Arians of all generations (who deny the divinity of the Son) jump on this verse and try to use it to prove their assertion that Jesus cannot be divine, it actually proves the reverse. Obviously, a created being would be less than God and would be only too aware of it—in fact, the holier a person is, the more aware he is of his own sinfulness and of how much greater is God than himself! If Christ were indeed a created being, this would be too obvious to require saying, and saying it would be ludicrous. It would be like a beggar saying, "I want to assure you that I am not running the country as king." No one ever thought he was! That the beggar thought it needed to be said would show that he was insane. Therefore, only a person who was in some way one with the Father (10:30) and who had some measure of equality with God (14:9) could without obvious absurdity make such a statement as "the Father is greater than I."

What then does this mean, and in what way was the Father greater than the Son? It is important to see that these words were not spoken as part of a dissertation on Christology. They were spoken before Christ and His disciples went into the lion's mouth, into mortal danger. Jesus as a man had no power, no recourse. His foes held all the cards and had all the power—the soldiers to arrest, the Sanhedrin prepared to deliver a guilty verdict by dawn, Pilate and the might of Rome to carry out the sentence. Jesus was but one man, with no armies, no powerful friends, no intercessors. He had only twelve men (now, only eleven!), with but two swords between them (Luke 22:38). How could He hope to triumph? Why should the disciples rejoice that He was to enter the garden of betrayal and depart this life to the Father? Because the Father was greater than He. He had no power, but the Father held all the world in His hand. The Father was able to turn defeat into victory and to glorify His co-eternal Son. That was why the disciples might still rejoice on that dark night.

In 10:29, the Father was said to be "greater than all" in the sense that the excommunications of the Jews could not overrule the blessing of God upon one who had become Jesus' disciple. He was "greater than all" in that He would overturn the Jews' sentences of condemnation. The same sense prevails here. The Father is here said to be "greater" than the Son in that He had power the Son did not and would overturn the plot of the Jews, vindicating His Messiah.

ॐ ॐ ॐ ॐ ॐ

31 "Arise, let us go from here.

Now the Lord says to His disciples, **"Arise, let us go from here."** This has puzzled some people, because after saying that it is time to leave, He seems to stay for another two chapters' worth of discourse and discussion. Did He tell them to go and they all remained where they were? Did they all stand up to leave and remain talking together for some time before exiting the room?

The puzzle can be resolved when we remember that the evening's discourse *took place within the context of a Passover meal.* That meal itself is not stressed in John (any more than in Matthew, Mark, or Luke) because it had no significance in itself. It was simply the framework for other things, such as the Institution of the Eucharist (which the other Gospels relate) and these discourses (which John relates). But the meal itself did occur and occupied the whole of the evening, stretching over two or three hours.

After the preliminary Passover course of bitter herbs and stewed fruit (with the giving of the sop), the meal itself opened with the blessing, breaking, and distribution of bread. (It was over this initial breaking of bread that the Lord spoke His word instituting the Bread of the Eucharist.) After that breaking of bread, the meal would continue, probably for two or three hours, until it ended with a third cup of wine, over which a long blessing was spoken. (It was over this post-supper cup of wine that the Lord spoke His word instituting the Wine of the Eucharist.) But it was up to the host to say when the meal should be concluded and that third cup of wine after the supper be drunk (1 Cor. 11:25).

The Lord's word to **arise** and **go**, therefore, *signals this conclusion of the meal.* Because it was a Passover meal, they would not respond by abruptly standing up and walking from the room. Before they could go after the meal, the post-meal cup of blessing had to be drunk, a fourth cup of wine filled, the conclusion of the Hallel sung (Ps. 115–118), and then the Great Hallel, Psalm 136, sung as well (the "hymn" of Matt. 26:30).

Granted that this is so, why does St. John mention this word about arising and going? He does not mention any other "housekeeping details" from that Passover meal. Why mention this one?

I suggest that he mentions this word about arising and going in order to stress that this teaching had to do with the Church's mission as it would go through all the world. The Lord's journey through the dark streets with His disciples which would follow the meal was an image of the Church's journey through the dark lanes of the world. Previously He had spoken mostly to reassure them. Now He must speak also of their mission to the world, and of the persecution and challenges that would accompany it.

This final part of their supper discourse (chs. 15; 16) took place, I suggest, after the meal proper, and after the third cup of wine. For after this third cup, a fourth and final cup would be poured, not to be drunk until after the singing of the Great Hallel. It was during this time that the Lord spoke of what they must do after they had left the safety of the Passover table and emerged again into the world.

༄ ༄ ༄ ༄ ༄

15 1   "I *Myself* am the true vine, and My Father is the farmer.

2   "Every branch in Me that does not bear fruit, He takes away, and every one that bears fruit, He cleanses it, that it may bear more fruit.

3   "You *yourselves* are already clean through the Word which I have spoken to you.

4   "Remain in Me, and I *Myself* in you. As the branch is not able to bear fruit of itself, unless it remains in the vine, thus neither can you, unless you remain in Me.

5   "I *Myself* am the vine, you *yourselves* are the branches; he who remains in Me, and I *Myself* in him, this one bears much fruit, for without Me you are not able to do anything.

6   "If anyone does not remain in Me, he is cast outside as a branch, and dries up, and they gather them and cast them into the fire, and they are burned.

7   "If you remain in Me, and My sayings remain in you, ask whatever you want and it will be done for you.

8   "By this My Father is glorified, that you bear much fruit, and become My disciples.

9   "As the Father has loved Me, I *Myself* have also loved you; remain in My love.

10   "If you keep My commandments, you will remain in My love, just as I *Myself* have kept My Father's commandments and remain in His love.

He begins by telling them another figure or parable. He is **the true vine**, they are **the branches**, and His **Father** is **the farmer** who tends the vine and its branches. Some branches do **not bear fruit**; these the farmer **takes away** and cuts off the vine. The ones that **bear fruit**, He **cleanses** or prunes, that it **may bear** even **more fruit**. This figure was probably suggested by the cup of wine which had been filled and which stood on the Passover table in front of them, the fourth cup, the *Hallel* cup (so-called because the *Hallel* hymn was sung over it).

The Lord then interprets this figure. The image of a farmer tending his vine was a familiar one: God was often described as the farmer who planted the vine of Israel His people (Is. 5:1f; Jer. 2:21; Hos. 10:1–2). Israel proved itself to be a false vine; Jesus is the true one. As God tended Israel of old, so the Father now tends Jesus' disciples, the branches of the true vine.

The disciples are like branches that have been cleansed (or pruned) and are ready to bear fruit. They have **already** been cleansed or made **clean through the Word** which He has **spoken** to them. That is, by accepting His teaching and becoming His disciples, they were made clean before God and ready to bear fruit for Him.

But they must take care to **remain in** Him and not fall away in the coming persecution. They must preserve their inner spiritual union with Him by loving and obeying Him (14:21). Just as a **branch** is organically a part of the vine and **not able to bear fruit of itself,** but only when it **remains** attached to **the vine,** so it is only as His disciples **remain in** Him that they will **bear fruit. Without** Him they are **not able to do anything.** All their spiritual success and their heavenly reward depend on their faithfulness to Him. If they **remain in** Him and His **sayings remain** in them and are obediently fulfilled in their lives, then they will indeed **bear much fruit.** That is, they can **ask** Him **whatever** they **want** and it **will be done** for them. Through this fruit-bearing, the **Father** will be **glorified** and they will **become** His **disciples** indeed.

What is this fruit-bearing? A life filled with love, the sign to the world that they are indeed His disciples (13:35). It was prophesied that Israel would blossom and fill the world with fruit (Is. 27:6). This will be fulfilled by Christ's disciples, the true Israel. The fruits of love—compassion, service, all the social works with which the Church has softened and enriched the world—this is the fruit which glorifies the Father. It is this to which the disciples are called.

Some branches in the vine will not bear fruit, and these the heavenly vinedresser will take away. Just as fruitless branches are pruned from a vine, so the Father will take those disciples of Jesus who do **not remain in** Him and His Word (compare 8:31) but fall away, and **cast** them **outside** the Kingdom. As a fruitless branch is cut away, left to **dry up** and then **gathered** and **cast into the fire** and **burned**, so the disciples of Jesus who do not persevere in His Word will be cast from the Kingdom. Branches only remain alive when they remain part of the life-giving vine.

It all depends on their perseverance. As **the Father loves** Jesus, so Jesus Himself passes that same love along and **loves** them. If they would be saved, they must **remain in** that **love**. It is a matter of obedience and of keeping His commandments. Jesus has **kept** His **Father's commandments**, fulfilling all that He required on earth. For this reason, He **remains** in the Father's **love**, abiding under His protection, sure of His ultimate vindication. The disciples must do the same. They must also **keep** Jesus' **commandments** to **remain** in Jesus' **love**, and so be sure of their ultimate salvation.

ॐ ॐ ॐ ॐ ॐ

11 "These things I have spoken to you, that My joy may be in you, and your joy may be made full.

12 "This is My commandment, that you love one another, as I have loved you.

13 "Greater love has no one than this, that one lay down his life for his friends.

14 "You *yourselves* are My friends, if you do what I *Myself* command you.

15 "No longer do I call you slaves, for the slave does not know what his lord is doing, but you I have called friends, for all things that I have heard from My Father I have made known to you.

16 "You *yourselves* did not choose Me, but I *Myself* chose you, and appointed you, that you *yourselves* should go and bear fruit, and your fruit should remain, that whatever you ask

> the Father in My Name, He may give to you.
> 17 "This I command you, that you love one
> another.

The Lord continues to teach them, saying that He has **spoken these things** about remaining in Him (vv. 1–10) that His **joy may be in** them and that their **joy may be made full**. The world may rage against them, but it cannot conquer or take away their joy. To remain in Christ is to remain in joy. Joy does not depend on outward circumstances, but on keeping one's focus on Jesus. The Lord's own joy that comes from His union with the Father, that same joy will be in the disciples and be made full.

This joy also depends on keeping His commandments (since the joy-bestowing union with Christ depends on keeping His commandments). The Lord repeats His **commandment**: that they **love one another, as** He has **loved** them. He loved them with a sacrificial, self-denying **love**, a love **greater** than all others: the love that would cause one even to **lay down his life for his friends**.

Christ is doing this for His disciples, for they, separated from the world (the **you** of v. 14 is emphatic, to stress this), are His **friends**, if they will obey this **command** to love which He has given them. They are no longer to be considered **slaves** and servants. **The slave** is not the confidant of his lord; he **does not know what his lord** and master **is doing**. The slave simply follows orders, happily oblivious to the big picture. The slave does not know; the intimate friend does know. The disciples now are to be considered **friends**, for **all things** that Christ has **heard from** the **Father**, He has **made known** to them. He has treated them like colleagues; He has held nothing back, kept no teaching secret. The entire Word that the Father gave Christ to share with His own, He has passed on to them (compare 17:6–8).

But though He loves them as friends, He is still their Lord, and His orders are to be obeyed. In the Israel of that day, most people who wanted to be specially taught chose their own rabbis and teachers, and attached themselves to whomever they wished. It was otherwise with Christ. *He* was the one who **chose** *them* (the pronouns you and I are emphatic in the Greek of v. 16). He moved sovereignly to claim them, to take control of their lives and use them for the Kingdom.

More than that, He **appointed** them to a certain task: to **go** into all the world as His representatives and **bear** enduring **fruit**. This **fruit** of love will **remain** and endure in the world, for the Church which manifests it in all the world will remain and endure. By being a community of love, the Church is able to call upon God with authority as His children. If the disciples will walk in love and let His sayings remain in them (compare v. 7), then **whatever** they **ask the Father** for in Jesus' **Name**, the Father will **give** it to them. And this is the foremost of His sayings—His **command** to **love one another**. For love is the essence of the Church. Without love, the branches remain fruitless, and the Church exists in name only.

ॐ ॐ ॐ ॐ ॐ

18 "If the world hates you, know that it has hated Me before *it hated* you.
19 "If you were from the world, the world would love its own, but because you are not of the world, but I *Myself* chose you from the world, for this *reason* the world hates you.
20 "Remember the word that I *Myself* said to you, 'A slave is not greater than his lord.' If they persecuted Me, they will also persecute you. If they kept My Word, they will keep yours also.

Their love for one another and their fruit-bearing in the world do not mean, however, that the world will love them. On the contrary, **the world hates** them—but that is not unexpected, for the disciples should **know** that the world already **hated** Christ **before** *it hated* them. The world's hatred for them is inevitable, for it is but another manifestation of the world's prior hatred for Christ. If they still belonged to the world, sharing its loyalties, agendas, and values, and were still from the world, then **the world** would still **love** them, and acknowledge them as its own. But all that is past. Now they are **not of the world**, since Jesus **chose** them **from the world**. Now they belong to Him.

Thus, the hatred the world has for Christ overflows to them also. This should not surprise them. They have only to **remember the word** that Jesus has just **said** to them, "**A slave is not greater than his lord**" (13:16), to know that they will receive the same treatment at the world's hands. If one despises one's enemy, one does not treat that enemy's messenger with deference. The disrespect one intends for the enemy is given to his emissary too. It is the same with the apostles, who are the Lord's emissaries. If the world **persecuted** Jesus, the world **will also persecute** the apostles. If **they kept** His **Word** and were open to His message, they **will keep** the apostles' word **also**. Whatever the world's attitude was to Jesus, that same attitude will be directed at His Church.

ॐ ॐ ॐ ॐ ॐ

21 "But all these things they will do to you because of My Name, because they do not know the One who sent Me.

22 "If I had not come and spoken to them, they would not have sin, but now they have no pretense for their sin.

23 "He who hates Me hates My Father also.

24 "If I had not done among them the works which no other did, they would not have sin, but now they have both seen and hated both Me and My Father.

25 "But *it is* that the word may be fulfilled that is written in their Law, 'They hated me without a cause.'

At first sight, this hatred toward Christ and His Church is surprising, especially in Israel. The Jews had been taught by the prophets for centuries to love God and to seek righteousness. Why should they react with such hostility to Christ's words and works?

The answer comes to the mysterious heart of the tragedy of Israel (a tragedy and mystery dealt with by St. Paul in Romans 9–11). The Jews would **do all these things**—persecuting Christ and His apostles who bore His **Name** and came as His representatives—**because they do not know the One who sent** Christ. That is, their hostility sprang from a fundamental ignorance of God and what He really wanted from men. Israel, through its unofficial teachers the Pharisees, came to a place where they did not understand their own Law. They had a distorted view of it and were convinced that the Law was an end in itself, that God was more concerned with the minutiae of complicated regulations than He was with the love of the human heart. Their whole sense of perspective had been skewed, and in their pride they refused to consider that they could be wrong. Thus, they regarded Jesus' teaching as a grievous apostasy from the Law and Jesus Himself as a dangerous deceiver, whose influence they had to stamp out at all costs.

Jesus says that Israel's rejection of Him (and His disciples) is nothing less than a hatred of the Father Himself. **He who hates** Him thereby **hates** Jesus' **Father also**, for Jesus is the visible embodiment of the Father (14:9). Israel has **seen** Him, experienced Him, heard all His words and all His message—and then **hated** and rejected Him. There is an air of finality to this: Israel has had its chance. They have seen the evidence and given their verdict. In their hatred and rejection of Jesus, they have thereby also seen and hated His **Father** as well. The nation that was created expressly to receive the divine Word has rejected its God.

In this they **have no pretense for their sin. If Jesus had not come and spoken to them**, speaking words such as no man ever before spoke (7:46), and **done the works which no other did**, they might have an excuse. National apostasy is indefensible in the face of such an overwhelming display of God's grace. It can only be explained as the judgment of God, long prophesied and **written in their** own **Law**: "**They hated me without a cause.**" In Ps. 69:4, David spoke of the perversity of those who opposed his royal house and dynasty. Jesus says that this **word** is being **fulfilled**

before their eyes. Israel has no cause to reject Him, but it is doing
so anyway.

ॐ ॐ ॐ ॐ ॐ

26 "When the Advocate comes, whom I *Myself*
will send to you from the Father, the Spirit of
truth, who proceeds from the Father, that One
will witness about Me,
27 "and you *yourselves* will witness also, because
you have been with Me from the beginning.

But though the Jews slander and malign Christ, the truth will
be manifest nonetheless. **When the Advocate**, the heavenly Helper,
comes (whom Jesus Himself will **send** to them **from the Father**;
the **I** is emphatic), then **that One will witness about** Him and tell
the truth—for He *is* **the Spirit of truth**. And He will do so through
the apostles, for inspired by the Spirit, they themselves (the pronoun **you** is again emphatic) **will witness also**. They know and can
share the truth, for they **have been with** Jesus **from the beginning**,
and know all.

The Spirit is here also described as He **who proceeds from the
Father**. A word may be added in view of the ongoing debate on the
filioque clause in the Creed (that is, the Western insertion into
the Creed which declares that the Spirit proceeds from the Father
and the Son—in Latin, *filioque*). The point of saying here that the
Spirit proceeds from the Father is that He is the Spirit of the Father,
the true manifestation of the Father's power and work on earth.
This is not to deny that the Spirit is a distinct *hypostasis* (or Person)
from Father, the Third Person of the Holy Trinity. It is simply to
assert that Christ's concern here is not to define the inner workings
of the Godhead, but rather to underscore the authority of the Spirit's
witness. Because the Spirit proceeds from the Father, the Spirit's
witness to Christ is that of the Father as well.

ॐ ॐ ॐ ॐ ॐ

16 1   "These things I have spoken to you, that you may not stumble.

2   "They will make you *banned* from the synagogue, but an hour is coming for everyone who kills you to suppose he is offering worship to God.

3   "And these things they will do, because they have not known the Father, or Me.

4   "But these things I have spoken to you, that when their hour comes, you may remember that I *Myself* told you of them. And these things I did not say to you from the beginning, because I was with you.

Our Lord continues to warn them of the persecution ahead. Things are going to get bad. The authorities will **make** them to be *banned* **from the synagogue**, just as the blind man was (compare 9:22, 34). More than that, they will hound them to death, even as they are now hounding their Master. Indeed, **an hour is coming for everyone who kills** them to **suppose** that he is **offering** sacrificial **worship to God**. In a Jewish commentary on Phineas (who slew the apostates during the time of Moses and was rewarded by God; Num. 25:13), it was said that "whoever sheds the blood of the godless is as one who offers a sacrifice." It is this deluded mindset that is to take hold of the Jewish authorities as they persecute Jesus' followers. With such an attitude, the apostles' persecutors will not cease until their deadly work is done. Dark and dangerous days are coming indeed!

Jesus **did not say these things** to them **from the beginning**. During all that time, He **was with** them and could guide them in their perplexity. Now He is going away from them, and foretells the coming storm so that **when** the **hour** of persecutions **comes**, the disciples **may remember** that He **told** them in advance and **not stumble**. Without the warning, they might be caught off guard and give in to the pressure to cease their witness to Jesus.

꙰ ꙰ ꙰ ꙰ ꙰

5   "But now I am going to Him who sent Me, and none of you asks Me, 'Where are You going?'

6   "But because I have spoken these things to you, sorrow has filled your heart.

7   "But I *Myself* tell you the truth, it is advantageous for you that I *Myself* go away, for if I do not go away, the Advocate will not come to you, but if I go, I will send Him to you.

8   "And when that One comes, He will reprove the world about sin, and about righteousness, and about judgment:

9   "about sin, because they do not believe in Me;

10 "about righteousness, because I go to the Father, and you will observe Me no longer;

11 "about judgment, because the ruler of this world has been judged.

12 "I have many more things to tell you, but you are not able to bear *it* now.

13 "But when that One comes, the Spirit of truth, He will guide you in all the truth, for He will not speak from Himself, but what He hears, He will speak, and He will announce to you the things to come.

14 "That One will glorify Me, for He will receive from Me and will announce *it* to you.

15 "All things that the Father has are Mine; therefore I said that He receives from Me and will announce *it* to you.

Over against all this persecution, Christ places the bestowal of the Spirit. The world may rage against them, but they have the power of God to keep them and make them invincible!

Christ said that He was **going to Him who sent** Him, and yet none of the disciples has **asked** Him, "**Where are You going?**" Peter's question about Jesus going away (in 13:36) was not really about where Christ was going; it was only about the fact of His departure. Their concern is only for their own grief at His absence and their panic at being abandoned. **Sorrow has filled** their **heart** and left no room in it for curiosity about Christ's future plans.

But, He tells them, they should not be sad. It is **the truth**, difficult as it is to believe—that **it is advantageous** for them that Christ **go away.** They need the Advocate, the power of the Holy Spirit, to help them through the coming dark days, and if Christ does **not go away**, the Spirit will **not come** to them. That is because the Spirit will only come if Christ first **goes** to the Father to be exalted at His right hand and then **sends Him** to His waiting Church (Acts 2:33).

When that One comes (on the Day of Pentecost), **He will reprove the world** for its condemnation of Jesus and its need to repent. That is, the Holy Spirit will reprove the world **about sin, because they do not believe** in Jesus as Messiah. Israel has disowned Him, thinking they are doing the will of God. By the working of the Spirit, they will be cut to the heart and see that this is sin (compare Acts 2:37).

The Spirit will also reprove the world **about righteousness,** because Christ is to **go to the Father** and all will **observe** Him **no longer.** That is, He is to be raised up and glorified to God's right hand, and thus be vindicated by God for His righteousness. Israel thought Jesus an unrighteous Law-breaker. By the working of the Spirit, they will see what true righteousness really is as they see Christ exonerated and glorified by the Father.

Finally, the Spirit will reprove the world **about judgment, because the ruler of this world has been judged**. That is, Satan and his instruments in the world (such as the Sanhedrin) have been judged and condemned by God. Their time of ascendancy is over; now is the time for Christ's victory. By the working of the Spirit, they will see that the time of lies is over; now is the time to repent.

When the Spirit comes, He will not just reprove the world. He will also guide the Church. On the night before His crucifixion, Christ has **many more things to tell** His disciples, but they are **not** able to bear *it* at that time. Christ is thinking of such things as the spiritual nature of the Kingdom and the inclusion of the Gentiles in it on equal terms with the Jews. These are things the disciples are in no position to understand, for they still look for the establishment of an earthly Kingdom.

But **when that One**, the Spirit, **comes**, He will **guide** the Church **in all the truth**, since He is **the Spirit of truth**. Like Christ, the Spirit will **not speak from Himself**, but **what He hears, He will speak** and **announce** to the apostles, giving insight into **the things** which at this time are still **to come**. That is, He will teach the apostles the truth, even as Jesus taught them the truth. He **will glorify** Jesus, in that **He will receive** from Him divine teaching and **will announce** it to the apostles. Christ stresses that these insights which the Spirit will give are truths from the Father, even as the precepts that *He* gave were truths from the Father. **All things that the Father has** belong also to Jesus, so when the Lord says that the Spirit **receives** from Him and **announces** this to the apostles, He means that the Spirit announces the truths from the Father.

The implication of this for the authority of the Church should not be missed. By saying that the Spirit will guide the Church in all the truth about God, Christ is assuring the disciples that they will not be left at the mercy of their own limitations. As men they are sinful and fallible, but they are not to be left alone. The Spirit will come to make up the deficiency, "healing that which is infirm and completing that which is lacking" (from the prayer for ordination). The Church therefore has all the authority of God, since it is guided by the Holy Spirit. Because of this, it is the pillar and firm buttress of the truth (1 Tim. 3:15), through which the manifold wisdom of God is revealed (Eph. 3:10).

❧ ❧ ❧ ❧ ❧

16 "A little *while* and you will no longer observe Me, and again a little *while* and you will see Me."

17 Some of His disciples therefore said to one

another, "What is this which He says to us, 'A little *while* and you will not observe Me, and again a little *while*, and you will see Me'; and 'because I go to the Father'?"

18 Therefore they were saying, "What is this that He says, 'the little *while*'? We do not know of what He speaks."

19 Jesus knew that they wanted to ask Him, and He said to them, "Are you debating with one another about this, that I said, 'A little *while*, and you will not observe Me, and again a little *while*, and you will see Me'?

20 "Amen, amen, I say to you that you *yourselves* will weep and lament, but the world will rejoice; you *yourselves* will be sorrowful, but your sorrow will become joy.

21 "When a woman gives birth, she has sorrow because her hour has come, but when she bears the child, she remembers the tribulation no more, for joy that a man has been born into the world.

22 "Therefore you *yourselves* also now have sorrow, but I will see you again, and your heart will rejoice, and no one will take away your joy from you.

As Christ began with a note of assurance (14:1), so He ends with one as well. He tells His disciples that in **a little *while*** they **will no longer observe** Him, but will be deprived of the sight of Him for a brief time. Then **again**, in but another **little *while***, they **will see** Him. His arrest, crucifixion, and burial will take Him away from them and throw them into confusion, but this will pass quickly. Soon enough, after His Resurrection, they will be reunited with Him. Let them be brave, and endure this brief trial!

Once again, the disciples are stumped as to what He can mean. They are still thinking that He will leave the country to go into the

Diaspora. How then can He go so far away and return again so quickly? What is **the little *while*** of which He is speaking? And how can He **go to the Father** in death and then return again? They cannot make sense of it. A quiet debate begins in whispers, but none can think how to organize their perplexity into a coherent question. **Jesus knew that they wanted to ask Him** this, and He moves to reassure them. He cannot dispel all their perplexity, for it is based on erroneous and carnal views of the Kingdom. But He moves to take away the sting of sorrow they still feel at the thought of His going away for **a little *while*.**

He acknowledges that they will certainly **weep and lament.** After His arrest, crucifixion, and burial, they will be sorely grieved. **The world**, on the contrary, **will rejoice.** But their **sorrow** will pass quickly and **will become joy.** It will be like the experience of **a woman** who **gives birth.** For a brief time, **she has** intense **sorrow** and pain **because her hour has come. But when she bears the child, she remembers the tribulation** and affliction **no more, for joy that a man**, another human being (Gr. *anthropos*), **has been born into the world.** The final joy completely swallows up all memory of the former pain. In the case of childbirth, the pain ends in joy and new life.

It will be the same here. The pain of the Cross and of their being deprived of Him will end in the joy of reunion and in the new life of the Resurrection. They **also now have sorrow** when His foes triumph. But He **will see** them **again**, and then their **heart will rejoice**, and **no one will take away** that **joy** from them. As in the case of childbirth, that joy will be worth the pain!

꒰ ꒰ ꒰ ꒰ ꒰

23 "And in that day you will not ask Me anything. Amen, amen, I say to you, whatever you will ask the Father in My Name, He will give *it* to you.

24 "Until now you have not asked for anything in My Name; ask, and you will receive, that your joy may be made full.

25 "These things I have spoken to you in figures; an hour is coming when I will no longer speak to you in figures, but will tell you openly of the Father.

26 "In that day you will ask in My Name, and I do not say to you that I *Myself* will ask the Father about you;

27 "for the Father Himself loves you, because you have loved Me, and have believed that I *Myself* came from the Father.

28 "I came from the Father, and have come into the world; I am leaving the world again and going to the Father."

Christ acknowledges that for now, their perplexity remains. But soon all will be clear. Now they want to ask Him many questions, but **in that day** which is soon coming, they **will not ask** Him **anything**. Now they are dependent on Him for teaching from God. But soon enough, they will have their own access to God, and **whatever** they **ask the Father in** His **Name**, the Father will **give** *it* to them. **Until now**, they have **not asked** God **for anything in** His **Name**, but have relied entirely upon Jesus. Now they may **ask**, and they will **receive** from God, **that** their **joy may be made full**.

These things He has **spoken** to them **in figures** and parables, for He cannot yet speak openly of the nature of the Kingdom. Until the Cross and Resurrection, they are in no position to understand the spiritual and hidden nature of the Kingdom. But soon they will be. **An hour is coming when** He **will no longer speak** to them **in** such **figures**, but will **tell** them **openly of the Father** and the Kingdom. After the Resurrection, for forty days, He will teach them plainly about the Kingdom of God and the Church (Acts 1:3).

In that day, they will **ask** God for themselves **in Jesus' Name**. He does **not say** to them that He will **ask the Father about** them or intercede on their behalf, as if they could not ask God for truth themselves. This will then be unnecessary, for the Father Himself loves them and will teach them truth. And **the Father loves** them because of their relationship to Jesus as His disciples—**because** they **have loved** Jesus **and believed that** He **came from the Father.** And not only did He **come from the Father** and enter **into the world,** He will also be **leaving the world again and going** back **to the Father** in His glorious Ascension (compare 20:17).

> ঌ ঌ ঌ ঌ ঌ
>
> 29 His disciples say, "Behold, now You are speaking openly and are no longer talking in figures.
> 30 "Now we know that You know all things and You have no need for anyone to ask You. By this we believe that You came from God."
> 31 Jesus answered them, "Do you now believe?
> 32 "Behold, an hour is coming and has come, for each one to be scattered to his own *place*, and to leave Me alone; and I am not alone, because the Father is with Me.
> 33 "These things I have spoken to you, that in Me you may have peace. In the world you have tribulation, but have courage! I *Myself* conquered the world."

Here at last the disciples think they understand, and that Christ is **now speaking openly and no longer talking in** obscure **figures.** He spoke about leaving the world and going to the Father, and they take this to mean Christ leaving the world in death, not seeing that He will triumph over death and return to the Father in His resurrected body in the Ascension. The Lord promised a new day would come, in which figures and veiled speech would not be necessary (v. 25). The disciples think that now this new day has come, since now (they think) they understand the Lord. **Now** they **know that** He **knows all things,** for He answered their unspoken question without **anyone** of them having to **ask** it (vv. 17–19). **By this** they **believe that** He **came from God.** That is, they profess their full

285

confidence in Him. This is not simply their confession of faith in Him as Messiah. It is their declaration of unshakable loyalty to Him.

Jesus knows how much they actually know, and how fallible their loyalty really is. He sadly asks if they **now believe** in Him with such tenacity as all that. For **an hour is coming and has come, for each one** of them **to be scattered to his own** *place*, **and to leave Him alone.** For all their profession of loyalty, they are about to abandon Him to His fate. Yet He is **not** truly **alone** or abandoned, **because the Father is with** Him.

This last saying seems to fill them with foreboding again. Some disaster is about to strike that will cause them all to scatter and run in fear back to the safety of their own homes. The Lord adds a final word of assurance. All **these things** He has **spoken** that **in Him they may have peace.** He has not spoken to alarm them, but to give them peace. **In the world,** they will **have tribulation** and affliction, to be sure (Gr. *thlipsis*; the same word used for the pain of childbirth in v. 21). But let them **have courage!** The world, with its tribulation, cannot deprive them of their peace. For He is the One (the pronoun **I** is emphatic) who has **conquered the world.**

§IV.4. Final Prayer for the Disciples

This prayer seems to have been offered by Christ as the conclusion of the supper evening, perhaps after singing the Great *Hallel* hymn that concluded the Passover meal. It sums up and expresses His love for His own (compare 13:1: "having loved His own, He loved them to the end"). After showing His love in preparing them for the things to come by giving them His final instructions (13:31—16:33), He also shows His love for them by praying for them and dedicating Himself to God.

17 1   These things Jesus spoke, and lifting up His eyes to heaven, He said, "Father, the hour has come; glorify Your Son, that the Son may glorify You,

> 2 "even as You gave Him authority over all flesh, that to all whom You have given Him, He may give eternal life.
> 3 "And this is eternal life, that they may know You, the only true God, and Jesus Christ whom You sent.
> 4 "I *Myself* glorified You on the earth, having perfected the work which You gave Me to do.
> 5 "And now, glorify Me beside Yourself, Father, with the glory which I had with You before the world was.

First of all, Christ prays for Himself, for the strength to offer Himself on the Cross—for even in His prayer for Himself, He is concerned only for the salvation of others, of His disciples.

Jesus **spoke** the words of His Passover night discourse, and then **lifting up His eyes to heaven**, prayed to His Father. Lifting up the eyes (and the hands) to heaven was the normal posture for prayer. John specifically mentions this here to stress that this was Christ's sole focus in this hour. Although facing His own torture and death, He is not frightened or concerned with His own well-being, but only with doing the Father's will. His focus is on heaven, since He is soon to return there (compare 13:1: "knowing that He would pass from the world to the Father"). He addresses the Most High God simply as **Father** (in Aramaic *Abba*, or "papa"), with all the confident familiarity of a child to his father.

His prayer for Himself now that **the hour** of His arrest and death **has come** and is upon Him is that the Father might **glorify** the **Son**. That is, Jesus prays for strength to carry out the Father's will by dying on the Cross, for this death is the way in which the Son will be glorified. In the Son's glorification, the Father will be glorified too, since the Father and the Son are one. By being glorified on the Cross, **the Son** will **glorify** the Father.

This is consistent with the plan of the Father up to that point. **Even as** God **gave** Jesus **authority over all flesh**, to **give** to any who would follow the Son the gift of **eternal life**, so God is asked now to

give Jesus this gift of strength also. God has given Him authority as
life-giver throughout His ministry; let Him now give Him power
not to shrink from His work of self-offering, that He might finish
His work of giving life. For it is only in this way that men can truly
know God and experience the eternal life which He alone can give
to men. Indeed, to **know** God *is* **eternal life**—and this knowledge
comes only through knowing **Jesus Christ** whom God **sent**.

Christ then prays that the Father will **glorify** Him **beside** Himself **with the glory which** He had with Him **before the world was**.
Prior to His Incarnation through the Virgin, the eternal Word shared
the heavenly glory of the eternal Father. Christ prays that such glory
might be restored to Him after He has fully **glorified** the Father **on
the earth** through His death on the Cross and **perfected the work
which** He **gave** Him **to do**. The humiliation and weakness He endured throughout His earthly sojourn were not to last forever, but
were always meant to give way to the restoration of the glory proper
to Him as the eternal Word.

> ൠ ൠ ൠ ൠ ൠ
>
> 6 "I manifested Your Name to the men whom
> You gave Me from the world; Yours they were,
> and You gave them to Me, and they have kept
> Your Word.
> 7 "Now they know that all things that You have
> given Me are from You,
> 8 "for the sayings which You gave Me I have given
> to them, and they themselves received *them* and
> truly know that I came from You, and they be-
> lieved that You *Yourself* sent Me.

Next, Christ prays for His disciples especially. He begins by assuring the Father that these are worthy of His blessing and protection. Christ **manifested** the Father's **Name** to those **men whom** He
gave Him **from the world**. They were truly the Father's possession
(**Yours they were**), in that they loved the Father and sought to follow

the Father's will, being taught by Him (compare 6:45). The Father indeed **gave them** to His Son to be the Son's possession as disciples and to **keep** the **Word** and teaching which the Father gave the Son. This they have done. They now no longer belong to the world, having been separated from the world by the Word and teaching of Jesus. They now **know that all things** that the Son teaches are truly from the Father, for the Son has **given** those **sayings** to them, and they faithfully **received** *them* and **truly know** that the Son teaches with divine authority.

ॐ ॐ ॐ ॐ ॐ

9   "I *Myself* ask about them; I do not ask about the world, but about the ones whom You have given Me, for they are Yours;

10 "and all things that are Mine are Yours, and Yours are Mine, and I have been glorified in them.

Christ stresses in His prayer that He **asks** the Father **about them**, that God bless them. Christ's concern here is **not** focused on or **about the world** which rejects Him. He asks blessing only for **the ones whom** the Father **has given** Him, for they belong to God (**for they are Yours**). Christ only asks that God should bless His own! Indeed, all things that God has also belong to Christ, since all these are jointly shared (**all things that are Mine are Yours, and Yours are Mine**), and Christ has **been glorified** in the disciples. So, in blessing them, the Father will glorify His Son also.

ॐ ॐ ॐ ॐ ॐ

11 "And I am no longer in the world, and they themselves are in the world, and I *Myself* am coming to You. Holy Father, keep them in Your Name, which You have given Me, that they may be one, even as We *Ourselves* are.

Christ especially asks that the Father keep His disciples from the power of the Evil One. While Christ was in the world, He kept them safe, like a Good Shepherd protecting His beloved flock (10:28). But now He is **no longer in the world**, but is **coming to the Father**, even though **they themselves** still have to remain **in the world**. Christ therefore asks the **Father** (who is **holy** and who therefore will delight to keep them holy as well) to **keep them** in His **Name**—this same Name **which** He has **given** to Christ. If the Father will do that, the disciples will **be one, even as** the Father and the Son are one.

By *Name*, Christ means the manifested power of God which the Father publicly revealed through the Son as a revelation of His faithfulness and love. In Psalm 20:1 and 54:1, we have the concept of the "Name" of God as the manifestation of His power on earth ("Save me, O God, by Your Name. . . . May the Name of the God of Jacob protect you"). The Father had given His Name to Jesus in that Jesus had manifested the power of the Father through His miracles. Christ here prays that His disciples would be kept by the Father in this Name—that the Father would powerfully preserve them, even as Jesus had.

If the Father will do this, the disciples will be one, even as the Father and the Son are one. This unity refers to the unity of love that exists between the Father and the Son, not to the consubstantial unity shared by the Persons of the Holy Trinity. If God will protect them from the world, the disciples will remain together, sharing the unity of love, remaining separate from the world.

ॐ ॐ ॐ ॐ ॐ

12 "While I was with them, I *Myself* was keeping them in Your Name which You have given Me, and I guarded *them*, and none of them was destroyed but the son of destruction, that the Scripture might be fulfilled.

13 "But now I am coming to You, and these things

> I speak in the world, that they may have My joy made full in themselves.

While Jesus was still **with them** during His ministry, He **was keeping them** and **guarded** *them*. Because of Christ's watchfulness and love, **none of them was destroyed** (Gr. *apollumi*) **but the son of destruction** (Gr. *apoleia*, cognate with *apollumi*), who had to be destroyed in order **that the Scripture might be fulfilled.** That is, all His disciples were preserved from the Evil One—all except Judas, the traitor. The lost one, of course, must be lost, for the Scripture prophesied the doom of the traitor. Christ is perhaps thinking of such passages as Psalm 109. In this passage, the one who "repaid evil for my love" (Ps. 109:5) receives such curses as "let a Satan [or Adversary] stand at his right hand; when he is judged, let him come forth guilty . . . his office let another take" (Ps. 109:6–8). (In Acts 1:20, this psalm is applied to Judas.) Christ here says that all that *could* be preserved *were* preserved.

But now He can preserve them thus no longer, for He is **coming** to the Father. He now wants to **speak these things in the world** and pray for them that they might have His **joy made full in themselves.** If the Father will preserve them by His Name and power, they will be preserved in the joy of united love. For in keeping the commandment to love is fullness of joy (15:11).

ॐ ॐ ॐ ॐ ॐ

14 "I *Myself* have given them Your Word, and the world has hated them, because they are not from the world, even as I *Myself* am not from the world.

15 "I do not ask that You take them away from the world, but that You keep them from the Evil One.

Christ had **given** the disciples the Father's **Word**, all of His teaching, and they received it faithfully. That is why **the world has hated**

them, because they are now **not from the world** any longer, any more than Jesus Himself was **from the world**. But though His disciples must remain behind to face cruelty and persecution from the world, Jesus does **not ask** that God **take them away from the world** and spare them that persecution. Rather, He simply asks that God **keep them from** the power of **the Evil One**. The Lord refers here to the power of Satan to divide the disciples, to sow discord and hatred and to tear down their love for one another. By the power of the Father, His followers are to remain united in love.

ॐ ॐ ॐ ॐ ॐ

16 "They are not from the world, even as I *Myself* am not from the world.

17 "Sanctify them in the truth; Your Word is truth.

18 "As You sent Me into the world, I *Myself* also sent them into the world.

19 "And for them I *Myself* sanctify Myself, that they themselves also may be sanctified in truth.

The disciples are now no longer **from the world**, the Lord repeats (compare v. 14), any more than Jesus Himself is. Therefore He asks the Father to **sanctify them in the truth** of His **Word**. By *sanctify* (Gr. *agiazo*, cognate with the word "holy," Gr. *agios*), the Lord means to make them holy, separate from the world. This separation is to be accomplished by His truth, the Word of teaching which He gave them. If they will abide in that, they will indeed be separate from the world, wholly dedicated to the Father. Furthermore, this dedication is thought of in terms of self-oblation and self-offering. One is **sanctified** in that one is prepared to be martyred for the sake of God. This willingness to die for the truth shows that one truly does not belong to the world, but to God.

This dedication is seen most clearly in the example of Christ. He **sanctifies** Himself **for them**, preparing to die on the Cross for the will of the Father. (Compare Deut. 15:19 LXX, which speaks of sacrifices being "sanctified" or consecrated to God.) By this saving self-offering, the disciples also will **themselves** be **sanctified in truth**, separated from the world and willing to make themselves living sacrifices to the Father. For they must follow in the path He will blaze. **As the Father sent Him into the world**, so Jesus will **also send them into the world**. They must carry out the same mission He was given and walk in the same steps. He is the saving and eternal Sacrifice to God, and they must also make offerings of themselves to the Father (compare Rom. 12:1). Their self-dedication is thus the fruit of His own saving self-dedication.

> ৯৯ ৯৯ ৯৯ ৯৯ ৯৯
>
> 20 "I do not ask about these alone, but also about the ones who believe in Me through their Word;
>
> 21 "that they may all be one, even as You *Yourself*, Father, *are* in Me and I *Myself* in You, that they themselves also may be in Us, that the world may believe that You *Yourself* sent Me.
>
> 22 "And the glory which You have given Me I have given to them, that they may be one, just as We *Ourselves are* one;
>
> 23 "I *Myself* in them, and You *Yourself* in Me, that they may be perfected in one, that the world may know that You *Yourself* sent Me, and loved them, even as You loved Me.

Finally, Christ prays for the Church throughout all the age. His prayer is not just about the Eleven alone, but **also about the ones who** will **believe in** Him **through their Word**. The unity and love that exist among the Eleven as they sit at table during that Passover night are to be given, by the Father's power, to all their future converts as well. The result is that they will **all be one, even as** the Father is one in the Son and the Son in the Father. They too will also be one in them, sharing the mutual love and unity that eternally exist between the Persons of the Holy Trinity. For if that love and unity remain, then **the world** will **believe** that the Father **sent** the Son to be the world's Savior (compare 13:35).

This longed-for unity is also effected by **the glory which** God **gave** to the Son, which the Son in turn **has given** to His Church. Through this glory they will all **be one, just as** the Father and the Son are **one**. What is this glory? St. John Chrysostom (in his *Homily 82* on John) says it consists of "miracles, teachings, and that they should be of one soul." That is, the Church will be enabled by Christ to do His works and proclaim His truth. The Church is thus to be His hands and His mouth in the world. More than this, the Church will abide as one family, united in love—which, Chrysostom goes on to say, is "greater even than miracles." Thus, the authority and transforming power of the Church are to be a spur and incentive to unity—one should behold such miracles and fear to divide such seamless unity by the sin of schism. The result will be that Jesus will be in His Church, even as the Father is in Jesus (**I in them, and You in Me**), and through this indwelling of Father and Son in the midst of His people (compare 14:23, which speaks of Them making Their dwelling-place with the disciples), the Church will be **perfected in one** (Gr. *teleioo*) and will reach its goal (Gr. *telos*) of unity. (The word *teleioo* is used in v. 4, where it describes Christ's finishing His work and accomplishing His goal.) Then **the world** will **know** that the Father **sent** the Son and **loved** the Church, **even as** He **loved** Jesus. The Church's glorious unity will demonstrate to all that the Church is of God, even as Jesus is.

ᘓ   ᘓ   ᘓ   ᘓ   ᘓ

24 "Father, I want that those also whom You have given Me be with Me where I *Myself* am, that they may observe My glory, which You have given Me, for You loved Me before *the* foundation of *the* world.

25 "Righteous Father, the world indeed has not known You, but I *Myself* have known You, and these have known that You *Yourself* sent Me,

26 "and I have made Your Name known to them,

> and will make *it* known, that the love with
> which You loved Me may be in them, and I
> *Myself* in them."

The Lord has one last petition for His Church throughout the age. He **wants that those whom** the Father **had given** Him should **be with** Him **where** He is, beside the throne of the Father, to **observe** His heavenly **glory**. The Father **loved** the Son **before** *the* **foundation of** *the* **world** and is about to manifest that love by restoring His former glory to Him. The Lord Jesus, bound to His own disciples with the cords of love, cannot bear to be separated from them. That is why His disciples are taken to heaven upon the death of the body and do not await the final resurrection in Sheol (the land of the dead) along with the rest of the world. Just as a loving parent cannot bear to be separated from his children, so Christ wants His own to be with Him. For by **observing** His **glory**, they share it as well. The word used for *want* is the Greek *thelo*, used not only for wanting and desiring, but also for willing. The use of this word here shows how strong Christ's desire is to have His beloved disciples with Him as He reigns at the right hand of the Father.

This desire is all the more intense because **the world** (in its unrighteousness) **has not known** the **Righteous Father**; only the Son has **known** Him. The world is not worthy therefore of seeing the glory of the Father in heaven. These disciples, however, have **known** that the Son was **sent** by the Father, and therefore out of the whole world, these disciples are worthy of observing the Son's heavenly glory. Christ has **made** the Father's **Name** (that is, His power) **known to them** through His miracles, and He **will** continue to **make** *it* **known** through His embrace of death on the Cross. It is through this self-dedication and saving death that **the love** with which the Father **loved** the Son **may be in them**, and the Son Himself **in them**. That is, Christ will not reject the approaching Cross, but will carry out the Father's will. Through this, the Church will share the love between the Father and the Son (compare vv. 11, 21) and remain in saving unity, knowing the Presence of Jesus within her.

In reflecting on the unity of the Church, which is the subject of

Christ's prayer and His will for His Church, we see that this unity is not so much something the *Church must create* (such as, for example, through ecumenism), but something *God sovereignly bestows as a gift*. That is, this unity is an objective reality, an inalienable mark of the Church, a characteristic without which the Church ceases to be the Church. It exists because Christ has prayed for it. It is not a coming reality, but a present fact. To be sure, there is an ethical component to it, in that human beings in the Church must strive to preserve this unity (compare St. Paul's exhortation in Eph. 4:3 to "keep the unity of the Spirit in the bond of peace"). But the basic thought here is that this unity is an organic reality, something the Body of the Church already has within it precisely because that Body is alive. We are thus called to "keep" that reality, to preserve it, not to create it. It does not need to be created, for it is already there. Our ethical task as Christians is to abide in the unity that already exists and to avoid schism, to remain in the one and already united Body. For to leave that fellowship of love is to leave the unity of the Trinity, to abandon the Father and the Son to return once more to the world.

❧ V ☙

THE PASSION
(18:1—19:42)

§V.1. The Arrest

> ☙ ☙ ☙ ☙ ☙
>
> **18** 1 When Jesus had spoken these words, He went out with His disciples across the Kidron ravine, where there was a garden, into which He Himself entered and His disciples.

After **Jesus had spoken these words** and all was done at that meal, **He went out** of the room **with His disciples** and went **across the Kidron ravine.** Assuming that the place of the supper was in the southwest part of the city, that means He went northeast towards the Temple and crossed the narrow ravine on the east side of the city. This was a wadi whose flowing winter stream was dry in the summer. On the other side, on the slopes of the Mount of Olives, was **a garden**, probably enclosed by a low wall (named by Matthew and Mark as Gethsemane). It is possible that this was owned by a rich supporter of Jesus who offered it to Him and His disciples as a place for private prayer and reflection, and which they used whenever in Jerusalem. Wanting a place for uninterrupted prayer (compare Matt. 26:36), Jesus **entered** this enclosure along with **His disciples.**

From the other Gospels, we know that Jesus entered this garden to pour out an agony of prayer to the Father (Matt. 26:37–39).

This agonized prayer is not narrated by St. John. Not only does he presuppose familiarity with this on the part of his readers (and so does not need to narrate it again), but it also forms no part of his purpose. John is more concerned to show that Christ's arrest and death were voluntary, and that He was never at the mercy of circumstances. Narrating His inner struggle at this point would contribute nothing to this purpose, and John passes over it in silence.

ॐ ॐ ॐ ॐ ॐ

2 Now Judas also, who was delivering Him up, knew the place, for Jesus had often gathered there with His disciples.
3 Judas therefore, having received the cohort, and attendants from the chief priests and the Pharisees, comes there with lanterns and lamps and weapons.

Judas, who was even then **delivering Him up** to His foes, **knew the place, for Jesus had often gathered there with His disciples** on their previous visits to Jerusalem. Judas knew that after the supper, they were all to meet in this garden, as they had before. It was the perfect location for his evil purpose, for it was private, and Jesus could be arrested with a minimum of outside attention or interference. Avoiding the attention of the Passover crowd was a big part of the total plan, for all Jesus' foes feared that the festal crowd would riot if they tried to arrest Him publicly (see Mark 14:2). The garden's enclosing walls would not only make it difficult for Him and His disciples to escape (for they were cornered in the enclosed space), but the walls would keep out the prying eyes of His supporters.

Judas is the guide and leader of the arresting group. After Judas went out of the room where Jesus had His final supper, he went to collect that prearranged posse. This was a mixed group, consisting of a Roman **cohort** as well as **attendants** and Temple police **from the chief priests and the Pharisees.** (Were some of these Temple police the same men who were sent to arrest Him on a previous occasion? Compare 7:32.) They expected armed resistance and came prepared for anything, arming themselves with **lanterns, lamps** (that is, torches), and **weapons** of swords and wooden clubs (Mark 14:43). The Jews among that posse perhaps remembered a similar posse sent to arrest the prophet Elijah, and the doom that fell upon them as a result (2 Kin. 1:9–10). It was not just armed resistance from the disciples they feared (the disciples, after all, were fishermen, not trained soldiers), but the more intangible threat of confronting One who was known for His miraculous power.

❧ ❧ ❧ ❧ ❧

4 Jesus therefore, knowing all the things that were coming upon Him, went out and says to them, "Whom do you seek?"

5 They answered Him, "Jesus the Nazarene." He says to them, "I *Myself* am *He*." And Judas also who was delivering Him up was standing with them.

6 When therefore He said to them, "I *Myself* am *He*," they went backward and fell on the ground.

7 Again therefore He asked them, "Whom do you seek?" And they said, "Jesus the Nazarene."

8 Jesus answered, "I told you I *Myself* am *He*; if therefore you seek Me, let these go away,"

9 that the word might be fulfilled which He spoke, "Of those whom You have given Me, I did not lose any of them."

John once again stresses Jesus' complete foreknowledge of the coming events (see also 13:1, 3; 16:30). He went into that enclosed corner from which there was no escape **knowing all the things that were coming upon Him**. His foes did not surprise Him, as they imagined. More than that, He **went out** of the garden through the enclosure's opening to meet them at the door, saying to them,

"**Whom do you seek?**" They did not find Him; He found them!

The arresting party answered Him, "**Jesus the Nazarene,**" no doubt thinking that He was someone else, perhaps the owner of the garden or one of His supporters. They seem to have expected Jesus to be hiding in some darkened corner, or at least seeking such a corner as He saw the approach of their torches, not striding forward boldly to meet them. When He announced confidently, "I *Myself* am *He*," with all the sovereign authority of God Himself (the Gr. is *ego eimi*, the same words He used when claiming to be God in 8:58), **they went backward and fell on the ground.** They came to the garden fearful of His authority as a true prophet, gripping their weapons and torches tightly in their nervousness, prepared to run if the fire of divine retribution started to fall. When this man emerged unexpectedly from the shadows and strode toward them, identifying Himself as the Nazarene, they were startled and unnerved, and jumped backward, falling over each other.

Jesus **again asked them** (after they got up hurriedly and recovered their torches and weapons!) **whom** they were **seeking.** They answered again, "**Jesus the Nazarene.**" Jesus answered again, "**I told you I** *Myself* **am** *He*; **if therefore you seek Me, let these go away.**" In their confusion and fear, the arresting party did not collect itself to jump on Jesus. Rather, Jesus retained the initiative. He asked the questions, not they! It is almost as if He had to force them to arrest Him. By focusing on this detail of the arrest, St. John shows how Jesus' arrest and death were indeed voluntary, and how He remained in command of the situation.

Even to the end, His concern was not for Himself, but for His own. This is why Jesus asked them who they were looking for—He knew they would answer that they were looking for Him. By evoking this answer, the Lord could use it, as an utterance from their own mouths, to make them take Him alone and let the others go. They said they were looking for Jesus—here He was! Their business was with Him, not with the disciples.

St. John also adds that this **fulfilled** the **word** which Jesus previously **spoke** to the Father in prayer (17:12). He had promised that **of those whom** the Father had **given** Him, He **did not lose any of**

them, and here He was fulfilling that word. For even as prophecy of necessity was fulfilled, so Jesus' word must be fulfilled also.

Throughout this, Judas **was standing with** the arresting party, showing by this how he now sided with Jesus' foes. It seems that it was after this exchange that he came forward to identify Jesus to the posse by greeting Him with a kiss (compare Matt. 26:47–50). Even after Jesus' words, this was thought necessary by the arresting party. Anyone could claim to be Jesus; how could they know that this confident stranger in the dark was not one of His disciples, falsely claiming to be Jesus so that the real Jesus could make His escape? So it was that Judas was required to make the identification. It was dark, with much movement and confusion. Pointing was not good enough. Judas was required to make the close physical contact so they could arrest the right man. This was, they thought, their one and only chance!

> ꙮ ꙮ ꙮ ꙮ ꙮ
>
> 10 Simon Peter therefore, having a sword, drew it and hit the high priest's slave and cut off his right ear; and the slave's name was Malchus.
> 11 Jesus therefore said to Peter, "Put the sword into the sheath; the cup which the Father has given Me, shall I not drink it?"

Simon Peter over the supper had pledged his loyalty to Christ, boasting that he was willing even to die for Him (13:37). Along with James and John, he had been drowsy and nodded off to sleep while His Master prayed in the garden (Matt. 26:40, 43, 45). The sudden arrival of an armed guard startled him wide awake, and he was prepared to make good his boast. **Having a sword** (one of the two swords they had found during the supper; see Luke 22:38), he **drew it** from its sheath and came out swinging. He no doubt intended to take off the head of **the high priest's slave** (who was probably armed and in the forefront of the posse). Being a better fisherman than a soldier, he merely **cut off his right ear** instead.

With an eyewitness' flair for detail, John adds **the slave's name was Malchus**. Did he know this because Malchus's friends in the posse cried out his name when he was hit? Or was it because one of Malchus's relatives used his name when challenging Peter at the charcoal-fire later that night (18:26)?

In defending his Master with the sword, Peter was still assuming that Christ's Kingdom would be of this world (compare 18:36), but this was not the case. The Kingdom of love could never be promoted with violence. **Jesus** therefore rebuked **Peter** for this act, saying, "**Put the sword into the sheath.**" **The Father** Himself had **given** Christ this **cup** of suffering—how could it be then that He would **not drink it**? He would allow Himself to be arrested and given over to death, since this was His Father's will.

ॐ ॐ ॐ ॐ ॐ

12 Therefore the cohort and the commander and the attendants of the Jews took Jesus and bound Him,

13 and led Him to Annas first, for he was father-in-law of Caiaphas, who was high priest that year.

14 Now Caiaphas was the one who had counseled the Jews that it was advantageous for one man to die for the people.

Accordingly then, **the cohort and the commander and the attendants** from the Temple police **took Jesus and bound Him**. They **led Him to Annas first**. Annas was formerly high priest, but like others, had been deposed by the Romans. Five of his sons had been appointed, one after the other, to that office, and **that** fateful **year** his son-in-law Caiaphas was high priest. Though no longer the official high priest, Annas was still very much the head of the dynasty and the power behind the throne. In the highly political world of Jewish Temple authorities, it had already been arranged that Jesus, once arrested, would be brought first to Annas. He is described as

father-in-law of Caiaphas, who is himself described as **the one who had counseled the Jews that it was advantageous for one man to die for the people.** This being the case, it was apparent that no fair hearing could be expected that night. The death of Jesus had already been prearranged among the powers manipulating the Sanhedrin.

§V.2. The Trial

In the other Gospels, we are told that Christ stands before the Great Sanhedrin (presided over by Caiaphas, the current high priest) and is condemned by them before being sent to Pilate. That is, Christ is tried, condemned, and disowned by Israel as the prelude to His official, legal trial by the Romans (who alone had authority to enforce the death penalty).

St. John once again assumes his readers' familiarity with this Synoptic Gospel tradition. Though he mentions Christ's being sent to Caiaphas for trial and condemnation by the Sanhedrin (in 18:24), he skips over that trial itself and jumps straight into Christ's transfer from the Sanhedrin to Pilate (18:28). In place of Christ's trial before Caiaphas, John narrates Christ's initial interrogation by the high priest emeritus, Annas.

In view of the fact that St. John is content to omit the trial before Caiaphas, why narrate the interrogation before Annas at all? It would appear that John does this for two reasons. Firstly, it provides the backdrop for Peter's denials. Though these denials actually took place *after* the interrogation before Annas and during the trial before Caiaphas, the denials are still narrated within the framework of that interrogation. This is to compare the inconstancy of Peter with the hostility of Christ's foes, and to show how Christ was let down by *everyone*, friend and foe alike. Behind closed doors, He was condemned by His foes (both before Annas and then by Caiaphas and the Sanhedrin), and outside those doors He was denied by His friend. The hostile interrogation before Annas therefore forms the counterpoint to Peter's denials and shows them to be of a piece with the rest of Christ's rejection by Israel.

Secondly, St. John narrates the interrogation before Annas rather than the trial before Caiaphas because the trial portrays Christ more as the victim of circumstances. He remains silent throughout (Matt. 26:63) and is physically abused at its conclusion (Matt. 26:67–68). John has less interest in showing Christ as the passive victim than he has in revealing Him as maintaining a serene composure and control throughout. Christ's interrogation before Annas was brief, but it was during this exchange that He more successfully defended Himself and resisted being bullied (John 18:21, 23). (It is for this reason too that John narrates Christ's startling effect on the soldiers in vv. 5–6 at the time of His arrest, rather than His being identified by Judas, for that identification shows Him to be passive rather than active.)

꒰ꕤ꒱ ꒰ꕤ꒱ ꒰ꕤ꒱ ꒰ꕤ꒱ ꒰ꕤ꒱

15 Simon Peter was following Jesus, and so was another disciple. Now that disciple was known to the high priest, and entered with Jesus into the court of the high priest.

16 But Peter stood at the door outside. Therefore the other disciple, who was known to the high priest, went out and spoke to the doorkeeper and brought in Peter.

17 The servant-girl doorkeeper therefore says to Peter, "Are you *yourself* one of this man's disciples?" That one says, "I am not."

18 Now the slaves and the attendants stood there, having made a charcoal-fire, for it was cold and they were warming themselves, and Peter also was with them, standing and warming himself.

St. John begins his narration of that final night with the story of Peter's denials. **Simon Peter was following Jesus,** intent no doubt on finding some way to help his Master. To this end, he was determined to avoid being arrested himself, since then he would be in no position to help Jesus further. Jesus had been taken **into the court of the high priest**. That high priest was previously identified (in v. 13) as Caiaphas, and so these denials actually took place before the (later) trial before Caiaphas and the Sanhedrin. (The matter is made less clear by the fact that Annas is also styled "high priest" in vv. 19–22 because of his having once been the high priest—which was, technically, a lifetime appointment.)

John draws the curtain aside a bit to reveal his own part in those events. Along with Jesus was **another disciple**—that is, John himself. Because he was **known to the high priest** (did his family deliver fish to them through their fishing business?), he was on a first-name basis with the doorkeeper, and was more easily admitted. Peter, however, **stood at the door outside** until John **spoke to the doorkeeper and brought in Peter**. John mentions this in the same way as he later mentions the precise movements of Peter and himself as they ran to the tomb (20:4–8). That is, John considers that he is giving testimony in an almost legal way and takes care to be absolutely precise.

On the way in, **the servant-girl doorkeeper** seems to recognize Peter as one of Jesus' disciples. (It seems likely that she knew that John was His disciple as well, but that her prior friendship with him was enough to seal her lips. Peter, however, had no such diplomatic immunity! Almost automatically, she asks him as he brushes by her, **"Are you** *yourself* **one of this man's disciples?"** The question in the Greek is phrased in such a way as to elicit a negative response: "*You* are this man's disciple, are you?" With brusque tones and in a low voice, he reflexively denies it, saying, **"I am not."** The Greek is a mere two words, *ouk eimi*, rendered idiomatically perhaps as "Not me!" Peter is not thinking in terms of meeting a direct challenge, nor in terms of confessing Christ before men. His attention is on what is happening to Jesus inside, and he simply wants to finish getting in.

He got as far in as he could. That is, he was with **the slaves and the attendants** who **stood there** in the outer court. They had made **a charcoal-fire** burning in a brazier, **for it was cold** that night, and they stood around it **warming themselves**. It was perhaps about midnight or somewhat after. Peter was tired (he had been dozing as Christ prayed in Gethsemane) and his body temperature had dropped. Accordingly, he joined the others at the fire and stood with them, **warming himself**. It would prove not to be a safe location.

ॐ ॐ ॐ ॐ ॐ

19 The high priest therefore asked Jesus about His disciples and about His teaching.

20 Jesus answered him, "I *Myself* have spoken openly to the world; I *Myself* always taught in synagogue and in the Temple, where all the Jews come together, and I spoke nothing in secret.

21 "Why do you ask Me? Ask the ones who have heard what I spoke to them; behold, these know what I *Myself* said."

22 And when He had said these things, one of the attendants standing by gave Jesus a slap, saying, "Do You answer the high priest in this way?"

23 Jesus answered him, "If I have spoken wrongly, witness to the wrong, but if *I have spoken* well, why do you beat Me?"

24 Annas therefore sent Him bound to Caiaphas the high priest.

St. John then narrates Christ's interrogation before Annas, picking up the thread of this story from v. 13. Annas (called **the high priest** because he once held that office) **asked Jesus about His disciples and about His teaching**. Annas was not asking because he wanted to learn; he was looking for ammunition to use against Jesus. So, when he asked Jesus about His disciples, he probably was hoping He would admit to their connections with the anti-Roman Zealot movement (one of them was a former Zealot; compare Luke 6:15);

when he asked about His teaching, he probably was hoping to find hints of a messianic plot to overthrow Rome.

Jesus refuses to provide him with the hoped-for ammunition. His public teaching contained no hint of future plans to violently overthrow Roman power. He had **spoken openly to the world**; He had **always taught in synagogue and in the Temple, where all the Jews come together.** There were no hidden plans, no secret agendas. He **spoke nothing in secret.** Annas does not have to take His word for this. He is invited to **ask the ones who have heard** what Jesus **spoke to them; behold, these know what** He **said.** They can corroborate the truth of Jesus' words.

Such upfront and forthright refusal to be bullied did not go down well. It was hoped that a private interrogation before Annas, the power behind the Temple authorities, would cow the Nazarene, or at least provoke Him into making some ill-advised reply. But Jesus was refusing to be bullied. So, **when He had said these things, one of the attendants standing by gave Jesus a slap**—probably across the face—and said, **"Do You answer the high priest in this way?"** That is, he accuses Jesus of being disrespectful and insubordinate. It was ever thus. A bully cannot abide being stood up to.

Jesus still refuses to be cowed. Though slapped in hostility, He does not retaliate in anger, nor respond with hostility. He maintains His inner peace and composure and simply says, **"If I have spoken wrongly, witness to the wrong, but if** *I have spoken* **well, why do you beat Me?"** That is, He calls the erring attendant to account and challenges him to repent.

The interrogation was proving to be fruitless, for they had not gained anything they could use before Pilate to substantiate a charge of treason. Giving up the attempt, **Annas therefore sent Him bound to Caiaphas the high priest.** Perhaps the official trial before the Great Sanhedrin could come up with something.

ॐ ॐ ॐ ॐ ॐ

25 Now Simon Peter was standing and warming himself. They said therefore to him, "Are you

> *yourself* not also one of His disciples?" That
> one denied and said, "I am not."
>
> 26 One of the slaves of the high priest, being a
> relative of the one whose ear Peter cut off, says,
> "Did I *myself* not see you in the garden with
> Him?"
>
> 27 Peter therefore denied again, and immediately
> a rooster sounded.

After narrating this brief scene, St. John returns again to the
fate of **Simon Peter** some time later. As he **was standing and warming himself** by the brazier, his face could be dimly seen in the light
of the fire. A number of people thought Peter's face was all too
familiar, and they asked, **"Are you *yourself* not also one of His disciples?"** Once again, the form of the Greek looks for a negative
answer, for this was the last place they had expected to find His
disciples. **That one** (Peter is referred to in this emphatic way—as
that one who was being truly identified) denied Christ once again,
with a terse **"I am not."**

This time, however, the crowd of bystanders was not so easily
put off. For one of them was **a relative of the one whose ear Peter
cut off** in the garden a few hours earlier. He is described as **one of
the slaves,** showing that although Jesus can withstand pressure from
the high priest Annas himself, Peter cannot withstand even the challenges of slaves and servant-girls. This slave, with dawning recognition breaking over his features, demands, **"Did I *myself* not see you
in the garden with Him?"** Peter, of course, remembers only too
clearly which garden he means, and is desperate to avoid detection
and arrest. He **denied again** (with a string of oaths; compare Matt.
26:74), and **immediately a rooster sounded.** St. John does not carry
his narration further. His readers knew the significance of that sound,
even as its significance crashed in upon Peter when the cock began
its continuous crowing at about 3:00 A.M. Out of consideration and
love for his friend, St. John draws a veil over the rest of Peter's actions that night (compare Matt. 26:75). Peter is not heard from
again in the narrative until the morning of the Resurrection.

ᖴᐠ EXCURSUS

ON PETER'S DENIALS

A number of people have attempted a harmony of the denials of Peter from the four Gospels. The Lord speaks of Peter denying Him three times (Matt. 26:34; John 13:38), and the attempt is made to count the three denials, identifying which denial in the Synoptic Gospels corresponds to which denial in John.

The self-assigned task is perhaps futile in being overly precise, for there were more than three denials that night. When the Lord spoke of Peter denying "three times," He meant "three" in the sense of "repeatedly." Compare Ps. 62:11: "once God has spoken, twice I have heard this"—i.e. "repeatedly I have heard this." Or compare Amos 2:1: "for three transgressions and for four I will not revoke punishment"—i.e. "for repeated transgressions I will not revoke it." The number three in Jesus' prediction is not used with mathematical exactitude. In fact, Peter spent that night denying his Lord, and it was this repeated disloyalty that Christ was predicting.

He predicted it would happen early. At the start of the Paschal supper, in the early hours of the evening, Christ predicted Peter's disloyalty (13:36–38). (Matthew and Mark narrate the prediction just prior to their entry into Gethsemane to heighten the ironic cowardice of the flight in the garden; Matt. 26:31f; Mark 14:27f.) At the beginning of the meal, Peter was asserting his constancy—a constancy which he promised would hold, even if that of all the others fell away. Christ replied that such confidence was ill-founded; before morning light, Peter would deny Him repeatedly.

Mark speaks of the rooster crowing *twice* (Mark 14:30). That is, it would happen before the rooster began its usual continuous and relentless crowing about 3:00 A.M. It might emit the odd crowing sound after midnight or so, but 3:00 A.M. was *the* time of cockcrow, when the rooster began its repeated crowing—a sound which Peter could not miss, however intent he might be on other things (such as escaping detection!).

I would suggest the following possible harmony of the four Gospels:

1. Peter first enters the courtyard of the high priest, passing through the door and being addressed by the doorkeeper servant-girl as he enters. He responds to her question, denying the Lord for the first time (John 18:17). (This is not mentioned in the Synoptic accounts.)

2. He then sits by the charcoal-fire to warm himself. One of the servant-girls approaches him as he sits there (a friend of the doorkeeper, possibly put up to it by her?) and again asks if he is not of the Nazarene's followers (Matt. 26:69–70; Mark 14:66–68; Luke 22:56–57; this is not related by John). Feeling unsafe in this present spot, Peter goes out to the outer gateway or vestibule.

3. A little while later (Luke 22:58) he is met again there by another servant-girl, who challenges him, being joined by others. He denies it again, addressing the man most specifically, possibly since the man was the most aggressive in his accusations (Matt. 26:71–72; Mark 14:69–70a; Luke 22:58; this also is not related by John).

4. After about an hour (Luke 22:59), Peter has returned to the charcoal-fire. (The retreat to the gateway did him no good, and there was a larger crowd in the courtyard into which he hoped to blend.) Once again, he is addressed by one of the attendants. He responds, only to have his distinct Galilean accent identified. The other bystanders by the charcoal-fire join in with accusations, and he continues his denials (Matt. 26:73; Mark 14:70b; Luke 22:59; John 18:25).

5. One of those joining in the accusation is a relative of

the man whose ear Peter cut off in the garden. He is especially keen to identify Peter and presses the accusation. The result of all this barrage of accusation, focusing on his undeniable accent and recognition of his face, is that Peter begins to invoke curses on himself if he ever even *knew* Jesus. As he tries to shout down the accusations, the rooster begins his continuous crowing (Matt. 26:74; Mark 14:71–72; Luke 22:60; John 18:26–27).

6. It would seem that the room where the trial is being held is above the courtyard (Mark 14:66), so that when the rooster begins to crow, Jesus is in a position to look around and see Peter surrounded by his tormentors, all dimly illumined by the charcoal brazier. He looks on Peter in compassion. Peter sees this—and realizes the significance of the rooster and of all his words that evening (Luke 22:61). He races from the courtyard, breaks down, and weeps.

༄ ༄ ༄ ༄ ༄

28 They led Jesus therefore from Caiaphas into the Praetorium, and it was early; and they themselves did not enter into the Praetorium that they might not be defiled, but might eat the Passover.

29 Pilate therefore went out to them outside, and says, "What accusation do you bring against this man?"

30 They answered and said to him, "If this man were not doing wrong, we would not have delivered Him up to you."

31 Pilate therefore said to them, "Take Him yourselves and judge Him according to your Law." The Jews said to him, "It is not permitted us to kill anyone,"

> **32** that the word of Jesus might be fulfilled which
> He said, signifying by what kind of death He
> was about to die.

John next narrates the official legal trial of Jesus before Pilate. Pilate was in **the Praetorium**, by which is meant the place the governor used as his temporary residence when he was in Jerusalem. (His permanent residence was in Caesarea.) This was probably the palace of Herod, in the northwest corner of the city, across from the Temple in the eastern part of the city. Courts were customarily open shortly after sunrise. Jesus' Jewish accusers hurried to bring Him to trial before Pilate at dawn's first light, at the first opportunity to have such legal cases tried.

They themselves, however, refused to **enter into the Praetorium** where Pilate sat to receive such cases, **that they might not be defiled, but might eat the Passover.** It was felt by devout Jews that to enter into the dwelling of a pagan brought ceremonial defilement (lasting at least until evening, and sometimes longer). If they entered the pagan premises of the Praetorium, they would be liable to such defilement, and would not be able to procure the obligatory sacrifice (the so-called *Hagigah*) which was to be offered on the day after Passover. (This sacrifice was reckoned as part of the Passover, being part of the required sacrifices that Passover week.) John narrates this detail with superb irony: Jesus' foes were so pious, they refused to contract defilement lest they be disqualified from the day's sacrificial requirement! Such good and devout Jews! In order to accommodate himself to their scruples, **Pilate therefore went out to them outside.**

He began with the usual legal requirement of asking with what the prisoner had been charged and **what accusation** they were **bringing against this man**. The evasive response is meant by John to show how flimsy their case was against Jesus. He was to be charged with treason against the Roman state, with making Himself a king in defiance of Caesar's authority, but they must have felt such a charge would ring somewhat hollow. They respond simply by saying, **"If this man were not doing wrong, we would not have**

delivered Him up to you." They do not make a concrete charge, but take refuge in such generalities as saying that He always does bad things.

Behind these words may possibly lurk a more secretive reference. It may be that the whole thing had been prearranged with Pilate—possibly through Annas or Caiaphas speaking with Pilate privately. Certainly Pilate's assent would have been necessary to gain the Roman cohort sent to arrest Jesus (18:3), and he must have been told about Jesus before that morning. It is possible that Pilate was therefore expecting Jesus to be brought to him at early morning, and that Jesus' accusers were hoping that Pilate would simply condemn Jesus on their say-so, with a minimum of legal formality. Pilate's insistence on due process caught them somewhat off guard, and they accordingly responded lamely to his question by saying if Jesus were not guilty, they would not have brought Him.

Whatever was or was not prearranged, Pilate now has little interest in hearing this case, as St. John makes plain. If the Jews have no substantive charge to bring against this man, but only accuse Him of a bad character, then they should not waste his time. He therefore responds that if that is the case, they should **take** Jesus themselves **and judge Him according to** their own Jewish **Law.** Certain infractions of the Law required flogging in the synagogues (compare Mark 13:9)—if this was one of those cases, let them handle it themselves!

Jesus' foes assure Pilate that this is not one of those cases, but involves a capital offense. It is, they wryly remind the Roman governor, **not permitted** the Jews under Roman occupation **to kill anyone** or to inflict the death penalty themselves. That is a right which Rome reserves to itself. Therefore Pilate must indeed hear this case. If the Romans executed any of the Jews, it was usually by crucifixion, not by the Jewish method of stoning. It was because of this, St. John adds, that Pilate heard the case, not because Pilate himself thought Jesus was a criminal. It was all due to the providence of God, **that the word of Jesus might be fulfilled**, when He was **signifying by what kind of death He was about to die.** Pilate heard the case, John insists, that Jesus might die by crucifixion, as He prophesied (12:32–33). Jesus' word was prophetic, like the Scriptures, and it too must be fulfilled.

> ৵ ৵ ৵ ৵ ৵
>
> 33 Pilate therefore entered again into the Praetorium, and called Jesus and said to Him, "You are the King of the Jews?"
> 34 Jesus answered, "Are you *yourself* saying this from yourself, or did others tell you about Me?"
> 35 Pilate answered, "Am I *myself* a Jew? Your nation and the chief-priests delivered You up to me; what have You done?"

The trial before Pilate was the legal and official one. Christ had been brought before Caiaphas and the Great Sanhedrin during the night (18:24) and been tried and condemned by the Jewish authorities. There He had been found guilty of blasphemously (as they thought) claiming to be the Messiah (Matt. 26:63–66). Such blasphemy made a man liable to death under Jewish Law. But blaspheming the Jewish God was of little consequence to the Romans (who alone could enforce the death penalty in Palestine). What the Romans *did* care about, however, was the threat of insurrection, of treason, of planning to overthrow Roman power. Many Jews considered that when Messiah came, He would do precisely this (even though Jesus Himself had pointedly refused such a role and such an interpretation of messianic redemption). But although Jesus had no intention of opposing Rome, He did claim to be the Messiah.

That was all they needed. The strategy of Jesus' accusers was therefore to portray Him as having claimed to be such a violent and military Messiah and a threat to the Roman power. His accusers knew that He was nothing of the kind, of course, but that was not the point. The point was how to get Rome to execute Jesus. They therefore came with an accusation against Him which, if true, would result in the death penalty.

Pilate entered again into the Praetorium and called Jesus so that he could investigate these charges. He begins by asking Him pointblank if He is guilty, if He is indeed the King of the Jews, the Messiah. This seems to him, however, incredible. He looks at the Nazarene standing before Him and asks incredulously, "**You are the King of the Jews?**" The **You** is emphatic, with the meaning, "*You*—bereft of power, weapons, armies, friends—*You* are this messianic firebrand?" Jesus had been charged with being a dangerous insurrectionist, but this seemed manifestly absurd.

The answer to the question of whether or not He was the Messiah, of course, depended entirely on what one meant by the term "the King of Jews." To the Romans, it could have only a military meaning, and the question would then mean, "Are you planning to defy and overthrow Roman power?" To the Jews, the question could have a more spiritual meaning: "Are you a teacher of truth and a bringer of eternal life?" Jesus therefore answers by asking if Pilate is **saying this from** himself, according to Roman understandings of the title, or if **others**—some Jews—**told** him about Him being King of the Jews, with a Jewish frame of reference.

Pilate derisively responds by asking, "**Am I a Jew?**" That is, obviously he could not care less about any Jewish frame of reference. He had no interest in a merely spiritual Messiah, only in a military one. Moreover, Jesus' own **nation and chief-priests** had **delivered** Him **up** to him. They wouldn't (he thought) have had Him sent on such a charge if all that were at stake was theological philosophy. He must have done something criminal, something smacking of insurrection. Let Him come clean! "**What have You done?**"

࿊ ࿊ ࿊ ࿊ ࿊

36 Jesus answered, "My Kingdom is not from this world. If My Kingdom were from this world, then My attendants would be fighting, that I might not be delivered up to the Jews, but now My Kingdom is not from here."
37 Pilate therefore said to Him, "So You *Yourself*

> are a king?" Jesus answered, "You *yourself* say
> that I am a king. I *Myself* have been born for
> this *reason*, that for this *reason* I have come
> into the world, that I might witness to the
> truth. Everyone who is of the truth hears My
> voice."
> **38** Pilate says to Him, "What is truth?"

Jesus responds by telling Pilate what he needs to know. Pilate is asking if Jesus has been involved in insurrection, and Jesus denies that He has any interest in overthrowing Rome. Indeed, His **Kingdom is not** at all **from this world.** It has nothing to do with armies, wars, secret plots, assassinations. **If** it *were* **from this world,** then He would not be standing before Pilate now! If His interest *were* in violently overthrowing Rome, He would not have so easily surrendered in the first place, but rather His own **attendants** (the apostles) **would** now **be fighting** that He **might not be delivered up to the Jews. But now,** as it is, His **Kingdom** is spiritual, transcendent, and **not from here** at all.

Pilate has trouble following such spiritual concepts. He leaps upon what he is familiar with, as a man of the world. Jesus talks about His Kingdom. If He has a kingdom, then He must be a king! Is He after all admitting the truth of the charge?

Jesus, with sublime composure, responds by agreeing with Pilate that He is indeed a king, saying, **"You** *yourself* **say that I am a king."** In English, this sounds as if Jesus is prevaricating, and avoiding affirming it Himself. It sounds as if He is saying, "You are the one who says I am a king, not Me." But there is no such meaning in the original. To say "the words are yours" is simply the formal and polite way of agreeing with a statement. There is no ambiguity in Jesus' answer in its original context. He affirms that He is a king, and moreover that He was born to be such. It was for this kingship and role that He was **born** and **came into the world,** that He might **witness to the truth.** His role as Messiah, the essence of His Kingdom, is to manifest the truth of God in the midst of the world of half-truths and lies, to shine the light of truth in the darkness. His

Kingship will be recognized and effective—**everyone who is of the truth hears** His **voice** and follows Him.

This talk of truth collides with Pilate's innate sense of worldly cynicism. He asks Jesus, "**What is truth?**" Truth for him is entirely a subjective thing, a pointless debate for philosophers and fools. It can have nothing to do with the real world. Pilate is denying that there is such a thing as objective truth. By implication, he is also saying that he thinks Jesus is an idealistic and deluded fool, a dreamer, someone who is not facing the hard realities of life. And John is not blind to the superlative irony of Pilate's dismissive and contemptuous question. Faced with Him who is the eternal truth of God (14:6), Pilate demands, "What is truth?" The governor is so blind, he cannot see truth when it literally stares him in the face.

ॐ ॐ ॐ ॐ ॐ

39 And having said this, he went out again to the Jews, and says to them, "I *myself* find no guilt in Him. But you have a custom, that I should release one *prisoner* for you at the Passover. Do you wish then that I release for you the King of the Jews?"

40 Therefore they clamored again, saying, "Not this one, but Barabbas!" Now Barabbas was a robber.

Though Pilate is a cynic, he can see that Jesus is no military threat to Rome. He realizes that the charges against Jesus have no substance. He therefore goes **out again to the Jews** waiting outside and delivers his verdict: "I *myself* **find no guilt in Him**," no cause to condemn Him to death. He should obviously be released. Now the Jews **had a custom** that the governor **should release one** *prisoner* for them **at the Passover**. At the major Jewish feast, Rome customarily made a big display of its clemency and declared an amnesty, dropping charges against one Jew to show how merciful and humanitarian Rome really was. Did they **wish** that he do this for Jesus now, and **release** for them **the King of the Jews**? For Pilate the politician, this only made sense. He had to release someone anyway. Jesus was obviously safe for Rome to release. Why not release Jesus!

If Pilate thought the Jews present at the feast would be happy to have one of their own released and would therefore say yes to his offer, he was sadly mistaken. The Jews wanted one released, all right, but not Jesus! **They clamored again** (for they had been noisily clamoring throughout) and cried out, **"Not this one, but Barabbas!"** John adds that Barabbas was a robber, a violent thief and an insurrectionist. Just the kind of man, in fact, that Jesus was falsely charged with being.

ॐ ॐ ॐ ॐ ॐ

19 1   Then Pilate therefore took Jesus and scourged Him.

2   And the soldiers plaited a crown of thorns and put it on His head, and threw around Him a purple garment,

3   and they were coming to Him and saying, "Hail, King of the Jews!" and were giving Him slaps.

4   And Pilate came out again and says to them, "Behold, I am bringing Him outside to you, that you may know that I find no guilt in Him."

5   Jesus therefore came out, wearing the crown of thorns and the purple garment. And he says to them, "Behold the man!"

The trial and investigation before Pilate was a long affair, lasting several hours, for they brought Jesus before him at sunrise, but He was not crucified until mid-morning. It would seem that early in these proceedings, Pilate attempted to foist the whole matter upon Herod, since Jesus was from Herod's jurisdiction of Galilee. Herod interrogated Him briefly, but quickly sent Him back to Pilate, dressed in the gorgeous robes of mockery (Luke 23:6–11).

In an attempt to win the crowd's sympathy, Pilate then **took Jesus and scourged Him**. (This scourging is narrated in Matt. 27: 27–31 and Mark 15:16–20 after the narration of His condemnation, as a kind of emotional climax to the Roman proceedings.)

The Roman punishment of scourging was severe indeed, and calculated to wring the heart of anyone. It involved having the victim tied to a post with his back and legs exposed. One (or two) soldiers then lashed the length of the victim with a leather *flagellum* or whip of several thongs, each thong of which had pieces of bone or metal inserted into it. These pieces actually removed the flesh from the victim's back and legs during the scourging, turning the back to a bloody pulp and exposing the bones, sinews and nerves within. It was not uncommon for some to die during scourging.

Not content with this brutality, the soldiers also indulge in some rough anti-Semitic horseplay (perhaps suggested and inspired by the robes of mockery He wore when He left Herod). Learning that the victim had claimed to be the King of the Jews, the soldiers take Jesus and force Him to play the lead part in a grotesque parody of Jewish messianic aspirations. They **plaited a crown** or royal cap from **thorns** growing nearby and **put it on His head**, so that its spikes pierced and lacerated His scalp. Forcing Him to sit down as on a throne, they **threw around Him a purple garment**, in imitation of the royal purple of the Emperor—possibly the short military cloak worn by soldiers. (The designation **purple** in those days denoted a range of colors from rose to true purple.) Whereas a Roman citizen would greet his true king and emperor by coming up to him, kneeling, saying "Hail, Caesar!" and then giving him the customary kiss of allegiance, these soldiers were **coming** up to Jesus and **saying, "Hail, King of the Jews!"** and then **giving Him slaps**.

Pilate allows this abuse and then brings Jesus out to show to all that he does not take His claims seriously, saying, "**Behold, I am bringing Him outside to you, that you may know that I find no guilt in Him.**" Pilate hopes that the crowd, seeing one of their countrymen so badly abused, will rouse themselves to His defense and ask for Him to be the one released. **Jesus therefore came out**, still **wearing the crown of thorns and the purple garment**, to face the assembling crowd. Pilate introduces Him to the crowd with the words, **"Behold the man!"**—that is, "Look at the poor thing!" His hope is that the spectacle will excite their pity for the Nazarene.

ॐ ॐ ॐ ॐ ॐ

6 When therefore the chief-priests and the attendants saw Him, they clamored, saying, "Crucify, crucify!" Pilate says to them, "You take Him and crucify Him, for I *myself* find no guilt in Him."
7 The Jews answered him, "We *ourselves* have a Law, and by that Law He ought to die because He made Himself to be *the* Son of God."

This strategy, however, badly backfired. The Jews had hoped that Jesus was indeed to prove their Messiah, the One who would overthrow the might of Rome and liberate Israel. When they saw Jesus so brutally humiliated, they concluded that they had been deceived in this hope, and that Jesus must have been a deceiver, as His enemies said. When Jesus came out and was presented to the crowd, **the chief-priests and the attendants** who had arrested Him **saw Him. They clamored, saying, "Crucify, crucify!"** in a (successful) attempt to stir up and win over the crowd.

Pilate, however, realizes that this is a matter of personal envy and vendetta (Matt. 27:18), and he is reluctant to carry out such an unjust sentence. He responds, **"You take Him and crucify Him** (the **you** is emphatic in the Greek), **for I *myself* find no guilt in Him."** The response is rather petulant, for the Jews had no legal authority to do anything of the sort.

The Jews (probably those of the delegation standing nearby) at this point let the truth slip out. **"We *ourselves* have a Law,"** they say, referring to such rulings as Leviticus 24:16, **"and by that Law He ought to die."** Pilate himself may not see any cause to put Jesus to death, but let him respect the local Jewish sensibilities. According to the customs and laws of the Jews, they insist, He ought to die for blasphemy, **because He made Himself to be** *the* **Son of God.** It is good politics, they imply, for Pilate to respect the local customs.

⚜ ⚜ ⚜ ⚜ ⚜

8   When Pilate therefore heard this word, he was the more afraid,

9   and he entered into the Praetorium again and says to Jesus, "Where are You *Yourself* from?" But Jesus did not give him an answer.

10 Pilate therefore says to Him, "You do not speak to me? Do You not know that I have authority to release You and I have authority to crucify You?"

11 Jesus answered, "You would not have authority over Me at all unless it had been given to you from above; for this reason he who delivered Me up to you has the greater sin."

Pilate was himself, however, not a Jew but a pagan—and like all pagans, prone to superstition. When he **heard this word, he was the more afraid.** Something there was about Jesus' demeanor, His serenity, His nobility, His freedom from fear, that made the idea of His being the Son of God more compelling. (Possibly also by this time Pilate's wife had sent her message to him, begging him to have nothing to do with Jesus, since she had suffered much in a dream that night because of Him; compare Matt. 27:19.) Pilate is, however, determined to get to the bottom of all this. He **entered into the Praetorium again** for a second private interview with Jesus and says to Him, **"Where are You from?"** (the historic present is used, to allow us to eavesdrop on their conversation). With doubt gripping his heart, Pilate begins to wonder if this strange Jew might not be somehow divine after all.

The question, however, does not come from a truly searching heart. The Lord knows that, regardless of what He answers, Pilate will not prefer principle to expediency. He therefore does **not give him an answer.**

This infuriates the governor, who is used to having his Roman authority respected. He says to Jesus, "**You do not speak to me? Do You not know that I have authority to release You and I have authority to crucify You?**" The double repetition of Pilate's authority should not be missed. Cannot Jesus see how important Pilate is?

Jesus knows where true authority is from, and that Pilate **would not have authority over** Him **at all unless it had been given** him **from** God **above.** Pilate is not the one in control, as he imagines. He is just a pawn, for all his outward show of might and authority. It is **for this reason** that **he who delivered** Jesus **up** to him **has the greater sin.** The chief-priests, led by Caiaphas, delivered Him up to Rome (18:30, 35). It is Israel that has ultimately disowned Him, and it is Israel that has the greater guilt and sin. It is they who must bear the judgment for this (compare Matt. 27:25). God, who truly has all authority, is the ultimate Judge here, not Pilate.

ॐ ॐ ॐ ॐ ॐ

12 Upon this Pilate sought to release Him, but the Jews clamored, saying, "If you release this one, you are not a friend of Caesar; everyone who makes himself a king contradicts Caesar."

13 When Pilate therefore heard these words, he brought Jesus outside and sat on the judgment-seat at a place called *the* Stone-pavement, but in Hebrew, Gabbatha.

14 Now it was Preparation *day* of the Passover, it was about the sixth hour. And he says to the Jews, "Behold your king!"

15 These ones therefore clamored, "Away! Away! Crucify Him!" Pilate says to them, "Shall I crucify your king?" The chief-priests answered, "We have no king but Caesar."

16 Then he therefore delivered Him to them to be crucified.

These words impressed Pilate, and in his heart he knew that Jesus was not guilty. He therefore **sought to release** Jesus, striving in his final exchanges with the crowd to secure His safety. **The Jews,** however, **clamored** and roared back, demanding Jesus' death. If Pilate would not grant this, they would inform his superiors in Rome about it. Jesus, they said, had claimed to be a king, and **if** Pilate chose to **release this one,** he was **not a friend of Caesar,** for all who made such treasonous claims **contradict** and oppose **Caesar.** The threat to Pilate's career was unmistakable.

Pilate was not prepared to risk career and safety for the sake of some Jew. **When he heard these words, he brought Jesus outside and sat on the judgment-seat** to deliver his final verdict. John, with his eyewitness concern for detail, identifies the location as the **place called** *the* **Stone-pavement,** or **in Hebrew, Gabbatha** (a word probably meaning "a rounded height," for its outlook over the people).

John's identification of the precise location shows how important this moment is for him. Here was the moment when the Son of God was disowned by the world. This is why John focuses more on Pilate than on Caiaphas and the Sanhedrin. Christ was indeed disowned by Israel, and Israel would pay the price. But the issue was wider than Christ's rejection by Israel. He was also rejected by the whole world. For this reason St. John turns the spotlight on Pilate, for Pilate was the representative of Rome and of the world. In the condemnation by Pilate, St. John sees Christ's rejection by the world He had made (1:10).

The day was hastening on. It was **Preparation** *day* of **Passover** week. (The word rendered **Preparation** *day* is the Gr. *paraskeue,* Friday on the weekly calendar, since Fridays were the times of preparation for the weekly Sabbath.) It was **about the sixth hour,** that is, approaching midday, perhaps about 10:30 A.M. in our time. Pilate **says to the Jews** assembled, **"Behold your king!"** Do you not want one of your own? **These ones clamored** and roared back over and over, like a mounting chant, **"Away! Away!** (That is, "Away with Him!") **Crucify Him!"** Pilate asked them if they really wanted him to **crucify** one who claimed to be their **king.** Here was one who was true to Israel, flesh of their own flesh. Did they really want Him to be turned over to torture and slaughter?

The crowd was working itself into a frenzy and a riot was on the verge of breaking out (Matt. 27:24). The mob was past reasoning. **The chief-priests** standing next to him answered his question, assuring him (with ironic loyalty) that they had **no king but Caesar.** They were loyal subjects of Rome; they were happy to turn over to Roman justice such a traitor. (For John, the irony is even heavier, for at this moment they spoke more truly than they knew. In disowning Christ, these Jews showed that they indeed had no king but Caesar, and no true loyalty to God.)

Pilate realized he had no choice. He **therefore delivered** Him to His foes **to be crucified.**

☙ EXCURSUS

Harmony of the Accounts of the Lord's Trial

The accounts of the Lord's trial in the Synoptic Gospels have rather less detail than that of John's Gospel. John is concerned to narrate details like an eyewitness (compare 19:35), and that makes for a more detailed account.

Matthew, Mark, and Luke narrate Christ's initial interview with Pilate (Matt. 27:2, 11–14; Mark 15:1–5; Luke 23:1–4). (Luke also narrates, which none of the others do, the interrogation before Herod, and how this contributed to a new cooperation between Herod and Pilate. Luke does this to set the stage for a more concerted persecution of the Church in the Acts of the Apostles; compare Acts 4:25–27.) The Synoptics also narrate the public tumult which results in Pilate handing down a death sentence (Matt. 27:15–26; Mark 15:6–15; Luke 23:13–25). John, however, gives a more detailed account. He narrates several public appearances of Pilate before the crowd as well as several private interviews Pilate has with Christ.

I would like to offer the following as a possible harmony

of the four Gospel accounts of the legal proceedings which together constituted Christ's trial:

1. Christ is brought before Pilate at sunrise by His accusers in the Sanhedrin, as Pilate meets the delegation outside his Praetorium (Matt. 27:2; Mark 15:1; Luke 23:1–2; John 18:28–32).

2. Pilate has his first private interview with Christ inside the Praetorium, asking Him if He is indeed the King of the Jews (Matt. 27:11; Mark 15:2; Luke 23:3; John 18:33–38a).

3. Pilate goes out of the Praetorium with Christ to talk to His accusers again, telling them that he finds no guilt in Him. His accusers respond with another barrage of accusations and ask for Barabbas, not Christ, to be granted freedom at the usual Passover amnesty (Matt. 27:12–14; Mark 15:3–5; Luke 23:4–5; John 18:38b–40).

4. Upon learning that Jesus belongs to Herod's jurisdiction, Pilate sends Him to Herod, hoping thereby to avoid the whole issue. Herod finds no guilt in Him and returns Him to Pilate (Luke 23:6–16).

5. Pilate then addresses the crowd that has gathered and proposes to scourge Christ and release Him. The crowd is stirred up by the chief-priests to resist this (Luke 23:13–22).

6. Pilate has Christ scourged, hoping to elicit enough sympathy for Him that the crowd will ask for Him rather than Barabbas (Matt. 27:27–31; Mark 15:16–20; John 19:1–3).

7. Pilate then goes out a second time before the crowd and brings Christ after His scourging, still wearing the crown of thorns. The crowd is insistent on His death (John 19:4–7).

8. Pilate goes back into the Praetorium for his second private interview with Christ, demanding that He speak to him (John 19:8–11).

9. Convinced of His innocence, Pilate continues to strive for His release, talking to the crowd. They insist on Jesus

being crucified, saying that if Pilate refuses, he is no friend of Caesar. Wanting to avoid a riot, Pilate gives in and sentences Jesus to death (Matt. 27:15–26; Mark 15:6–15; Luke 23:24–25; John 19:12–16).

§V.3. The Crucifixion

ॐ ॐ ॐ ॐ ॐ

17 They took Jesus therefore and He went out, bearing His own cross, to the *place* called Place of a Skull, which is called in Hebrew Golgotha,
18 where they crucified Him, and with Him two others, one on either side, and Jesus in the middle.
19 And Pilate wrote a notice also, and put it upon the cross. And it was written, "Jesus the Nazarene, the King of the Jews."
20 Therefore many of the Jews read this notice, for the place where Jesus was crucified was near the city, and it was written in Hebrew, Latin, and Greek.

The crucifixion is narrated with an economy of words. The soldiers **took Jesus** and **He went out** from the city, **bearing His own cross**, as was customary. (From the Synoptic Gospels, we learn that He had to be helped in this by Simon of Cyrene.) By *cross* is meant the horizontal crossbeam. During the actual crucifixion, the hands would be nailed to the ends of the crossbeam, which would be hoisted up and secured to the vertical post already planted in the earth. The feet would then be nailed to the bottom of the vertical beam, often with one foot overlapping the other. The victim would sit on a small seat which carried much of his weight, though he would slump forward and would have to press up with the feet to draw each breath. If the legs were broken, the victim would not be able to push up and draw a breath and would then die by asphyxiation.

Jesus went out to the hill where executions usually took place, called **Place of a Skull** (or **in Hebrew, Golgotha**)—so called probably because its bare rounded height resembled the top of a skull. This name was made all the more apt by its being the local site for crucifixion. It was there **they crucified Him, and with Him two others, one on either side, and Jesus in the middle.** By stressing His location in the midst of the thieves, St. John shows how great an indignity Christ endured for us. He was indeed numbered among the transgressors (Is. 53:12) and treated like a common criminal.

John also stresses that He died as the Messiah. **Pilate wrote the notice** (in Latin, the *titulus*) of Jesus' crime. This notice was a white board written with black or red letters that stated the offense for which the victim was being punished. The placard was carried in front of the victim on the way to execution and affixed to the cross. Jesus' notice read, **"Jesus the Nazarene, the King of the Jews."** By this, the Romans meant to identify Jesus as an insurrectionist, a traitor to the Roman state. For St. John, the writing revealed the truth of God, and proclaimed the true messiahship of Jesus. He was indeed the Messiah, the King of the Jews, and it was as the Messiah that He was dying for the sins of the world. Here was a proclamation that all the world could see. Certainly all the local populace could read this, **for the place where Jesus was crucified was near the city,** so that all the crowds who came to Jerusalem for Passover week could see the sight. Moreover, **it was written in Hebrew, Latin, and Greek,** in all the international languages of the world. All the world could read and know the truth.

ॐ ॐ ॐ ॐ ॐ

21 Therefore the chief-priests of the Jews were saying to Pilate, "Do not write, 'the King of the Jews'; but 'that one said, "I am the King of the Jews."'"

22 Pilate answered, "What I have written I have written."

The chief-priests of the Jews, however, took offense at the wording of the notice. They had emphatically repudiated Jesus as their Messiah, and it was offensive to them for Him to claim such a title, even in death. They lodged a complaint with **Pilate,** saying to him, **"Do not write, 'the King of the Jews'** as the charge, **but** rather **'that one said, "I am the King of the Jews."'"** Christ's foes were concerned to heap scorn upon Him in every way possible. It was not enough that He be tortured and killed. He must be disgraced by the charge itself too. For them, that Jesus claimed "I am the King of the Jews" from the cross was its own refutation and showed that He was wrong. The true King of the Jews, they felt, would never allow himself to be crucified. If Jesus had been crucified, He was obviously not the true King of the Jews.

Pilate, however, had had enough of Jewish envy and spite. Though not believing in Jesus, he had no time for the chief-priests and their malevolence. He dismissed their request, simply saying, **"What I have written I have written."** He had no intention of changing it for them. St. John stresses this refusal, for he sees it as part of the overriding providence of God. Jesus was proclaimed the messianic King of the Jews from the cross, and not even Jewish backroom politics could change it.

ॐ ॐ ॐ ॐ ॐ

23 The soldiers therefore, when they had crucified Jesus, took His garments and made four parts, a part to each soldier, and the shirt; now the shirt was seamless, woven from above through the whole.

24 They said therefore to one another, "Let us not split it, but cast-lots for it, *to see* whose it will be," that the Scripture might be fulfilled, "They divided up my garments for themselves, and for my apparel they cast lots."

25 Therefore the soldiers did these things.

John is concerned to show how Jesus' death proves Him to be the Messiah. The unchanged notice proclaimed this truth. The circumstance of His despoiling proves it as well, for it fulfilled the ancient prophecies. Jesus had five pieces of clothing, and these were removed when He was crucified, leaving Him but a simple loincloth for modesty. He had His outer cloak, His belt, His sandals and His head-covering. He also had an inner long shirt or tunic. There seem to have been four soldiers in attendance at this execution. His cloak, belt, sandals, and head-covering **made four parts** to be distributed, one to each soldier. The long inner **shirt**, however, **was seamless**, all of one piece, **woven from above through the whole**, and could not be **split** or torn without ruining it. They decided therefore to **cast-lots for it,** *to see* whose it would be.

Though the soldiers could not know it, their callous actions **fulfilled** the ancient Jewish prophecy, for it had been written in Ps. 22:18, "**They divided up my garments for themselves, and for my apparel they cast lots.**" In its original Davidic context, this verse was a lament that the Psalmist had been plundered by his foes of all that he had. In its prophetic fulfillment, this verse shows how the messianic Son of David is indeed plundered of all that He has in death. The strikingly literal way in which this verse is fulfilled in Christ shows Him to be the true Son of David. It was because of the ancient Jewish prophecy that the Roman **soldiers did these things**. They had no choice but to unwittingly fulfill the prophecy about Jesus.

ॐ ॐ ॐ ॐ ॐ

25 But there were standing beside the cross of Jesus His Mother, and His Mother's sister, Mary the *wife* of Clopas, and Mary Magdalene.

26 When Jesus therefore saw *His* Mother and the disciple whom He loved standing by, He says to *His* Mother, "Woman, behold your son!"

27 Then He says to the disciple, "Behold your

> Mother!" And from that hour the disciple took
> her into his own *place*.

St. John then narrates a brief exchange between Christ, His Mother, and himself. **There were standing beside the cross of Jesus His Mother, and His Mother's sister,** namely, **Mary the *wife* of Clopas, and Mary Magdalene.** (The second-century Jewish historian Hegesippus, quoted by Eusebius in his *History of the Church*, 3.33, identifies Clopas as the brother of St. Joseph, the foster-father of Christ. This would mean that Clopas was Christ's uncle and Mary wife of Clopas was Christ's aunt, the sister—i.e. sister-in-law—of Christ's Mother.) Thus, Christ's close family stood by the Cross. (Mary Magdalene is mentioned as being in such close proximity to Christ's cross to prepare the way for the story of His appearance to her at the empty tomb in 20:1f.)

John focuses upon Mary the Lord's Mother. **When** He **saw** her **and the disciple whom He loved** (that is, John himself) **standing by,** Jesus **says to *His* Mother, "Woman** (a formal address, like our "Madam"), **behold your son!" Then He says to the disciple, "Behold your Mother!"**

This is the first time Mary has been mentioned since the wedding of Cana in chapter 2—during which Christ also addressed her formally as "Woman." This form of address was a polite way of distancing Himself from her and her authority. He was then withdrawing from her maternal authority and obeying the superior authority of the Father as He began His ministry. He again refers to her with the same distant formality here, for He is still under the authority of the Father. But He lovingly takes thought for His Mother, arranging that she be henceforth cared for by John the beloved disciple. From that time, John **took her into his own *place*,** assuming responsibility for her care. (This confirms that Mary had no other children, for if she had, Christ would certainly have let them care for her, and not given her over to the care of His friend. Christ's actions are only explicable as the actions of an only child dying and leaving a widowed mother.)

Christ was motivated, then, by love for His Mother. But St.

John has another and deeper reason for including this incident here. The other time John referred to Mary, in the miracle at Cana, Mary functioned as an image of Israel. For though flesh and blood with Jesus, Mary came to submit to Him as her Lord, and Israel, though Jesus' brothers after the flesh, also must come to submit to Him (see commentary on 2:1–11). Throughout the years, John had plenty of time to reflect upon the significance of the woman he was caring for. For him, Mary was not simply Christ's Mother; she was an embodiment of sacred history, the living Daughter of Zion (Zeph. 3:14), the true Israel, the Woman clothed with the sun (Rev. 12:1). As Mary found a home with the disciple of Jesus, so Israel must find its true home in the Church. When John talks about Mary in his Gospel, he does so with an eye on Israel, and presents Mary as pointing the way.

ॐ ॐ ॐ ॐ ॐ

28 After this, Jesus, knowing that all things had already been finished, that the Scripture might be fulfilled, says, "I thirst."
29 A jar full of vinegar was lying there; therefore they put a sponge full of the vinegar around a hyssop and brought it to His mouth.
30 When Jesus therefore had received the vinegar, He said, "It is finished!" And He bowed His head and delivered up *His* spirit.

St. John has more to narrate in the circumstances of Christ's death that point to Him as the true Messiah. Death on the cross could take a matter of days if the victims were left to expire on their own. Jesus had only been on the cross a few hours. Nonetheless, He knew that it was time to die and **that all things had already been finished** and accomplished. His lips were parched, however, and He could not speak. He needed to wet His lips in order to speak and be heard. **A jar full of vinegar was lying there**—that is, a jar of refreshing sour wine (Gr. *oxos*), which was the drink of the poor (compare Ruth 2:14). Jesus **says, "I thirst"** in order to ask for some of the drink, and **they put a sponge full of the vinegar around a hyssop and brought it to His mouth** for Him to drink and moisten His throat. **When** He **had received the vinegar,** He was able to speak, and He lifted up His voice to cry, **"It is finished!"** in a final shout of triumph. After saying this, **He bowed His head and delivered up *His* spirit.** That is, He died voluntarily, as an act of His will. His life was not taken from Him so much as it was freely given up (compare 10:18). Having accomplished all that the Father willed, He dismissed His spirit.

This was an extraordinary way to die. First of all, John points out that the request for vinegar and the saying that He was thirsty was a way that **the Scripture** was **fulfilled.** Psalm 69 spoke of the suffering of the one who for the sake of God bore reproach (Ps. 69:7), the suffering of the one who was consumed with zeal for God's House (Ps. 69:9; John 2:17). This sufferer declared that for his thirst, his enemies gave him vinegar to drink (Ps. 69:21). In its original context, this referred simply to how the Psalmist's foes took every opportunity to hurt him. In its prophetic fulfillment, it is a striking anticipation of the actual sufferings endured by Jesus, when He actually was given vinegar for His thirst.

Secondly, John points out how Jesus **knew that all things had already been finished** and how He therefore chose to die at that moment. The request for vinegar was only so that He could give His final victory shout and give His life to the Father. The request for vinegar reveals Jesus' complete control over His own life. He did not die involuntarily; He died because He chose to do so *and at the moment He chose to do so*. Only the Messiah could have such authority over His own life and death.

ॐ ॐ ॐ ॐ ॐ

31 The Jews therefore, because it was Preparation *day*, that the bodies should not remain on the cross on the Sabbath (for that Sabbath was a high *day*), asked Pilate that their legs might

be cracked and that they might be taken away.

32 The soldiers therefore came and cracked the
legs of the first, and of the other who was crucified with Him,

33 but coming to Jesus, when they saw that He
had already died, they did not crack His legs,

34 but one of the soldiers stabbed His side with a
spear, and immediately there came out blood
and water.

35 And he who has seen has witnessed, and his
witness is true, and he knows that he speaks
truly, that you *yourselves* also may believe.

36 For these things happened that the Scripture
might be fulfilled, "A bone of him shall not be
broken."

37 And again another Scripture says, "They will
look on him whom they pierced."

St. John has one final proof of Jesus' messiahship: the way in
which, *contrary to what should have happened and what happened to
the others*, His legs were not broken. John's point is not just that
Jesus' legs were not broken after death; it is that everything con-
spired to make this happen, and *yet it did not*. John sees in this the
overriding providence of God (just as in Pilate's refusal to change
the notice above Jesus' head; v. 22) and another proof that Jesus is
the Messiah.

John set up this ending earlier in the chapter, when he narrated
that "it was Preparation day of the Passover, about the sixth hour"
when Christ was condemned (v. 14). That is, it was hastening to
noon when Pilate gave his verdict, and so it would soon be evening.
In Jewish reckoning, the day began with the evening, and since it
was Friday of Passover week, that next day would be the Sabbath.
That meant that if steps were not taken, the bodies would **remain
on the cross on the Sabbath**—and not just any Sabbath, but the
high and important **Sabbath** of Passover week. This was not accept-
able to Jewish piety, which decreed that a body hung on a tree (as

was the case with crucifixion) should not remain there after sunset
(Deut. 21:22–23).

So it was that **the Jews asked Pilate** that the **legs** of the three
might be cracked. With their legs broken, they would not be able
to push up with their feet and draw their next breath. They would
therefore immediately expire and would **be taken away** from the
cross, so that Jewish piety might be satisfied. **The soldiers therefore
came and cracked the legs of the first and of the other.** They should
have cracked the legs of Jesus also and were ready to do so. But
coming to Jesus, they saw that He had already died and, contrary
to what all expected, **did not crack His legs.** Deprived of the opportunity to kill by breaking this victim's legs as well, **one of the soldiers**, in an act of sheer brutality, **stabbed His side with** his **spear**
instead **and immediately there came out blood and water.**

John stresses these two aspects of the treatment of Christ's corpse.
Firstly, they did not break Christ's legs, as a providential sign of
Jesus' messiahship, despite all the circumstances that converged to
compel it. This **fulfilled** the **Scripture** that said, **"A bone of him
shall not be broken."** This may refer to several things in the Scrip-
tures. The Passover lamb was to have been preserved unbroken. In
Exodus 12:46, Israel is told not to break any bone of the sacrifice.
The unbroken bones of Jesus point therefore to Him as the true
Passover sacrifice, the Lamb that takes away the sins of the world.

John stresses a second aspect of the treatment of Jesus' corpse.
In place of cracking His legs, one of the soldiers stabbed His side
with a spear, so that there came out blood and water. John especially mentions the blood and water, for it had special significance.
Just as blood and water were poured on the altar as part of the
sacrifice, so blood and water poured from Jesus' side, revealing Him
as the true Sacrifice. This also was prophesied in Scripture, for **another Scripture says, "They will look on him whom they pierced."**
The passage in Zechariah 12 refers to the final redemption of Jerusalem and of all Israel, the time when God would "pour out" on His
people "the Spirit of grace and supplication." It is during this time
of repentance that the prophet predicts that they "will look" on
Him "whom they pierced and mourn for him as one mourns for an

only-begotten son" (Zech. 12:10). It was in that day that a fountain would be opened for God's people to cleanse away their "sin and impurity" (Zech. 13:1). St. John sees this fountain as the blood and water that flowed from the side of the Savior, present perpetually in the Church's sacraments and able to cleanse away all sin and impurity.

John sets forth all the facts of Christ's death as evidence that He is indeed the Messiah. In this the beloved disciple presents himself as one who has **witnessed** the events firsthand and who gives his evidence as a trusty witness whose **witness is true. He knows that he speaks truly** and that his evidence is reliable. He presents his case **that you**, the readers (the **you** is emphatic), **also may believe** and join the Church, the community of faith.

§V.4. The Burial

ॐ ॐ ॐ ॐ ॐ

38 And after these things Joseph of Arimathea, being a disciple of Jesus, but secretly, for fear of the Jews, asked Pilate that he might take away the body of Jesus, and Pilate allowed *it*. He came therefore and took away His body.

39 And Nicodemus came also, who had first come to Him by night, carrying a mixture of myrrh and aloes, about a hundred pounds.

40 Therefore they took the body of Jesus and bound it in wrappings with the aromatic *spices*, as is the custom of the Jews to bury.

41 Now in the place where He was crucified there was a garden, and in the garden a new tomb, in which no one had yet been laid.

42 Therefore because of the Preparation *day* of the Jews, because the tomb was near, they laid Jesus there.

After Christ's death, **Joseph of Arimathea** came forward. As his name indicates, he had his ancestral home in Ramathaim-zophim, about twenty miles northwest of Jerusalem (compare 1 Sam. 1:1). Though a member of the Sanhedrin (Mark 15:43), he too was **a disciple of Jesus**, but was one **secretly, for fear of the Jews.** That is, he did not come forward to declare himself to be one of Jesus' followers, lest he be banned from the synagogue. After Christ's death, however, he took courage and **asked Pilate that he might take away the body of Jesus.** Normally the bodies of those who had been executed for treason were not granted to family and friends. Burial in such cases involved getting special permission from the governor. For Joseph to come forward with this request meant not only placing himself at odds with his Jewish colleagues in the Sanhedrin, it also meant identifying himself to the Romans as a supporter of the treasonous Galilean. Nonetheless, **Pilate allowed** his request, and he **came** and **took away** Jesus' **body.**

Joseph was accompanied in this errand by a fellow-member of the Sanhedrin Council, **Nicodemus.** Nicodemus is identified by John as the one who **had first come to** Jesus **by night** (3:1f)—that is, as one who had received some of Christ's teaching and had some measure of loyalty to the fallen Nazarene.

Nicodemus came **carrying a mixture of myrrh and aloes, about a hundred pounds'** weight. This was a large amount of **aromatic** *spices* for burial, and shows the greatness of their devotion to the Lord. St. John also mentions it to show the great dignity of Christ, who was worthy of such royal treatment. As the sun was setting, **they took the body of Jesus** with great haste and **bound it in wrappings with the aromatic** *spices.* The aromatic spices were granular in form, and though it is difficult to be certain, they were probably spread over the place where the corpse was to be lain to form a kind of bed. The purpose, of course, was to offset the odor of decomposition. St. John mentions for his non-Jewish readers that this was **the custom of the Jews** when they came **to bury** their dead. Unlike the Egyptians, they did not embalm the dead or mutilate the corpses.

In the immediate locale and **place** where Jesus **was crucified there was a garden, and in that garden a new tomb, in which no**

one had yet been laid. The tomb was the property of Joseph (Matt. 27:60), and he decided to bury Christ there **because** it was **the Preparation** *day* **of the Jews** and **because the tomb was near**. That is, there was a need for haste, for it was Friday, and if Christ was to be buried before the coming Sabbath (that is, before that evening), this was the only way to accomplish it.

John makes a point of saying that it was a new tomb, in which no one had yet been laid. It was the custom to bury more than one person in a tomb, laying each body within its own niche. In this case, the tomb was entirely empty, with the result that there would be no possibility of mixing up the corpses lying within, or of mistakenly thinking that Jesus' body had gone when it was one of the enshrouded bodies still lying there. Jesus' body was the only one in the tomb, and they would easily be able to know that it was no longer there if the tomb should later prove to be empty.

❧ VI ❧

THE RESURRECTION
(20:1—21:24)

§VI.1. The Empty Tomb

> ❧ ❧ ❧ ❧ ❧
>
> **20** 1 Now on the first *day* of the week, Mary Magdalene comes early to the tomb while it is still dark, and sees the stone taken away from the tomb.
>
> 2 She runs therefore and comes to Simon Peter and to the other disciple whom Jesus loved, and says to them, "They took away the Lord from the tomb, and we do not know where they have laid Him!"

St. John now comes to the climax of the case he has been building to prove that Jesus is the Christ. He narrates the first finding of the empty tomb, and then several appearances to Mary Magdalene and to His disciples.

Mary Magdalene came to the tomb as part of a larger group. In the closing minutes of the day Christ died, amidst the confusion occasioned by darkness settling over the land and by an earthquake (Matt. 27:45, 51), Mary Magdalene arranged with some other women to buy spices as soon as the coming Sabbath was over and go to the tomb to anoint Christ's body as a final act of devotion (Mark 16:1). These arrangements were doubtless made in haste, as each agreed to come from her respective location in Jerusalem and meet at the tomb at sunrise.

On the first *day* **of the week,** therefore, **Mary Magdalene comes early to the tomb while it is still dark.** (The historic present is used throughout the account.) Perhaps the same zeal that compelled her to remain by the Cross (19:25) also compelled her to arrive at the tomb earlier than the rest of the women. From whatever cause, however, she preceded them to the tomb and was alone there before they arrived.

She immediately **sees the stone taken away from the tomb** and concludes (not unnaturally) that a theft has taken place. In panic, **she runs therefore and comes to Simon Peter,** the leader of the disciples, who was with his friend John, **the other disciple whom Jesus loved.** We can almost hear her breathless and terse announcement, her voice full of grief at this latest catastrophe: **"They took away the Lord from the tomb, and we do not know where they have laid Him!"** Who this *they* might be is not specified, nor perhaps did she have any real idea herself. All she knows is that the Lord she loves is gone, and she is now no longer able to perform the last sad rites of devotion.

ॐ ॐ ॐ ॐ ॐ

3   Peter therefore went out and the other disciple, and they were going to the tomb.

4   And the two were running together, and the other disciple ran ahead faster than Peter and came first to the tomb,

5   and stooping *and looking*, he sees the wrappings lying *there*, but did not enter.

6   Simon Peter therefore also comes following him and entered into the tomb, and he observes the wrappings lying *there*,

7   and the neckerchief which had been upon His head, not lying with the wrappings, but rolled up in one place apart.

> 8 Therefore the other disciple who had first come to the tomb entered then also, and he saw and believed,
> 9 for as yet they did not know the Scripture, that it was necessary for Him to rise from the dead.
> 10 The disciples therefore went away again to their *places*.

Peter and John are distressed themselves, and take instant action. Despite their fear of detection and arrest (when they would meet later, it would be behind doors which had been shut and locked; v. 19), they bravely **went out** and ran to see for themselves. At this point in his narrative, St. John takes care to specify every detail, as a careful witness should. He says that he and Peter **were running together**, but that he **ran ahead faster than Peter and came first to the tomb, stooping** *and looking*. He **sees** the burial **wrappings lying** *there*, **but did not enter.** Then **Simon Peter comes following him and entered into the tomb**, and also observes the empty tomb.

Why such precision in narrating this running to the tomb? Later interpreters such as Gregory the Dialogist saw allegorical significance in the account, making John a symbol of the synagogue (because he did not enter the tomb) and Peter a symbol of the Church (because he did). This seems contrary to John's previous approach, for if John himself had any mystical or symbolic significance, it would be as the believing Church, not the unbelieving synagogue (see the commentary on 19:25–27).

What *is* consistent with John's previous approach is a concern to present an eyewitness account, something which could stand up in court. John narrates that he came quickly and first to the tomb to stress that he came before anyone and so can vouch for the fact that no one else was there who could have stolen the body or returned the burial wrappings. Their leader Peter could not have done so, because John got there before him and would have seen it if Peter had removed the body. John's testimony that the disciples did not steal the body therefore was reliable. Moreover, he did not enter the tomb, and so he himself cannot be accused of placing the burial wrappings in the tomb. He saw them there, but could not have planted them there.

Peter also came following him, breathlessly arriving shortly after. With his usual impulsiveness, he *did* enter the tomb, and observed the wrappings lying there. Together Peter and John constitute two legal witnesses. This is important for the building of St. John's case for the Gospel, for according to the Law, it is "on the evidence of two or three witnesses that a matter will be confirmed" (Deut. 19:15).

John states that what he and Peter saw in the tomb was not simply the absence of the only body that had been placed there. They also saw **the wrappings lying *there*, and the neckerchief which had been upon** Christ's **head, not lying with the wrappings, but rolled up in one place apart.** As with the burial of Lazarus, Christ's head was wrapped with a neckerchief. This neckerchief (*soudarion* in the Greek) was rolled up and folded upon itself so as to form a long piece of cloth which was then wrapped around His head (to keep the jaw closed). A knot was tied at the top of the head to hold the neckerchief in place. The body was then wrapped in a large linen sheet (*sindon* in the Greek), which covered the front, came up over the head and then came down to cover the back. This was held in place by bandages or linen strips, which tied and secured both the feet and the arms. The apostles saw these wrappings lying there (both the large *sindon* and the bandage strips) as well as the *soudarion* or neckerchief. This last was still rolled up and tied in a knot, as it had been when it was upon the Lord's head. It was not lying with the wrappings, in a big tangle, but was in a place apart.

That is, the tomb did not look as it would have if thieves had come to steal the corpse, tearing off the wrappings and leaving them scattered everywhere. If thieves had come, they would hardly have removed the wrappings or the neckerchief and left them there, nor taken time to refold the neckerchief itself. Grave-robbers usually steal valuables from the grave and leave the body, not steal the body and leave the valuables!

John came into the tomb then also, and he too **saw and believed**. That is, he believed Mary's story, that the Lord was not there.

He did not immediately conclude that his Lord had been raised, for Luke 24:10–11 says that the apostles did not believe any of the stories told by the myrrh-bearing women, but considered them to be nonsense. But they did believe that Christ was no longer in the tomb, which was the beginning of their faith in His Resurrection.

St. John says that they believed in Christ's absence from the tomb because they saw for themselves the tomb was empty, and that this was only necessary because **as yet they did not know the Scripture, that it was necessary for** Christ **to rise from the dead.** For them also it was necessary to see before they could believe. If they had properly understood the prophecies of Scripture, they would have believed that the tomb was empty even without seeing. After this, **the disciples went away again to their** *places* in Jerusalem. (There they would soon be met by the other myrrh-bearing women and by a late-arriving Mary Magdalene; Luke 24:9–10; John 20:18.)

§VI.2. Appearance to Mary Magdalene

ॐ ॐ ॐ ॐ ॐ

11 But Mary was standing at the tomb outside weeping. As she wept therefore, she stooped *and looked* into the tomb,

12 and she observes two angels in white sitting *there*, one at the head and one at the feet, where the body of Jesus had been lying.

13 And those ones say to her, "Woman, why are you weeping?" She says to them, "They took away my Lord, and I do not know where they have laid Him!"

Peter and John had returned to the safety of their places, to remain in hiding. **Mary,** however, was lost in her grief, and remained **standing at the tomb outside weeping. As she wept, she stooped** *and looked* **into the tomb,** perhaps because she could scarcely believe that her Lord had been taken from her. This time, however, as she peered into the tomb, **she observes two angels in white sitting** *there*, as if keeping vigil at the holy place **where the body of Jesus had been lying.** The angels address her formally, saying, **"Woman, why are you weeping?"** For the angels, this is the time of joy and triumph. The question is not so much a request for information (they could guess why she was weeping) as it was a summons to rejoice.

Mary, blinded by tears, stunned by grief (and possibly dizzy with lack of sleep), does not discern that these are two angels, only that they are two men in white. If she thinks anything about it, she probably thinks they are Temple guards. She answers the question, blurting out words of childlike grief and pain—**"They took away my Lord, and I do not know where they have laid Him!"** The words are almost identical to the ones she spoke to the disciples earlier (v. 2), but the small changes are significant. Then she spoke of "*the* Lord" and also said that "we" women (in the plural) did not know where they had laid Him; now she speaks of "*my* Lord," and also uses the singular, saying that she herself does not know where to find Him. She is here more focused on her own relationship with Jesus and on her own grief.

ॐ ॐ ॐ ॐ ॐ

14 When she had said these things, she turned behind her, and observes Jesus standing, and did not know that it was Jesus.

15 Jesus says to her, "Woman, why are you weeping? Whom are you seeking?" That one, supposing Him to be the gardener, says to Him, "Lord, if you *yourself* have borne Him away, tell me where you have laid Him and I *myself* will take Him away."

16 Jesus says to her, "Mary!" That one turns and says to Him in Hebrew, "Rabboni!" (which is to say, "Teacher").

Having **said these things, she turned behind her**, possibly because she saw the angels look at Someone behind her, and she turned to follow their gaze and see who this was. Was this the one she should talk to in order to find the body of Jesus?

There she saw the Lord. In His resurrected body, Jesus was subtly changed and not immediately recognizable, and though she **observes Jesus standing**, she **did not know that it was Jesus**. Rather, she supposed Him to be **the gardener**—for who else would be in a garden that early? The Lord asks her the same sort of questions the angels did. He addresses her formally, calling her "**Woman**," and asks, "**Why are you weeping? Whom are you seeking?**"

For Mary the answer was obvious: she was seeking the one from the now-empty tomb. She asks Him, "**Lord**" (*Kurie* in the Greek, meaning in this case, "sir"), "**if you *yourself* have borne Him away** (the **you** is emphatic), **tell me where you have laid Him and I *myself* will take Him away**." She thinks perhaps that Jesus' corpse was moved because it was not permitted to lie in this tomb, and she fears that it may be left in a common grave. If this is the case, she will take loving custody of the body. Having said this, she turns back to the tomb, in agitated distraction.

Christ can no longer contain His compassionate love for her. He bursts out with her name, "**Mary!**" At the sound of Him calling her name, she recognizes her Lord at last. (Did not Jesus Himself say that He calls His own sheep by name and they know His voice?—10:3, 4). She **turns** back to Him again and calls out to Him, "**Rabboni!**" (literally, "my **Teacher**"). John mentions the actual **Hebrew** title, for in using this title, Mary joyfully supposes that her Teacher has returned to her, and that all will now be as it was in the earlier days. He will return with them to Galilee and there will be many happy healing nights when they can sit at His feet and drink in His Presence and be at peace. She rushes to embrace Him and hold Him forever.

ৡ৾ ৡ৾ ৡ৾ ৡ৾ ৡ৾

17 Jesus says to her, "Do not touch Me, for I have not yet ascended to the Father, but go to My

> brothers and say to them, 'I ascend to My
> Father and your Father, and My God and your
> God.'"
> 18 Mary Magdalene comes, declaring to the dis-
> ciples, "I have seen the Lord," and that He had
> said these things to her.

Christ, however, has not been raised to return with them and live in the coziness of Galilee. He has to go where they cannot follow to prepare a place for them (13:33; 14:2). He therefore says to her, "**Do not touch Me,**" do not cling to Me or suppose that all will return to the way it was. He has **not yet ascended to the Father,** and He must indeed ascend to that place for the sake of His disciples. But when He goes there, He will send the Spirit to them, through whom they will cry, "Abba! Father!" (16:7; Gal. 4:6). This depar-ture will therefore effect a glorious change of status for them, for the relationship which He has with His Father and God, He will share with them. The Father will treat the disciples as His beloved sons also (compare 16:26–27). That is why Christ tells Mary to **go** to the disciples and **say to them, "I ascend to My Father and your Father, and My God and your God."** The disciples are now the **brothers** of the Lord, sharing the Lord's access to the Father.

Mary Magdalene obeys her Lord and returns to the disciples, declaring to them that she has **seen the Lord** and that **He had said these things to her.**

§VI.3. Appearance to the Disciples

> ॐ ॐ ॐ ॐ ॐ
>
> 19 When therefore it was evening on that day, the
> first *day* of the week, and when the doors were
> shut where the disciples were for fear of the
> Jews, Jesus came and stood in their midst, and
> says to them, "Peace to you!"
> 20 And having said this, He showed them both

His hands and His side. The disciples therefore rejoiced when they saw the Lord.

21 Jesus therefore said to them again, "Peace to
you! As the Father has sent Me, I *Myself* also
send you."

22 And having said this, He breathed into them,
and says to them, "Receive *the* Holy Spirit.

23 "Whose sins you forgive, they have been forgiven them; whose sins you retain, they have
been retained."

The Lord first revealed Himself to Mary Magdalene, as a reward to her for her loyalty and as a healing to her grief. He also
revealed Himself that day to Simon (compare 1 Cor. 15:5; 24:34).
He would reveal Himself to His disciples as a group too (compare
Luke 24:36–43 for a parallel account).

This occurred when it was **evening on that** very **day, the first**
day **of the week** (that is, Sunday evening). The disciples still feared
detection and arrest, and so **the doors were shut** and locked **where
the disciples were for fear of the Jews** (the plural *doors* probably
indicates that both the outer and inner doors were locked). The
resurrected Christ was now no longer bound by the limitations of
time and space, and so despite the locked doors, **Jesus came and
stood in their midst.** He greeted them, saying, **"Peace to you!"**
Though this was the usual Jewish salutation of *Shalom*, St. John
sees in it a deeper meaning. Their hearts had been troubled and
filled with uncertainty and fear; they had sorrow like a woman in
childbirth (14:27; 16:22). Now was the time for all that anguish to
melt away and to give place before the Lord's invincible peace. The
Lord was not just greeting them; He was bestowing His peace—a
peace such as the world could never give and which it could never
take away.

The disciples could hardly believe their ears—and so Christ used
their eyes. Condescending to their need to see before they could
fully believe, He **showed them both His hands and His side.** In the
resurrected bodies of men, all wounds will be healed and all diseases

overcome. The physical body dies and is sown in weakness, but it will be raised in power (1 Cor. 15:43). In the case of the Lord, however, His wounds were not defects to be overcome, but trophies to be treasured. Thus His wounds remain—no longer gaping and ugly injuries, but marks of glory. As the hymns for Thomas Sunday declare, to touch those wounds meant to touch fire.

So it was that Christ's wounds remained even in His resurrected body and that He showed them to the disciples there to prove that it was He. (This was the more necessary, since some were frightened and supposed that He was a ghost; Luke 24:37.) **The disciples therefore rejoiced when they saw** that it was **the Lord**—even as He said they would rejoice (16:22). John mentions this joy as the fulfillment of Christ's words, and as the vindication of all that He said. This was the joy in which the Church was to live perpetually—an unshakable joy, not of this world.

Christ once more bestows His peace, saying again, "**Peace to you!**" But this present bestowal is for a reason. They are being given the gift of peace because they are being given a mission, for that peace is the power with which that mission will be carried out. As the disciples now will share His relationship with the Father, so they will now share His mission from Him. **As the Father** sent Christ, so Christ **also sends** them. It is just as He prayed to the Father at their last meal together (17:18). Now they too must go out into all the world with the Father's saving Word to be His Church. The torch the Father gave to Jesus He has passed to them in turn.

In order to equip them for this mission, He **breathes into** them and says to them (the historic present is used), "**Receive *the* Holy Spirit. Whose sins you forgive, they have been forgiven them; whose sins you retain, they have been retained.**"

This experience of the Holy Spirit should not be misunderstood. Some have thought that this was meant by John to describe the fulfillment of Christ's promise to send the Spirit, and have called this event "the Johannine Pentecost." This seems unlikely, for John wrote his Gospel with full knowledge of the Synoptic traditions, and there is no suggestion that he dissented from the interpretation which saw the Day of Pentecost as the fulfillment of the

Lord's promise of the Spirit. Indeed, John's narration of Christ talking about leaving them in order to send the Spirit presupposes this interpretation (16:7).

What then was happening here? A clue may be gathered from the verb rendered *breathed into* (Gr. *emphusso*). It is a comparatively rare verb and is used in Gen. 2:7 LXX to describe how God "breathed into his face the breath of life" so that the lifeless clay "became a living soul." That is, it describes the infusion of life into man.

The word is also used in the prophecy of Ezekiel about God's breath/Spirit/life coming into His people in the last days. In the vision of Ezekiel 37:8–10, Ezekiel sees a similarly lifeless Israel, reconstituted from "a valley of dry bones" and restored to "flesh and sinews and skin," but yet still dead and devoid of life. He then sees the divine *Ruach*, the Wind, the Breath, the Spirit, come into them so that they "came to life, an exceedingly great army."

The same meaning obtains here. Christ breathed the breath of eternal life into His disciples, granting them the Holy Spirit that they also might come to true life and stand on their feet as a mighty army. He had promised that after the Resurrection He would give eternal life to His own, making them alive from the dead (5:25). That promise could only be completely fulfilled after His Resurrection, for it was the new and eternal life of the resurrection that He was to bestow on them.

In giving new resurrection life to His apostles, He restores them and reconstitutes them as the new Israel. As leaders of this community of new life, they are given authority to admit men to this Church and to expel men from it. If one comes to the apostles and church leaders in penitence, that apostle or leader can forgive the penitent man his sins and readmit him to the fellowship of the forgiven, confident that his sins will truly be forgiven him. If one in the Church sins grievously and without repentance, the apostle or leader will retain that man's sins, expelling him from the Church, knowing that his sins will be retained in heaven also. Receiving the Spirit and new life made the apostles the authoritative gatekeepers for the Kingdom of God. They were thus able to bind and loose, and know that their decisions had all the authority of heaven (compare Matt. 18:18).

It is difficult today not to read back into these words our present pastoral practice of Holy Confession or the Sacrament of Penance. It is important, however, to see that our present pastoral practice stands at the end of a long history of development. In the early days of the Church, the Mystery of Penance presupposed formal and public excommunication. If a Christian sinned grievously, that one would be expelled from the eucharistic community. If he later repented, he was forgiven and publicly readmitted after penance and the prayer of absolution.

The Sacrament of Penance usually has a more private and pastoral application now. The apostolic authority of the bishop to readmit penitents to the Church community has largely devolved on the presbyter or parish priest. Furthermore, the public and once-in-a-lifetime character of penance has also been transformed. The sacrament is now not given only for the purpose of admitting the excommunicated back into the Church; it is also given privately to aid the faithful communicant as he struggles with his sinfulness.

Nonetheless, despite these developments, it is the same sacrament and the same authority to forgive that is manifested, whether given publicly and infrequently (as in the early Church) or whether given privately and regularly (as now). The apostles were given authority to prevail with heaven by their prayers, and to admit men to a community in which new life from God flowed to the faithful. These words of Christ to His apostles are truly applied to our present Sacrament of Confession. Like Holy Baptism, that sacrament too is a way of receiving life and forgiveness.

ॐ ॐ ॐ ॐ ॐ

24 But Thomas, one of the Twelve, the one called the Twin, was not with them when Jesus came.
25 The other disciples therefore were saying to

him, "We have seen the Lord!" But he said to them, "Unless I will see in His hands the mark of the nails and put my finger into the place of the nails and put my hand into His side, I will never believe."

This experience of resurrection life was not shared by all of the apostles, for **Thomas was not with them when Jesus came** that Sunday evening. John considers the evidence of Thomas to be important, and so he takes care to thoroughly identify his witness. It was Thomas, **one of the Twelve, the one called the Twin,** who was meant. Where Thomas was is not said, but in those chaotic days of danger and confusion, it would have been easy to have missed gathering together. Perhaps he was with some other friends of their movement in Jerusalem. Nonetheless, when **the other disciples** joyfully reported to him, **"We have seen the Lord!"** he refused to believe them.

The reason for his lapse is not stated. Though history has stigmatized him as "Doubting Thomas," this is perhaps a little unfair. Certainly it was not because he did not love his Lord enough. When Christ said that He was going back to Judea to rejoin the recently dead Lazarus, it was Thomas who rallied the others, and who was prepared to die with Him (11:15–16). It was perhaps this great love for Christ that ironically accounted for his lapse now. Thomas had been so hurt and bruised by his Lord's death that he was emotionally numb. He could not stand another disappointment, and so refused to believe his comrades' story lest it should prove false. On this, he was adamant. **"Unless I will see in His hands the mark of the nails and put my finger into the place of the nails and put my hand into His side, I will never believe."** This last negative is a strong one—not just "I will *not* believe," but the stronger "I will *never* believe" (Gr. *ou me pisteuso*). The amount of detail Thomas demands is impressive. He wants a thorough examination of all Christ's wounds. Only then will he believe the disciples' story.

§VI.4. Second Appearance to the Disciples and to Thomas

> ❧ ❧ ❧ ❧ ❧
>
> 26 And after eight days His disciples were again inside, and Thomas with them. Jesus comes, the doors having been shut, and stood in their midst and said, "Peace to you!"
>
> 27 Then He says to Thomas, "Bring your finger here and see My hands, and bring your hand and put *it* into My side—and do not be unbelieving, but believing."
>
> 28 Thomas answered and said to Him, "My Lord and my God!"
>
> 29 Jesus says to him, "Because you have seen Me, have you believed? Blessed *be* the ones who have not seen, and have believed!"

St. John focuses especially on this appearance to Thomas, making it the climax of his case, for the depth of Thomas' skepticism would become the strength of the proof for Christ's Resurrection. It is after this appearance that John sums up his Gospel, saying that all was written that his readers might believe that Jesus is the Christ (20:31).

This appearance took place **after eight days**, by Jewish reckoning, counting each Sunday as one day. It is liturgically significant that these first Resurrection appearances took place on a Sunday. Sunday, the first day of the week, became *the* Christian day, "the Lord's day" (compare Rev. 1:10), the day when the defining act of Christian worship, the Eucharist, took place. Jews might continue to meet on the Sabbath, but Christians, *as Christians*, met on the first day of the week to commemorate the Resurrection.

As can be seen from John's designation of this as **eight days** later, the *first* day is also the *eighth* day—not just mathematically, but symbolically as well. For Sunday is the eighth day in the sense that it transcends the other seven days. In this age, the week has only seven days, and after counting seven days, one returns to the first day again. The eighth day is therefore the day outside of time, outside of this age, the day of eternity, the day of the Kingdom. The Christian Sunday is the eighth day in that during this day we ascend to the Lord in our worship and enter the Kingdom, transcending the limitations of this age.

On this second Sunday after the Lord's Resurrection, **His disciples were again inside** a secure room where **the doors** had **been shut** and locked. This was probably still in Jerusalem, for such security precautions would not be needed in Galilee. Once again the Lord transcended the limits of this age and **stood in their midst**, despite the locked doors. Once again He bestowed the peace that His Presence alone can give, saying, **"Peace to you!"**

He especially turns to Thomas. Thomas' refusal to believe was born from pain and hurt, from a bruised heart, not from a hardened one. Christ therefore seeks him out to bring healing. The peace that He had bestowed upon the others, He would give to His beloved Thomas as well. He knows all things, and knows only too well what Thomas said to the others. He says to him, **"Bring your finger here and see My hands, and bring your hand and put** *it* **into My side—and do not be unbelieving, but believing."** In His compassion for Thomas, Christ does not disdain such a test, but is willing to do whatever it takes to bring Thomas home to faith with the others.

It is not stated whether Thomas takes the opportunity to probe the Lord's hands and place his hand into His side. The feeling given by the text is that such tests are no longer necessary for Thomas, and he bursts forth in a joyful and relieved confession, **"My Lord and my God!"** Here is the high-water mark of faith in the Gospel. Others had confessed Jesus to be Lord and showed faith in His power (e.g. 9:38; 11:27). Here Thomas confesses Jesus not only to be his Lord, but his God as well. The confession with which John began his Gospel in 1:1 (saying "the Word was God") finds its fulfillment here in the Church's confession of this truth, when Thomas confesses that Jesus is indeed God. This is the climax of John's Gospel, the point to which all has been leading.

St. John ends his narration with a blessing. Christ does not so much rebuke Thomas for his need to see, as He offers a blessing to future generations who would believe without such proof. Has Thomas **believed** because he has first **seen**? There is a blessing in store for all those others—Christians through the ages, who will **believe** even though they have **not seen!**

§VI.5. The Purpose of the Gospel

꣠ ꣠ ꣠ ꣠ ꣠

30 Many other signs therefore Jesus also did before the disciples, which are not written in this book,
31 but these have been written that you might believe that Jesus is the Christ, the Son of God, and that believing you may have life in His Name.

John concludes his case by saying that he could have written much more. The sign of His glorified wounds which Christ offered to Thomas was one thing, but there were **many other signs** which **Jesus also did before the disciples, which are not written in this book.** The forty days following the Resurrection was a time when Christ ate and drank with His **disciples** and taught them many things, offering them (as St. Luke says) "many convincing proofs" (Acts 1:3). John has made a selection of them and given them to the Church in his Gospel so that it might proclaim Jesus to the world. As the Church shares what John has written, John hopes that the reader **might believe that Jesus is the Christ, the Son of God, and that believing** the reader **may have life in His Name.** The Christ proclaimed by the Church was a controversy for the world. John wrote his Gospel that the controversy might be resolved in the Church's favor, and that the reader might have eternal life within that fellowship.

§VI.6. Third Appearance to the Disciples and the Fate of Two Friends

Although St. John brings his case for the Church's Gospel to a climax with the sign given to Thomas, this is not the end of his Gospel. The story he has been telling still needs to be brought to a conclusion by telling how Peter was restored after his threefold denial of Christ and how a rumor began to be circulated about John himself.

To some, it would seem odd that John would (as they think) put the finishing touch on his story by saying "these [things] have been written that you might believe" (20:31), and then go on for another chapter. (This perceived oddness has led some scholars to deny that John wrote this chapter, or to say that, if he did, it was added afterwards.) But this ending only seems odd because of a modern prejudice regarding how a Gospel "should" end. John ends his Gospel, in fact, in the same way as he ended his First Epistle. In that Epistle, he wrote, "these things [i.e. the Epistle] I have written to you who believe in the Name of the Son of God, that you may know that you have eternal life" (5:13). Then, after this seeming "finishing touch," he goes on to write another eight verses. The statement of purpose (for both the Gospel and the First Epistle) comes near to the end, but not at the absolute end. There is still room in both documents to tie up loose ends.

ॐ ॐ ॐ ॐ ॐ

21 1 After these things, Jesus manifested Himself again to the disciples at the Sea of Tiberias, and He manifested Himself in this manner.

2 There were together Simon Peter and Thomas called the Twin and Nathanael of Cana in Galilee and the *sons* of Zebedee and two others of His disciples.

3 Simon Peter says to them, "I am going fishing." They say to him, "We *ourselves* will also

> come with you." They went out and got into the
> boat, and that night they took hold of nothing.
>
> 4 But when it was already early, Jesus stood on
> the beach; however, the disciples did not know
> that it was Jesus.
>
> 5 Jesus therefore says to them, "Children, have
> you *caught* anything to eat?" They answered
> Him, "No."
>
> 6 And He said to them, "Cast the net on the right
> side of the boat, and you will find some." They
> cast therefore, and then they were no longer
> strong enough to draw it in because of the mul-
> titude of fish.
>
> 7 That disciple therefore whom Jesus loved says
> to Peter, "It is the Lord!" And so when Simon
> Peter heard that it was the Lord, he girded his
> cloak about (for he was naked), and cast him-
> self into the sea.
>
> 8 But the other disciples came in the boat, for
> they were not far from the land, but about two
> hundred cubits away, dragging the net of fish.

After the first two appearances to the group of the disciples (in 20:19f and 20:26f), St. John narrates the time that **Jesus manifested Himself again to the disciples at the Sea of Tiberias** (that is, the Sea of Galilee). It began with a gathering of **Simon Peter, Thomas, Nathanael** (that is, Bartholomew; see commentary on 1:45), **the *sons* of Zebedee** (that is, John himself and his brother James), and **two others of His disciples** (who were probably not from among the Twelve, since they are not named). They have returned to the safety of Galilee, but since they are deprived of their Leader, they remain without direction and purpose. They still need to earn a living in order to eat, and so **Simon Peter says to them, "I am going fishing."** The others have nothing else to do, and since they are fishermen by trade, they respond, **"We *ourselves* will also come with you."**

The group of seven men worked hard all **that night** and yet **they took hold of nothing** in their nets, despite the fact that nighttime was the best time for fishing. The frustration of working hard and getting nothing for it added to their general sense of malaise.

When they were just about to give up, **when it was already early** and the day was just breaking over the lake, **Jesus stood on the beach**, about one hundred yards or so away (or a little over **two hundred cubits** by ancient measurement). **The disciples**, however, **did not know that it was Jesus.** Both because of the fact that the Lord's resurrected form was subtly different from His previous earthly one, and also because of the dim light, they could not see that their Lord had once again come to them. As they struggled with the cold and with their empty growling stomachs, a figure appeared on the shore and called out to them, **"Children, have you *caught* anything to eat?"** (The question in the Greek is phrased so as to expect a negative answer.) The word rendered *anything to eat* is the Greek *prosphagion*. It is a synonym for *fish* (Gr. *opsarion*) in vv. 10 and 13, both of which words properly mean "a dainty, something to eat with bread." In all New Testament usage, it denotes fish. Jesus hails them in an affectionate and hearty manner, calling them *children* (Gr. *paidia*)—a term closer in feel to our English "lads" or "boys."

The disciples' reply is a brief shouted **"No"**—natural enough, since they are shouting their conversation over a hundred yards of water. The mysterious figure, however, has some fishing advice for them: **"Cast the net on the right side of the boat** (that is, to the opposite side from where they were fishing) **and you will find some."** Having nothing to lose, they decide to take the advice. To their astonishment, such a **multitude of fish** swam obediently into the nets they had just lowered that **they were no longer strong enough to draw it in.**

This event had an eerily familiar feel to it, since it recalled the day Jesus had first called them to be His disciples. On that day too, they had fished all night and taken nothing, and on that day too Christ had bid them let down their nets for a catch (Luke 5:4–5).

Just like on that now far-off day, their nets had now enclosed an astonishing multitude of fish. As this came shortly after the previous unexpected appearances of Christ, the **disciple whom Jesus loved** instantly knew who this mysterious figure was. He cried out **to Peter, "It is the Lord!"** His friend **Simon Peter** also realized that this must be so, and the second he **heard that it was the Lord, he girded his cloak about** him (for he was stripped **naked** for work, wearing possibly only a loincloth or undergarment, as was customary for such fishing) **and cast himself into the sea.** (Decorum dictated that to formally greet someone, one must be clothed.) With his characteristic impulsiveness, Peter could not wait to see the Lord, but jumped off the boat and waded ashore as fast as he could. **The other disciples came in the boat** at a slower pace. They came **dragging the net** crammed with **fish,** since they were **not far from the land, but about two hundred cubits** (or one hundred yards) **away.** They did not want to lose the fish the Lord had provided for them. Peter did not want to lose the fish either, but all his thought was on meeting the Lord.

ॐ ॐ ॐ ॐ ॐ

9   Therefore, when they got out upon the land, they see a charcoal-fire laid and a fish lying on it, and bread.

10   Jesus says to them, "Bring some of the fish which you have now taken hold of."

11   Simon Peter went up therefore and drew the net onto the earth, full of big fish, a hundred and fifty-three *of them*; and although there were so many, the net was not split.

12   Jesus says to them, "Come, eat *breakfast*." No one of the disciples dared to inquire of Him, "Who are You?" knowing that it was the Lord.

13   Jesus comes and takes the bread and gives *it* to them, and the fish likewise.

14   This is already the third *time* that Jesus was

> manifested to the disciples after He was raised
> from *the* dead.

It was a strange meal. The stranger had prepared **a charcoal-fire**, and upon it were **a fish** (Gr. *opsarion*, a small fish, to be eaten as a dainty) and **bread**. He had taken thought for their cold and hunger and had prepared the beginnings of the first meal of the day (called *ariston* in the Greek). The Jews of the first century usually ate two meals a day—this first meal (usually eaten before going to work, though it could be eaten later as luncheon) and the main meal or supper of the day, eaten toward evening (called *deipnon* in the Greek). There was one fish cooking on the fire, and more would be needed to feed the seven tired and hungry men. He **says to them,** "**Bring some of the fish** (Gr. *opsarion*) **which you have now taken hold of.**"

Simon Peter went up therefore and drew the net onto the dry **earth.** No doubt the others helped him (it was too big a load for one person), but Peter is singled out as the leader of the fishing expedition—and also because it was he whom Christ would soon recall to his task of fishing for men. The net was **full of big fish, a hundred and fifty-three** *of them.* They took some of the fish and obediently brought them to the stranger, who added them to the fish and bread already there. When the air was full of the smell of cooked fish, He **says to them, "Come, eat** *breakfast.*" The hungry men gratefully received the meal provided. Despite the fact that they did not recognize the outward appearance of their Host, **no one of** them **dared to inquire of Him, "Who are You?"** (The **You** is emphatic in Greek.) They **knew that it was the Lord.** They therefore all came up to receive the miraculous food from His hand, as He **takes the bread and gives** *it* **to them, and the fish likewise.**

They all looked closely at their host between mouthfuls, yet the question about identity remained unasked. The miracle of the catch, the way He broke and served them the bread, all identified Him to them as the Master.

It is characteristic of Christ that He revealed Himself to His own disciples, whom He loved as His own children (v. 5), by providing them a breakfast to eat when they were cold, hungry, and tired. Here we see the care of Christ for all His children. He sees us as we toil and strive and wrestle with disappointment, and takes thought for us.

There is a further meaning in this miracle, besides the loving care of Christ for His own. Christ had first called His disciples to be fishers of men as they fished on that very lake—perhaps using that very boat (Matt. 4:19). They had seen from their fruitless night of fishing that without Him, they could do nothing (compare 15:5). Now He comes to redirect them once again to their original calling. As with the first miraculous catch of fish on that lake, once again with His power they were able to catch a supernaturally large multitude of fish.

The excitement of that catch survives in the report of the number of fish taken. A group of fishermen must always count the catch, since it must be equitably divided up among them. We can almost hear their voices rising with excitement as the count rises ever higher—"one hundred and fifty, one hundred and fifty-one, one hundred and fifty-two—one hundred and fifty-three!" And these were not just any size fish, but big fish. The final number of such a catch is recorded as a testimony to the power of Christ to enable the fishermen in their task.

For Christ came not simply to help them catch fish—He had long since called them to catch men (Luke 5:10). And now, with the power of His Resurrection, He would help them to do it. The first time they caught such a multitude of fish from that lake, the nets began to break (Luke 5:6). But now, St. John emphasizes, **although there were so many, the net was not split.** This was a sign of how Christ would help them to "bring the world into their net" (as the Troparion for Pentecost says), and how there was to be room for all there. The love of Christ is strong enough to bring all of us fish safely ashore.

St. John summarizes the events of that early morning meal by saying that this was **already the third** *time* **that Jesus was manifested to the disciples** (that is, as a group) **after He was raised from** *the* **dead.** That is, this was the very next appearance to the group after the appearances narrated in the previous chapter. By narrating a third appearance in Galilee, far to the north of the previous appearances in Jerusalem, John shows how Christ appeared to them over and over. The appearances in Jerusalem were not symptoms of some post-traumatic stress disorder on the part of the apostles. The Lord truly was appearing to His disciples as a group—and would continue to do so over the period of forty days (Acts 1:3).

ॐ ॐ ॐ ॐ ॐ

15 When therefore they had eaten *breakfast*, Jesus says to Simon Peter, "Simon, *son* of John, do you love Me more than these?" He says to Him, "Yes, Lord, You *Yourself* know that I love You." He says to him, "Feed My lambs."

16 He says to him again a second *time*, "Simon, *son* of John, do you love Me?" He says to Him, "Yes, Lord, You *Yourself* know that I love You." He says to him, "Shepherd My sheep."

17 He says to him the third *time*, "Simon, *son* of John, do you love Me?" Peter was sorrowful because He said to him the third *time*, "Do you love Me?" And he said to Him, "Lord, You *Yourself* know all things; You *Yourself* know that I love You!" Jesus says to him, "Feed My sheep.

After this third appearance, St. John narrates a conversation which Christ had with Peter during the course of that early morning breakfast on the beach. This conversation is the main reason for narrating the third appearance at all. For the case John had been building came to a climax with the appearance to Thomas. It was during that appearance that Christ proved He was alive from the dead by offering to show Thomas His wounds, as He had shown them to the others. It was this sign that clinched the case for the Resurrection and for Jesus being the messianic Son of God.

By comparison, this third appearance does not add much to the case for Christ's Resurrection. Indeed, the disciples did not actually recognize Him visually as the Lord at all, though they concluded that it was the Lord from the miraculous catch of fish. This appearance then is not narrated so much to prove Christ's Resurrection as to set the scene for Christ's conversation with Peter.

There are two parts to that narrated conversation. The first has to do with the fate of Peter, and the second with the fate of his friend John.

Peter had thrice denied his Lord during that final night when he huddled with the others around a charcoal-fire to warm himself in the cold wee hours of the morning. It would seem that by these denials Peter had irreparably shattered his calling and forsaken his apostolic leadership. John narrates this conversation to show that this was not so, but that Christ was to restore Peter to his original calling. In narrating the restoration of Peter, John also reveals the meaning of Christ's Resurrection to *all* sinners. In the dawn of the resurrection light, there is forgiveness available to all. No matter how grievous our sins, no matter how damaging our betrayals of God's calling in our lives, Christ comes with the morning light to forgive, heal, and restore.

St. John stresses in this story that Christ had built a charcoal-fire (Gr. *anthrakia*). This word is used only twice in the New Testament: in this present narrative and in the story of Peter's denials (18:18). John uses the word here to hearken back to the scene around that earlier charcoal-fire when Peter denied his Lord, to show how his threefold confession now cancels out that denial.

The conversation occurred after they **had eaten** *breakfast*. In the silence that followed (and perhaps in a space a little bit away from the others?), **Jesus says to Simon Peter, "Simon, *son* of John, do you love Me more than these?"** The form of address is significant. Jesus does not address him as "Peter" (Gr. *Petros*, rock), for he had defected from any rocklike stability. He addresses him formally as Simon, son of John, using his full legal name. It is the same name He used when He first bestowed upon him the apostolic leadership, giving him the keys to the Kingdom of Heaven (Matt. 16:17–19). And He has a question for him: "Do you love Me more than these?"

The comparison is also significant. Jesus does not just ask Simon if he loves Him; He asks him if he loves Him more than these other disciples. Earlier, Peter had brashly declared that he did love Jesus more than those others did, and that even if they forsook Him, he never would, but would even die for Him (13:37; Mark 14:29). His denials have taught him the folly of such overconfidence. Peter no longer claims a superiority over the others. He does, however, affirm that he **loves** the Lord—as He Himself **knows**. The Lord responds by restoring him to his original role as leader, telling him to **feed** His **lambs**. Peter has trouble forgiving himself and accepting this commission. Has he not just proven utterly unequal to the task and unworthy of the Lord's trust in him? So (after perhaps a pause of some minutes) Jesus speaks to him a second time. "**Simon, *son* of John, do you love Me?**" Peter replies in exactly the same words, saying, "**Yes, Lord, You *Yourself* know that I love you.**" Christ restores him a second time, telling him to **shepherd** His **sheep**.

Still Peter cannot forgive himself and accept this restoration. So, to complete his restoration (doubtless after another pause), Jesus asks Peter **the third *time***, saying, "**Simon, *son* of John, do you love Me?**" Peter's threefold denial has been met with a threefold call to confess Him again. The poor heart of Peter finally breaks before this onslaught of love and grace. He has been unwilling to forgive himself and accept again the apostolic leadership, even as he was reluctant to follow Him in the first place, aware, as he was, of his inner weakness (compare Luke 5:8). Now he is sorrowful and grieved that Christ seems not to trust his affirmation of love, and he blurts out from his heart, "**Lord, You know all things; You know that I love You!**" Christ replies again with His call to **feed** His **sheep**. For Peter to love Christ means that he must forgive himself and again take up the mantle of apostolic leadership. Does he truly love Christ? Then let him obey Him and shepherd the flock, as originally appointed him. Now that Peter has turned again, he must strengthen his brothers (Luke 22:32).

The inner heart of Peter in this exchange is revealed, we think, by the choice of verbs used, for the Greek uses two different verbs, both rendered by the English word *love*. Christ first asks Peter, "**Do** you love Me?" (Gr. *agapao*), and Peter replies, "**Yes, Lord, You know I love You**" (Gr. *phileo*). Christ asks Peter the second time, "**Do you love Me?**" (Gr. *agapao*), and again Peter replies, "**Yes, Lord, You know I love You**" (Gr. *phileo*). In the third instance, the verb in Christ's question changes, so that John says that Christ asks the third time, "**Do you love Me?**" (Gr. *phileo*), and Peter replies using the same verb, "**Lord, You know I love You**" (Gr. *phileo*). What is the significance of these changes of verb form?

Scholars are divided. Some say that *agapao* is a stronger verb than *phileo*, so that Christ asks Peter if he loves Him with true devotion, while Peter responds in a chastened way with a weaker affirmation of loyalty. Other scholars say that *phileo* is a stronger verb than *agapao*, so that Christ asks Peter if he is loyal to Him, while Peter responds with a stronger and heartfelt confession of devotion. When scholars disagree about something so fundamental, we may think the matter cannot be decided from a dictionary. Certainly St. John uses the verbs as synonyms, since he describes himself as the disciple whom "Jesus loved," using both the verb *agapao* (13:23; 19:26; 21:7) and the verb *phileo* (20:2).

It would seem that the change cannot be merely stylistic. If one is asked a pointblank question (for example, "Do you hate me?") and one responds not with either a simple "yes" or "no" but also with a change of verb (for example, "I loathe you"), one not unnaturally looks for some distinction or nuance between the two verbs. For if there was no distinction to be found, why not simply reply using the same verb?

I would suggest that the distinction is not to be found in the *actual meaning of the verbs* (we have seen that John uses them interchangeably in other contexts), but *in the inner attitude of Peter*. That is, Peter wanted to answer the question in the affirmative. But there is still an inner deflection present, a turning aside from the implication of a simple affirmative answer. Christ has asked, "Do you love Me?" and Peter's inner reluctance and sense of unworthiness will not allow him to look Christ straight in the eye and answer, "Yes, I do love You." He therefore answers "yes," but looks away in pain as he does so. This act of saying "yes" while simultaneously not accepting the implications of that affirmation is expressed by John by the use of a different verb. *This change of verb form allows Peter to answer affirmatively, but still not agree with exactly what Christ has said.*

Thus, Christ asks Peter if he loves Him, and Peter replies that he does, while still deflecting the implication. This question and answer is repeated. Christ then relentlessly pursues Peter, not allowing him to escape the implications of his affirmation. Christ takes up the chase and catches up with Peter. This is expressed by Christ taking up the same verb as Peter had used, changing *agapao* to *phileo*. Christ's exchange with Peter therefore is a study of the heart. Christ counters Peter's threefold denial by eliciting a threefold confession—and by this confession restoring Peter to his original calling and role. Peter's sense of shame and unworthiness finally gives way before His Master's loving perseverance, and he accepts again the mantle of apostolic leadership.

ॐ ॐ ॐ ॐ ॐ

18 "Amen, amen, I say to you, when you were younger, you girded yourself and walked where you wanted, but when you are old, you will stretch out your hands, and another will gird you and bring you where you do not want *to go.*"

19 Now this He said, signifying by what kind of death he would glorify God.

This role would come at a cost. No sooner had Peter been reinstated than Christ prophesied his martyrdom. With great solemnity (saying **Amen, amen, I say to you**), the Lord used a parabolic image of being tied to depict Peter's future martyrdom, **signifying by what kind of death he would glorify God**. His future when he is **old** is contrasted to his past when he was younger. In the days of his strength and independence, he **girded** or tied himself with his belt and **walked where** he **wanted** to. But at the end, he would **stretch out** his **hands** and **another** would **gird** and tie his hands to the horizontal beam of a cross and **bring** him **where** he did **not want to go**.

The parable had to do with the inevitability of his martyrdom. Old age and dotage are characterized as a time when one is too old to dress oneself properly, and when one is dressed by others and led about by them, wherever they decide. Youth is characterized as a time when one dresses oneself and goes about wherever one wants. Just as old age inevitably follows youth, so Peter's martyrdom would inevitably follow his life's service also.

By prophesying of his martyrdom, Christ means to reassure Peter. Peter might have been afraid that his strength would once again fail, and that he might again deny his Master. Christ no sooner restores Peter to his office than He reassures him that he will be equal to this task. The test will come again, but Peter will not fail, as he did that night by the charcoal-fire. In the days to come, he will hold to his faith until the end, and by his death will **glorify God**. By this parable, Christ is not simply predicting the manner of Peter's death; He is also assuring Peter of his final perseverance.

ॐ ॐ ॐ ॐ ॐ

19 And having said this, He says to him, "Follow Me."

20 Peter, turning back, sees following the disciple whom Jesus loved, the one who also had leaned back on His breast at the supper and said, "Lord, who is the one who is delivering You up?"

21 Peter therefore, seeing this one, says to Jesus, "Lord, and what about this one?"

22 Jesus says to him, "If I want him to remain until I come, what *is that* to you? You follow Me!"

23 This word therefore went out among the brothers that that disciple would not die; yet Jesus did not say to him that he would not die, but, "If I want him to remain until I come, what *is that* to you?"

> **24 This is the disciple who witnesses about these things and wrote these things, and we know that his witness is true.**

It would seem that after this exchange, Jesus wanted to talk more with Peter about his future. This further conversation was apparently to be of a more private nature, and so Jesus says to Peter, **"Follow Me,"** leading him to withdraw with Him a little way down the beach. (This would seem to be not just a metaphorical "following" or a call to discipleship, for **Peter, turning back, sees the disciple whom Jesus loved**—that is, John himself—**following** them to the place where Jesus was leading. "Following" in this context apparently indicates a literal following behind in one's footsteps.)

John is described further as **the one who also had leaned back on His breast at the supper and said, "Lord, who is the one who is delivering You up?"** That is, he is described as the Lord's confidant, the one close enough to Christ to know His secrets.

Peter, turning back then, sees John behind them. John is his closest friend, and Peter not unnaturally is concerned about John's fate too. John occupied such a place of trust with the Lord that Peter cannot imagine John not sharing the same glory he is to have. He inquires if John is to join him in a martyr's death, saying, **"Lord, and what about this one?"**

Jesus refuses to discuss the fate of John with Peter. John's end is not Peter's concern. Christ closes the door to such inquiries, saying simply, **"If I want him to remain until I come, what** *is that* **to you? You follow Me!"** That is, whether John was to inherit a martyr's crown, or whether he was to die in peace of old age, or whether he was to remain alive until the Lord finally came—that was no business of Peter's. His only concern was to follow Christ.

John adds an historical note and a clarification. **This word** of Christ about John remaining until He came **went out among the brothers**, and they concluded that John **would not die.** This was incorrect, however, for Jesus **did not say** to John **that he would not die,** but only, **"If I want him to remain until I come, what** *is that* **to you?"** The Church at large (or in Asia Minor at least, where John

367

lived) was drawing unwarranted conclusions from this saying, and they should cease.

Why was John so concerned to clarify and correct this misunderstanding? For though their thinking was incorrect, it was not obviously destructive like a heresy, and would anyhow be corrected naturally by the eventual death of John.

I suggest that John is at pains to correct this error because he sees in it the seeds of a personality cult. At the time of writing (about AD 85 or so) John had been working for many decades, and many in the Church had come to revere him. This reverence was good in itself, but if left unchecked, it could mutate into an unhealthy regard for John as a personality in himself (much the same as the much later reverence for St. John of Kronstadt, who died in 1908, mutated in some circles into an unhealthy idolization of the man). The suggestion of personal immortality was setting a trajectory along these lines. St. John the Evangelist is concerned that he be valued and loved only because of his apostolic connection with his Lord, because he was the one **who witnesses about these things and wrote** about them, and because all **knew that his witness** was **true.** That is, he wanted to be reverenced only because of his status as an apostolic witness, not as the potential founder of a new religion or as Christ's successor.

It was the same with his First Epistle. John's abiding concern was that his flock draw near to Christ, their true God. He concluded that First Epistle by pointing to Jesus Christ as "the true God and as eternal life" (1 John 5:20), and then by finishing with the words "little children, keep yourselves from the idols" (1 John 5:21). In the context of that Epistle, St. John was not simply warning his flock to avoid the idolatrous rites of the pagans, but also *to avoid anything which would set itself up as a rival to their love for Christ.* This is the same way he concludes his Gospel. He would have his readers not fasten their devotion on him, as if he were a locus of holiness in himself, but to keep their eyes on the Lord. St. John was concerned that he not become an idol to well-meaning but misled Christians in Asia Minor.

❧ VII ☙

FINAL NOTE
(21:25)

☙ ☙ ☙ ☙ ☙

25 And there are also many other things which
Jesus did, which if they were written one by
one, I suppose that even the world itself would
not have room for the books which would be
written.

John adds a final note. Having finished his Gospel, he is clear
that the case he has presented is not exhaustive. There were many
other proofs he could have presented, and did not. For there were
many other things Jesus did, and he had chosen not to relate them.
This was inevitable, for **if they were** all **written one by one, the
world itself would not have room for the books which would be
written.** May he be pardoned, then, for omitting some of these
glorious works. He had beheld the Lord's glory and had done his
best to witness to it.

Appendix

Harmony of Chronological Events in the Four Gospels from Jesus' Infancy to His Final Entry into Jerusalem

This is but one possible harmony of the events in the four Gospels.

Of the four Evangelists, John is the most rigorous regarding temporal connections (e.g. "Jesus then left this place and went to that place"), with attention being given to the cycle of Jewish feasts. This provides an annual framework into which the other Synoptic material can be fitted.

Matthew also has many temporal references and connections, as does Mark. Luke has the least, and because of this, references to events in Luke's Gospel have often been omitted. Many of the parables and teachings given in Luke could be placed anywhere in Jesus' ministry.

The years given (AD 27–29) are consistent with traditional computations. There is no indication in the text as to which years saw these events take place, however, and the years 27 to 29 are given only to provide a notion of the passage of time.

Infancy and Childhood	
Annunciation	Luke 1:26f
Jesus' birth	Luke 2:1f
Jesus' circumcision at 8 days (in Bethlehem)	Luke 2:21
Jesus' presentation in Temple at 40 days	Luke 2:22f
Visit of Magi in Bethlehem at 1 year(?)	Matt. 2:1f
Flight into Egypt	Matt. 2:13f
Return to Nazareth	Matt.2:19f; Luke 2:39
Jesus in Jerusalem at age 12	Luke 2:41f

Early Work

Jesus baptized in Jordan in Judea	Matt. 3:13f; Mark 1:9f
40 days temptation in wilderness of Judea	Matt. 4:1f; Mark 1:12

Week of Witness, at end of 40 days:

Jesus returns on Day 3 of week	John 1:35f
Jesus gathers disciples	John 1:43f
Water to wine in Cana	John 2:1f
To Jerusalem	John 2:13

March/April AD 27—Passover:

Cleanses Temple	John 2:14
Does miracles	John 2:23
Nicodemus in Jerusalem	John 3:1f
To Judea, to continue with John's movement	John 3:22f
John arrested	(not recorded)

May AD 27:

Jesus returns to Galilee; Samaritan woman	John 4:1f

Early Galilean Ministry

Calls disciples in Capernaum	Matt. 4:18f; Mark 1:16f; Luke 5:1f

June AD 27:

Heals demoniac in synagogue	Mark 1:21f; Luke 4:31f
Heals Peter's mother-in-law	Matt. 8:14f; Mark 1:29f; Luke 4:38f

Appendix

Visit to Nazareth synagogue	Luke 4:16f
Cleanses leper	Matt. 8:1f; Mark 1:40f; Luke 5:12f
Heals centurion's servant	Matt. 8:5f; Luke 7:1f
Tells would-be follower "birds have nests"	Matt. 8:18f; Luke 9:57f
Stills storm	Matt. 8:23f; Mark 4:35f; Luke 8:22f
Heals Gadarene demoniac	Matt. 8:28f; Mark 5:1f; Luke 8:26f
Heals paralytic and forgives his sins	Matt. 9:1f; Mark 2:1f; Luke 5:17f
Calls Matthew and eats with sinners	Matt. 9:9f; Mark 2:13f; Luke 5:27f
Woman with flow of blood and Jairus' daughter	Matt. 9:18f; Mark 5:21f; Luke 8:40f
John sends delegation to Jesus	Matt. 11:1f; Luke 7:18f
Jesus' disciples pick grain in field	Matt. 12:1f; Mark 2:23f; Luke 6:1f
Heals man with withered hand in synagogue	Matt. 12:9f; Mark 3:1f; Luke 6:6f
Family calls to see Him; Jesus accused of using Satan's power	Matt. 12:22f; Mark 3:20f; Luke 11:14f

Mission of 12	Matt. 10:1f; Mark 6:7f; Luke 9:1f

To Jerusalem
February/March AD 28—Purim

Healing of man by pool	John 5:lf

Later Galilean Ministry

Multiplies loaves for 5000	Matt. 14:13f; Mark 6:30f; Luke 9:10f; John 6:lf

March/April AD 28—Passover:

Walks on water	Matt. 14:22f; Mark 6:45f; John 6:16f
Teaches Pharisees about true cleanness	Matt. 15:1f; Mark 7:1f
Heals Syro-Phoenician woman's daughter	Matt. 15:21f; Mark 7:24f
Multiplies loaves for 4000 in Decapolis	Matt. 15:32f; Mark 8:1f
Heals blind man in 2 stages	Mark 8:22f
Caesarea Philippi	Matt. 16:13f; Mark 8:27f; Luke 9:18f
Transfiguration; healing of demoniac boy	Matt. 17:1f; Mark 9:1f; Luke 9:28f
In Capernaum to pay shekel tax	Matt. 17:22f; Mark 9:30

Sets child in midst to teach humility	Matt. 18:1f; Mark 9:33f; Luke 9:46f
Mission of 70	Luke 10:1f
Upbraids Galilean cities	Luke 10:13f; Matt. 11:20f
70 return	Luke 10:17f
Jesus' joy	Luke 10:21f; Matt. 11:25f
Disciples blessed to hear	Luke 10:23f; Matt. 13:16f

To Jerusalem
September/October AD 28—Booths:

Healing and controversy	John 7:1—10:18

Judean Ministry

Into Judea/Perea	Matt. 19:1; Mark 10:1f
Teaches on divorce	Matt. 19:3f; Mark 10:2f
Blesses children	Matt. 19:13f; Mark 10:13f
Challenges rich young ruler	Matt. 19:16f; Mark 10:17f

To Jerusalem
late December AD 28—Dedication:

Controversy	John 10:22f
To Perea area	John 10:40f

January–March AD 29:

To Bethany; raising of Lazarus	John 11

early March AD 29:	
To Ephraim north of Jerusalem	John 11:54f
To Jerusalem through Jericho	Matt. 20:17f; Mark 10:32f

March/April AD 29—Passover:	
Triumphal Entry into Jerusalem	Matt. 21:1f; Mark 11:1f; Luke 19:28f; John 12:12f